# FROM COFFIN TO HEAVEN

# From Coffin to Heaven

## A Psychological Study of Christian Conversion in Drug Rehabilitation

Ho-yee Ng

**The Chinese University Press**

*From Coffin to Heaven: A Psychological Study of Christian Conversion in Drug Rehabilitation*
By Ho-yee Ng

© **The Chinese University of Hong Kong**, 2004

ISBN 962–996–151–2

**THE CHINESE UNIVERSITY PRESS**
The Chinese University of Hong Kong
SHA TIN, N.T., HONG KONG
Fax: +852 2603 6692
        +852 2603 7355
E-mail: cup@cuhk.edu.hk
Web-site: www.chineseupress.com

Printed in Hong Kong

In loving memory of Erik Kvan
(5 March 1917 – 11 February 2003)

My irreligiously religious friend who walks with me in conversations

# Contents

**TABLES**

**DIAGRAMS**

# Foreword

The Chinese University of Hong Kong is committed to training students of the highest calibre for the increasingly sophisticated needs of society. In pursuance of this goal, the University has, from its inception in 1963, attached great importance to research and to the development of postgraduate programmes. A large number of research postgraduate programmes are now offered, spanning a broad spectrum of disciplines, and nearly a thousand students are now enrolled. Doctoral programmes were launched in 1980, and since then some 799 doctorates have been awarded; this number increased very significantly, reflecting the larger intake in recent years.

The theses, which report the findings of research, represent the fruit of the students' work. Much of the material in these theses have already found their way into journals and conference presentations, from which fellow researchers world-wide can have access. However, it would be of interest to the wider public, and also a source of encouragement to aspiring doctoral students, if some of these theses could be published in the form of monographs. It is therefore a matter of much delight that this idea can be realized with the generous support of The Chinese University of Hong Kong Alumni Fund. Under the *Young Scholars Dissertation Awards* scheme, Ph.D. students graduating from 1993 onwards may apply, or may be nominated by their Faculty Deans, to have their theses published by The Chinese University Press. The theses are scrutinized by external assessors of high international standing, and three of the best theses each year are then selected for the award. This monograph is one of the 1998 theses so selected. It is hoped that, through this book, readers may share the research results of the student, and also get a glimpse of both the toil that went into the work, and the joy of bringing novel ideas and results to light. We hope that the thesis will be found to be intellectually stimulating, and will provoke further discussions on the topic, and further in-depth research in related areas.

I take this opportunity to congratulate Dr. Ho-yee Ng on her work. The University also wishes to express its deepest gratitude to the CUHK Alumni Fund, without whose generous support this publication would not be possible. The Chinese University Press has rendered most useful advice and assistance in the assessment, editing and publication.

Kenneth Young
*Dean, Graduate School*

# Acknowledgements

This book is based on research undertaken at the St. Stephen's Society drug rehabilitation centre in Hong Kong.

Thanks to St. Stephen's Society and to all the participants who have generously shared their stories of grief and joy.

Thanks to Lily Yau for her patience in proofreading the manuscript, to Pat Chan, Vivien Chan and Tim Sim for their assistance in making the completion of the book possible.

Thanks to my children, Erik Lau and Clarence Lau with whom I share the joy and pain of growing together while apart.

# Introduction

This is the story of a group of men who called themselves "heroin-coffins" (白粉棺材). This is the story of their ascension from the styxian shore of heroin addiction to a new found heaven within a Christian brotherhood. The research study which has given rise to this story falls within the area of social sciences, in particular, social work and psychology, which immediately raises the question of the apparent antagonism between science and religion. Can religious faith be studied from a scientific viewpoint? Is scientific skepticism not spiritually destructive in its demand for objectivity, quantification, and repeatability? At some point, scientific communication has been deliberately made devoid of human passion, the longings and despairs of the human condition. However, a research orientation, which opens up avenues to reconcile the antagonisms, is found in George Kelly's Personal Construct Theory (1955), which also offers a theoretical framework for understanding drug addiction and drug rehabilitation.

The substantive areas discussed in this book are drug addiction and rehabilitation, religion and healing, religious conversion in a Christian context, and Kelly's (1955) Personal Construct Theory, all situated against the background of postpositivist psychology.

The research study centres on an investigation of the psychological changes that take place after Christian conversion in chronic heroin-addicted individuals attending a religious drug rehabilitation programme. Specific to the problem of addiction, the study throws light on questions such as: "How do people account for their use and abuse of drugs?" And, "Can drug addiction really be treated, given the perennial problem of relapse?" Indeed, the inevitability of relapse has been taken by some researchers to be a hallmark in defining drug addiction (Gorski, 1986; McAuliffe et al., 1986). This belief is also vividly embodied in the label "heroin coffin" which the participants in the study gave themselves, and in other clichés popular among addicted persons, such as "once an addict, always an addict" (既成道友，終生道友). Perhaps the question that should be asked is whether relapse after treatment should be regarded as treatment failure? What should the aims and objectives of drug rehabilitation be? While the study primarily targets the role of the social work profession, the outcome of the study also has implications for other professionals concerned with addiction work, such as psychologists, psychiatrists, family doctors, counsellors, ministers and administrators.

The study begins by noting the dramatic changes recorded in heroin-addicted persons who have undergone drug rehabilitation programmes run by St. Stephen's Society, a voluntary organization founded in Hong Kong by the Christian missionary Jackie Pullinger (1980). As one of her converts said:

> My pain went away and I felt really changed, and — well — sort of new. I got this strength like — it's called the Holy Spirit and I spoke in a new language and I didn't have any pain at all. (p. 18)

How does one begin to understand the change reported here? What are the Holy Spirit and the new language that have healed the convert? The significance of the investigation is two-fold: a) it throws light upon questions regarding drug addiction, relapse and treatment issues, in particular, upon the possible role of counselling work in drug rehabilitation, and, b) in a wider context, it examines the role of religion in therapy work.

Speaking about the relationship between science and religion, a religious leader, Pope John Paul II (1989, p. 21), once declared: "Science can purify religion from error and superstition, and religion can purify science from idolatry and false absolutes". This book represents an attempt, made jointly by the author and her research participants, to close the apparently insurmountable gulf of understanding between the mysteries of religious faith and the vigour and discipline of the social sciences. The more technical aspects of the study are outlined in Appendix I for those readers who would like to further explore the theory and the methodology used. For authenticity, verbatim transcriptions of the participants' conversations in Cantonese, the language they speak, are given along with an English translation. The literature reviews have also been updated since the study which took place during June 1996 to March 1997.

# CHAPTER 1

# Drug Addiction

Drug use can take many forms. It ranges from experimental use by young people through to regular or controlled use, such as that by social drinkers who manage to keep their substance intake "under control", and finally to drug-addicted individuals whose drug habit is characterized by tolerance, craving, and withdrawal symptoms that signify their psychological and physical dependence on drugs.

How shall we begin to understand drug addiction? Historically, addiction has been seen as either a sin or a disease. As research into addictive behaviour reveals more and more of its complexity, addiction is increasingly regarded as the learning of maladaptive behaviour with multiple determinants.

## The Moral Model

The moral model (Siegler & Osmond, 1968) sees addiction from either a religious or a legal perspective. The former regards addiction to be related to a lack of spiritual understanding resulting in sin, and the addictive behaviour is seen as freely chosen, irresponsible and morally wrong. From a legal perspective, addiction violates social rules and norms, and punishment is deemed necessary for such wrongful behaviour. Relapse is considered the evidence of evil, resulting from moral decay either in society or in the individual, so that a return to traditional and family values is needed.

Research, however, strongly suggests that the origin of addiction is multi-factorial, involving pharmacological, biological, psychological, and social factors. Instead of drug abuse being a freely chosen behaviour, drug abusers appear to have lost control of their drug use. Punishment through law enforcement has been found to be ineffective in reducing the prevalence of addiction and its related problems, and has had unintended outcomes such as creating underground markets and perpetuating organized crime and drug trafficking. The disease model has subsequently overshadowed the moral view, as research on addiction has begun in earnest.

## The Disease Model

The disease model sees drug abusers as victims of a disease that has a cause (drugs), produces physical signs and symptoms (compulsive drug use), has a clinical course (loss of control in drug use, presence of withdrawal symptoms), and is harmful to health. The disease may have possible genetic origins, and is progressive and irreversible. Without medical treatment, it is fatal. Yet over the years, this formulation has been found wanting in accounting for the enormous complexity of addictive behaviours like switching between drugs, voluntary and involuntary periods of abstinence, spontaneous remission, and even "maturing out" of the habit entirely (Peele, 1985). These kinds of behaviour are incompatible with the central thesis of the disease model that the person loses control of their drug use because of the body's habituation to drugs. Attention has, therefore, turned to psychosocial factors for explanations of such a diverse range of drug use behaviours.

## The Psychoanalytic Perspective

The psychoanalytic approach sees addiction as defensive behaviour to protect a person from overwhelming psychic pain due to intra-psychic conflicts that result in poor ego functioning (Wurmser, 1974). Typical correlations between drug types and affect types are postulated: narcotics and hypnotics are for rage and shame; stimulants for depression; psychedelics for boredom and disillusionment; and alcohol for guilt, loneliness, and related anxiety. More recent formulations have identified opiates for victims of traumatic abuse and violence, as the opiates have a calming effect on such victims who typically suffer from acute and chronic feelings of anger and hostility, and can become perpetrators of violence themselves (Khantzian, Halliday, & McAuliffe, 1990).

As addiction is seen by psychoanalysts to result from ego deficiency, treatment would have to be aimed at improving a person's ego strength. However, insight therapy has been found to have very poor outcomes

(Brickman, 1988; Gerald, 1992), as ironically, for self-analysis to be effective, it requires a client to have significant ego strength to begin therapy. Analytic theories' sole emphasis on the intra-psychic origins of addiction has not been supported by empirical evidence, which suggests that most addictive behaviours are multi-determined, involving biological, psychological, behavioural, and cultural factors. The learning model pays due attention to the environmental forces relevant to addiction.

## The Learning Model

The learning model, in terms of classical conditioning, says that people continue with a habit because of the rewards it brings. A narcotic like heroin is said to produce an inherent euphoria that serves as a reward or reinforcement. Yet, when naïve subjects were exposed to narcotics, usually in hospitals, they neither found the drug pleasant nor did they get addicted (Beecher, 1959; Smith & Beecher, 1962). It was also found that volunteer participants who were given amphetamines for positive mood effects over several days whilst continuing with their daily routine did not become addicted (Falk, 1983). Hence, the nature of a reinforcer is not confined to the intrinsic effects of a particular drug, and physical dependence is neither a necessary nor sufficient condition for developing an addiction. For drugs that do not produce physical dependence, other types of reinforcers or rewards would be more potent, e.g. stress reduction. While studies have been conducted which largely support the Tension Reduction Model (S. A. Brown, 1985; Stockwell, 1985), other studies have found that individuals under stress respond in different ways. What works for one individual may not apply to another. The search for the reinforcing properties of drugs has caused researchers to look beyond the chemical effects of drugs to the context of drug use. The rituals involved in drug use, such as self-injection, or the environment in which drugs are taken, such as a bar, or the presence of special music or drug mates, may all become conditioned stimuli that elicit craving. However, Robins, Helzer, & Davis's (1975) study found that while half of their addicted Vietnam soldiers used narcotics at home, only a minority became re-addicted on returning from Vietnam. This suggests that actual drug use in the home environment was not sufficient to lead to their relapse. Researchers, therefore, have widened their perspective to look for answers from the entire socio-cultural environment surrounding the individual.

## The Socio-cultural Model

This model focuses on forces in a person's interpersonal environment that bring about or support addiction. These include their family, peer group, social values, beliefs and the norms surrounding drug use, as well as macro forces like government, laws, and organized crime. A short detour into history illustrates how macro forces have brought about heroin addiction as a social concern in Hong Kong.

Prior to 1946, the then Hong Kong Government monopolized the sale of opium at a time when opium was being taken as a medium for social interactions and recreation. The legalized opium trade ended in 1946 when the British Government conceded to international pressure and abolished official opium distribution. Opium was declared illegal overnight in Hong Kong. However, years of tolerance of the opium trade left a high prevalence of opium addiction, which was replaced soon after by heroin addiction, as heroin was much easier to conceal by both seller and consumer (Traver, 1992). The influx of refugees from China in the 1950s helped spread heroin smoking quickly among manual labourers and the unemployed. Heroin addiction has since remained the dominant drug of abuse in Hong Kong (Narcotics Division, 2002a). Once the opium trade became illegal, government attention was directed to the problem of drug trafficking, which had caused underground markets and organized crime to flourish. The history of Hong Kong's heroin problem shows that socio-political factors have an important role in generating the problem.

Aside from macro forces, research has also linked drug use to socio-demographic characteristics. For example, in North America, alcoholism has been found to relate to age, sex, ethnicity and social status (Cahalan, 1970; Valliant & Milofsky, 1982). For Hong Kong, the latest statistics on drug abusers indicate that addiction is also related to such variables as age, sex, education, marital and employment status (Narcotics Division, 2002b).

While socio-cultural variables might predispose a person to drug use, the impact of sub-cultural influences also play a role in translating this potential into actual drug use, or even determining what type of drugs to use. Such influences may come from the family, peers, news media, schools, etc.

The impact of a subculture mediated through the peer group has been found to play a prominent role in the initiation of experimental drug use. A person usually comes into contact with drugs through friends who are taking drugs. Then he/she is taught what to look for in terms of the drug experience and also how to enjoy the effects of drugs (Becker, 1953). Surveys in Hong

Kong on young people experimenting with drugs found that they repeatedly cite peer influence/pressure as one of the reasons for their first contact with drugs. Other reasons given are curiosity and relief from boredom. (Narcotics Division, 1994; 1997a; 2002c; 2002d). Research data also indicated that drug-using youths tended to be less satisfied with life, lacked life goals, and had poorer academic performance and poorer family relationships when compared with non-drug users (Narcotics Division, 1994). In other words, there are psychosocial factors that may account for why some people continue with drug use beyond the first attempt. While drugs are chemical agents, the impact of the total drug experience is mediated by a host of non-chemical factors. This is elaborated within the cognitive model of addiction.

## The Cognitive Model

Cognition refers to mental processes like thinking, sensing, perceiving and remembering, or expectations and beliefs a person holds that influence their perception of events and subsequent behaviour. The cognitive model thus stresses a person's active interpretation of environmental events.

In the past two decades, research has shown that addiction does not occur during a person's first contact with drugs. Drug use develops over time and is linked to a variety of risk factors such as gender, age, socio-economic status, and ethnic/religious affiliation (Glantz & Pickens, 1992; Hawkins, Catalano, & Miller, 1992). Individual factors like temperament and personality have also been linked to eventual drug addiction. High risk factors include antisocial personality, sensation-seeking, and reward-seeking characteristics (Sher, Walitzer, Wood, & Brent 1991; Zucker & Gomberg, 1986). At the physiological level, the search for biological markers relating to addiction continues (Gordis, 2000; Newlin, 1989; Swan, Carnelli, & Cardon, 1996). Yet, the identification of high risk factors does not explain actual vulnerability to addiction. One must ask what it is about gender or ethnic affiliation that could lead to eventual addiction; or how a person's need for excitement, or the inheritance of a particular gene, could actually cause drug use. In other words, human behaviour must be seen as a continuous reciprocal interaction between genetic, behavioural, cognitive, and environmental determinants. The consequences of behaviour (reinforcement) do not act automatically to shape behaviour in a mechanistic manner. Rather, internal cognitive processes mediate the impact of environmental events on behaviour.

Lindesmith (1968) was one of the first to recognize the role of cognition in addiction. He argued that to be addicted, the heroin user must be aware that his suffering from withdrawal pain is due to cessation of drug use and that re-taking the drug will ease this pain. He also noted that hospital patients did not become addicted to the narcotics they took because they associated the drug effects with their illness and believed that any discomfort would be temporary. Further, Zinberg (1974) found that people who recovered from illnesses almost never developed a craving for narcotics outside the hospital setting.

In Marlatt, Demming, and Reid's (1973) landmark study in which subjects were randomly told that they would be given either vodka and tonic or tonic only, it was found that both alcoholic and non-alcoholic men drank significantly more when they thought their drinks contained alcohol. It was the subjects' belief (expectancy) about the beverage content rather than the actual content that was crucial in influencing their behaviour. Thus, cognition could create expected drug effects.

Beck, Wright, Newman, and Liese (1993) further sharpened the formulation of the cognitive model of addiction by pinpointing the role of belief. Addiction and relapse are seen as a function of dysfunctional or addictive beliefs. In other words, drug users learn to associate drugs with certain effects. Peele and Brodsky (1991, p. 42) presented this position neatly by saying: "The addictive potential of a substance or other involvement lies primarily in the meaning it has for a person". People become attached to the addictive experience because they believe drugs bring them certain rewards, such as the lessening of pain and tension, or an enhanced sense of control, power, self-esteem etc. That people choose to satisfy themselves with an addiction signifies a *value choice*, in that they choose what they consider to be rewarding to them. In this sense, addiction follows all the ordinary rules of human behaviour as people act to maximize the rewards they perceive as available to them. As a function of such perceptions, a variety of drug taking behaviours from controlled use to addiction can be accounted for based on an individual's habitual adjustment to his/her environment, with the extreme case of addiction becoming self-defeating behaviour that will eventually change a person's whole lifestyle. This is the familiar story of Waldorf's (1973) "dope fiend". As long as people believe the drug experience can help them in certain ways (addictive beliefs), drug use will continue. As drug tolerance sets in, more drugs are needed to get the required "high", so more money is needed to sustain the habit. At the same time, the drug habit interferes with daily routines, resulting frequently in job loss. Desperate, these chronic drug abusers turn to the crime-related underground market for dope and easy money. They get incarcerated for a period. Upon being released, they find it difficult to face the stress of life, and run back to the drugs that they believe can help them "escape reality". The instant relief encourages them to continue, while relapse brings them back into contact with old associates in the drug world. And so drug use sets in as a habitual style of coping, a revolving door of arrest, detoxification, relapse, incarceration, release, and re-addiction. Given such a negative lifestyle, addiction and poor mental health is to be expected.

## Drug Addiction and Psychopathology

One of the most stringent studies for estimating the prevalence of psycho-pathology in heroin-addicted persons was conducted by Rounsaville, Weissman, Kleber, and Wilber (1982), who found that in a sample of 533 subjects, the lifetime incidence of any psychiatric disorder was 86.9%, with 23.8% diagnosed with current major depressive disorders.

Many researchers have since documented the presence of depressive symptoms in opiate abusers (Croughan, Miller, Wagelin, & Whitman, 1982; Dackis & Gold, 1983; Weissman, Slobetz, Prusoff, Mezritz, & Howard, 1976). Narcotic-addicted persons were found to be easily depressed, lacking in confidence, and pessimistic about the future (Gilbert and Lombardi, 1967). They suffered from hypochondria, depression, and hysteria (Haertzen and Hooks, 1969); they showed feelings of inadequacy and alienation (Lombardi, O'Brien and Isele, 1968); and they reported more neurotic symptoms in the form of depression, pessimism, anxiety, and concern for bodily ailments (Sutker, 1971). Berzins, Ross, English, and Haley (1974) also found that their sample of 1,500 subjects displayed high levels of subjective distress and confused thinking. They postulated that this group used drugs to control feelings of anxiety, depression, and distress. Robins (1974) found depression with a sense of hopelessness to be an important feature in his sample of 114 subjects, with suicidal attempts reported in a few cases. He considered that the following factors contributed to depression: a) early childhood depression; b) a life pattern prior to drug use characterized by boredom, frustration, and lack of future expectations; c) an addictive lifestyle which deprived the person of normal gratifications; and d) repeated treatment failures. In other studies, affective personality type as well as mood and anxiety disorders were found in mixed groups of narcotic-addicted persons (Geerlings et al., 1990; Sheppard, Fracchia, Ricca, & Merlis, 1972;

Sheppard, Ricca, Fracchia, & Merlis, 1973; Van Limbeek et al., 1990). Likewise, methadone patients were reported to be moderately to severely depressed (Dorus and Senay, 1977; Steer, Emery and Beck, 1980). Brooner, King, Kidorf, Schmidt, & Bigelow (1997) found a prevalence of around 16% for incidence of depression in 716 opiate abusers seeking methadone maintenance, while Brewer, Catalano, Haggerty, Gainey, & Fleming (1998) identified depression as one variable predictive of continued opiate use.

Changes in psychopathological symptoms have been recorded as a result of drug treatment (DeLeon, Skodol, & Rosenthal, 1973). In a drug-free residential programme, DeLeon (1974) assessed psychiatric symptoms in 208 opiate-addicted persons and found the cross-sectional results revealed a significant decrease in psychopathological signs with increased time spent in the treatment programme. There was a gender difference, however, with females scoring consistently higher than males in psychiatric indices. Sutker, Allain, and Cohen (1974) found that as a result of both short-term and long-term hospitalization, their sample of 58 males all showed lower scores on almost every clinical scale on the Minnesota Multiphasic Personality Inventory (MMPI). More recently, Bennett and Rigby (1991) also found that amongst other changes, there were significant reductions in anxiety, depression and hopelessness, and an increase in self-esteem in a group of 50 females who underwent residential drug rehabilitation.

Research evidence clearly indicates that heroin-addicted persons manifest significant psychiatric symptoms, noticeably that of depression (Regier et. al, 1990; Holmes, 1999). Treatment programmes, particularly of the residential type, are found to reduce such symptoms by a significant degree. What are the objectives and roles of drug treatment and rehabilitation?

# CHAPTER 2

# Drug Treatment and Rehabilitation

The objectives of the treatment of addiction differ according to the perspective of the vested party, such as that of the therapists, clients, their families, or the treatment agency. There are, however, some common goals. The primary goal is to eliminate or reduce a client's drug use. Secondary goals often include decreasing criminal activity, increasing educational standards or improving vocational skills, gaining steady employment, achieving stable social and familial relationships, developing coping and communication skills, improving physical and psychological health, and eliminating or reducing the client's health risk behaviour such as HIV transmission and infection. These goals can be achieved in different ways, depending on the perspective one takes in understanding addiction.

## Treatment Perspectives

When addiction is seen as an illness, pharmacological treatment is used, mostly for detoxification. For psychoanalysts, insight therapy is the treatment of choice. However neither approach is found to be very effective when used in isolation (N. S. Miller, 1995; Washton, 1995). Behaviour therapies, derived from the learning model, aim at helping clients to learn more effective ways of behaving through behavioural interventions such as aversion therapies that use chemicals or electric shocks as negative reinforcers; covert sensitization that pairs verbal aversion with the unwanted behaviour; extinction that blocks the effects of drugs by narcotic antagonists; contingency contracting that uses contracts to reinforce positive behaviour; and finally community-based behavioural treatment programmes that extend the contingency contract beyond the individual into the vocational, recreational, social and familial settings. Biofeedback and relaxation therapy have also been tried to reduce stress for those who use drugs to counteract anxiety and tension. Although these behavioural interventions have been found to be effective, their effects are however, usually not long lasting (Rotgers, 1996).

While the socio-cultural model has provided a valuable framework for understanding the environment within which a person learns socially transmitted rules of drug use, it has very little practical value in guiding addiction treatment, since social systems are extremely difficult to manipulate. For example, while abstinence from drinking and drugs is demanded in many drug rehabilitation programmes, the mass media may provide cues for drinking for pleasure and encourage taking drugs for quick relief of all kinds of ailments, physical or psychological. Harsh economic and social realities, such as unemployment and drug policy, are simply beyond the control of both therapists and clients.

As for cognitive-behavioural approaches derived from the cognitive model, W. E. Miller's (1983) motivational interviewing and Marlatt and Gordon's (1985) relapse prevention treatment package are the better-known ones. Through confrontation and persuasion, W. E. Miller (1983) aims to help clients reach a state of self-examination of their drug taking behaviour, while Marlatt and Gordon (1985) teach people to identify, and then cope in constructive ways with high-risk situations which can lead to relapse. The search for relapse determinants in high-risk situations and skills training are therefore important procedures. Specific interventions may include cognitive remediation (positive self-statements, coping imagery), skill building (role-playing, relapse rehearsal), and lifestyle modification (relaxation, effective time management). Other researchers in relapse prevention have emphasized different cognitive dimensions, for example, enhancing clients' expectations of success through learning self-regulatory and social skills (Annis, 1986).

While psychotherapeutic techniques derived from the various models of addiction continue to expand, there is also a move towards using these techniques in a multi-component treatment programme, or as adjuncts to pharmaco-therapies, as there is little evidence that the sole use of psychotherapy is effective, particularly with acutely addicted or recently detoxified persons (Rawson, 1995). As a result, several major forms of treatment modalities are currently in use, either as stand-alone techniques or in combination within different treatment modes.

## Major Treatment Modes

### *Detoxification*

Detoxification, carried out within an inpatient or an outpatient setting, stops a client's physical dependence on drugs. The length of time in detoxification depends on the withdrawal syndrome associated with a specific drug. It provides a means of breaking up the cycle of addiction to allow for the chance to enter long-term treatment, since when used alone, it has not been found to be effective in reducing or eliminating subsequent drug use (Hubbard et al., 1989). Detoxification programmes usually serve as adjuncts to other treatment regimes.

### *Methadone Maintenance*

Methadone maintenance programmes originated in the 1960s as a treatment for opiate-dependent clients (Dole & Nyswander, 1965). Methadone is a long-acting synthetic opiate substitute administered orally in varying doses. It eliminates withdrawal symptoms without producing euphoria. Kreek (1991) stated the goals of methadone maintenance as: a) reduction or cessation of drug use; b) voluntary retention in treatment; c) reduction or cessation of other drugs, including alcohol; d) reduction in diseases transmitted by the use of un-sterile needles; e) reduction in criminality and antisocial behaviours; and f) improvement in productivity. Therefore, methadone may be used in three treatment phases: stabilization, maintenance, and detoxification, each according to the clients' needs and their readiness for change, since some of them may prefer to remain on methadone for years without becoming drug-free.

   While some studies have found methadone to be effective (Hubbard et al., 1989; McLellan, 1986; Tims, Fletcher, & Hubbard, 1991), others have found it to be more addictive and more difficult to withdraw from than heroin, and concerns have been raised about its long-term use (Allison, Hubbard, & Rachal 1985; Seivewright, 2000). Furthermore, methadone maintenance programmes vary in their provision of supportive and social services. There also tend to be specific client predictors of successful outcome, such as employment, stable family relationships, the ability to stabilize on low dosages of methadone immediately before detoxification, and longer times spent on methadone (McLellan, Luborsky, Woody, O'Brien, & Druley, 1983). Nevertheless, having reviewed 30 years of methadone use, Platt, Widman, Lidz and Marlowe (1998) are of the opinion that it can at least stabilize certain client groups although the percentage of individuals who successfully detoxify from methadone is very low.

## *Outpatient Drug-free Treatment*

Generally speaking, this form of treatment is for clients with less severe drug-related problems, those who are re-entering the community after residential treatment, or for clients who have relapsed. Apart from medication, individual counselling or group therapy is used to enhance clients' self-image and to provide support. In addition, a variety of services catering to educational, vocational and legal needs are available, either within the programme, or through referral to other service agencies. Price et al. (1991) identified the following treatment goals: a) abstinence from drugs; b) steady employment; c) stable social relationships; d) positive physical and mental health; e) improved spiritual strength; and f) adherence to legal requirements if applicable. However, retention of clients remains a problem due to frequent defaults (Hubbard et al., 1989).

## *Self-help Groups*

The self-help movement provides non-professional support for people with a variety of problems. It originated from the setting up of Alcoholics Anonymous (AA) in the United States in 1935, when two alcoholics found that they could maintain sobriety by sharing their experiences and by following a set of principles that eventually came to be known as the Twelve Steps (AA World Services, 1952). In 1953, Narcotics Anonymous (NA) began in California along similar lines. The movement has now spread to most countries in the world, including Hong Kong.

AA and NA see addiction as a progressive illness without a cure, but where recovery is possible if the sufferer remains abstinent from drugs and enters into the Twelve Steps Programme which deals with, firstly, the paradox of gaining control over one's behaviour by giving up control to a higher power; secondly, a self-examination through which guilt is alleviated by making amends to those the person may have wronged; and finally, sustaining sobriety through prayer, meditation, helping others, and propagating the AA philosophy.

Several outcome studies indicate the success of AA in promoting recovery from alcoholism (Hoffmann, Harrison & Belille, 1983; McLatchie & Lomp, 1988; Shereen, 1988). However, relapse is also found to be common (Blum, 1991). More recent debates centre on whether the programme refers to religion or spirituality in essence (Chappel, 1990; Warfield & Goldstein, 1996). Further, the factor of self-selection in people who join the fellowship probably means that some people are more likely to benefit from such a programme than others.

### *Residential Treatment*

The primary residential treatment model is the Therapeutic Community (TC) that follows the philosophy of the self-help movement in its emphasis on group processes.

Therapeutic communities are longer term (usually six to twenty-four months) residential treatment communities for people with long-standing problematic behaviour associated with drug taking, particularly those with repeated relapses. Within the TC framework, addiction is seen as "a deviant behaviour, reflecting impeded personality development and/or chronic deficits in social, educational and economic skills" (DeLeon, 1986, p. 7). The goal of TCs involve global lifestyle changes, aimed at developing a responsible, drug-free lifestyle through a process of resocialization. This is achieved by simulating a model family with a hierarchical structure. Explicit rules for behaviour are given and clients progress through stages of treatment giving them increasing responsibilities, privileges and status within the TC. Confrontational encounters, individual and group counselling, remedial and formal education, are all provided by staff members who are mostly ex-drug addicted persons.

Follow-up studies support the effectiveness of TCs in reducing drug use and criminality, and in increasing employment among graduates of the programme (DeLeon, 1984). However, this form of treatment requires a total commitment which many chronic drug-addicted persons are unable to make, hence drop-out rates are high (Bale et al., 1980).

## Treatment Effectiveness

The question of whether there are differences in treatment effectiveness across treatment modes is an important one, not only for practitioners, but also for the policy makers responsible for decisions in funding treatment programmes. However, outcome measures are affected by a wealth of factors that are difficult to control in outcome research. These include the different effects of drugs on a user; different clientele with differing goals in seeking treatment; differences in programme aims and duration; different definitions of therapeutic success; and lack of comparability between programmes (Roman, 1992).

Furthermore, many drug users have been found to alter their lifestyles and behaviour for reasons unrelated to treatment (Wells, 1990). Research suggests that there are people who are able to stop using drugs on their own (Prugh, 1986). Therefore, for any treatment to be considered successful, it should produce higher success rates than what would be expected from self-cure, spontaneous remission and untreated cases. If abstinence is taken as the criterion of success as in many treatment programmes, then is relapse after treatment to be seen as treatment failure? According to Gorski (1986), relapse is almost universal. Most people achieve partial recovery and then experience one or more relapses over time. Total abstinence may then be too idealistic a goal; minimizing the adverse consequences of relapse may be more important. Indeed, many experts in the addiction field have regarded relapse as a determining characteristic of addiction (Lindesmith, 1968; McAuliffe et al., 1986).

## Relapse

When Hunt, Barnett, and Branch (1971) published their relapse curve, it sparked off a torrent of interest in the phenomenon of relapse. They indicated that about 60% of heroin, alcohol, and smoking relapses occur within the first three months. After that there is a negative acceleration in relapse rates for up to six months, but which levels off at twelve months. However, Litman, Eiser, and Taylor (1979) later considered this as a cumulative survival curve showing only how many survivors (abstainers) are left at a given point in time, and using group means as an index can obscure individual patterns of relapse. Moreover, there is the question of what constitutes a relapse.

The meaning of relapse may range from any drug use after a period of abstinence, to a return to pre-treatment level of drug use. However there are many dimensions involved in assessing improvement or deterioration in drug taking behaviour, such as drug dose, number and type of drugs used, frequency and mode of drug taking, criminal involvement, and indices of psychosocial adjustment in the form of work performance or social adjustment. This makes determination of treatment success highly dependent on one's definition of relapse.

If the criterion of recovery is entirely contingent upon total abstinence, then any form of relapse would mean treatment failure. However, if the actual drug use is seen as secondary to other circumstances in a person's life, then outcome measures may best be seen in terms of improved quality of life. There is therefore a need to consider when relapse occurs. Does it occur at the very first use of drugs after treatment and if so, how soon? Can it occur after one day of abstinence? Does it involve intoxication? In this aspect, Marlatt's (1985) distinction between a *lapse* and a *relapse* is helpful. He sees a lapse as a single episode in which restraint is violated, and which is regarded as a mistake, whereas a relapse marks the unsuccessful end of the whole attempt to change behaviour, which is then a more significant deterioration. Relapse for Marlatt and Gordon (1985) is a breakdown or failure in a person's attempt to change or modify any target behaviour. For Marlatt (1985), a lapse presents an urgent opportunity for intervention that might prevent a relapse.

Apart from clarification of the concept of relapse, the search for precipitants, and models of lapse and relapse, are also major concerns in addiction literature.

### Lapse and Relapse

Gossop, Green, Phillips, & Gradley (1987) identified cognitions (intentions, planning of drug use), moods (unpleasant states such as boredom, anger, sadness, loneliness), and leaving a protected environment, as the most common initial factors leading to the first lapse. Cognitive and mood factors were also judged to be most important in terms of relapse. In studies of high-risk situations, Cummings, Gordon, and Marlatt (1980) found three general factors which accounted for 70% of relapse: a) an interpersonal situation: peer pressure to use drugs; b) negative emotions of an intrapersonal nature: feelings of depression, anxiety, loneliness, boredom, and lack of structure in time use; and c) interpersonal conflicts.

Shiffman (1989) organized the different relapse factors into three models of relapse, each emphasizing different factors: a) The constant-risk model, referring to personal characteristics and individual vulnerability such as demographic or personality differences; b) The cumulative-risk model, emphasizing background factors in a person's experiences during the maintenance period such as work stress or marital status; and c) The episodic-risk model, focusing on fast-changing antecedents of a particular relapse episode such as financial changes or exposure to drug cues.

Each of the relapse models must necessarily be limited, since each deals only with part of a very complex process in which variables may be additive or interactive, and the potential combinations among the variables involved are numerous and complex. For example, chronic stress may make a person more vulnerable to drug cues, but it will only have effects for those whose drug use is tied to stress reduction. Against a background of low stress and high life satisfaction, exposure to drug cues may interact with high life satisfaction for those who take drugs for its pleasurable effects, thereby further enhancing life satisfaction. Shiffman (1989) therefore suggested that maintenance of a drug-free state could be seen as a continuing struggle between the temptations offered by drugs and one's resistance towards using them. It is the balance between temptation and resistance to temptation that determines whether relapse occurs. Therefore one should look for relapse-promoting and relapse-protecting factors. This is in line with Stimson and Oppenheimer's (1982) view. They see a person's decision to continue drug taking or to quit it as the eventual outcome of the conflict between the reasons to continue and the reasons to stop, this is, in itself, a source of tension.

This brief review of the relapse literature highlights the difficulties involved in treatment outcome research. Perhaps Valliant's (1983) view serves as a reminder that a wider perspective is needed in the definition of treatment effectiveness. He stated, "It must be remembered that abstinence is a means, not an end. It is justifiable as a treatment goal only if moderate drinking is not an alternative and only if sight is not lost of the real goal — social rehabilitation" (p. 215).

The overview so far, regarding addiction treatment, suggests that individual psychotherapy is probably ineffective, or not as effective as combined approaches. The use of a single treatment modality is probably also inadequate to cover all kinds of drug abusers. Nor is any single treatment modality or technique found to be the most effective (Mejta, Naylor & Maslar, 1994). Thus Straussner and Spiegel (1996) recommended that 12-steps groups may be combined with formal psychotherapeutic treatment to provide drug abusing individuals the opportunity to work through life issues. Furthermore, religious programmes, though the least studied, have also been found to have an efficacy comparable to other secular treatment regimes. There is some indication that religious programmes may produce longer periods of abstinence. In view of the many studies pointing to a negative correlation between religiousness and drug abuse, Gorsuch (1995) has called for improvements in religious treatment research, such as in the measurement of "religiousness", or in monitoring the spiritual/religious change in participants in religion-based treatment programmes. If being religious is an inhibiting factor for drug abuse, then research should be designed to provide an understanding of how the effect occurs.

## Religion-based Drug Treatment and Rehabilitation

The TC model has been adopted by some Christian communities as a form of rescue mission for the destitute, including drug-addicted persons, the Salvation Army and National Teen Challenge Inc. in the United States being the better-known ones (Bahr and Hawks, 1995). These programmes are seen to be less strict in discipline and in hierarchical structure than the TCs. Instead, interpersonal problems are dealt with in the context of a Christian-based belief system through Bible reading, prayer, worship and religious discussion.

Not much is known about the religious/spiritual dimensions of addiction treatment since religious/spiritual variables have been neglected in research (W. R. Miller, 1990). However Maddux and Desmond's (1981) review of 63 heroin-addicted persons who entered programmes with varying degrees of religious content found that these programmes were more effective in maintaining post-treatment abstinence beyond one year. Nine of their subjects did not join a formal programme but attributed their three years or more of abstinence from drugs to religious conversion or to involvement in church activities. They concluded that religious programmes are an effective alternative to conventional therapies for some people. Likewise, Muffler, Langrod, and Larson (1992) evaluated four religion based treatment programmes and concluded that these are "neither a panacea nor a perfect solution ... in the very few studies conducted, these programs have demonstrated successful outcomes comparable to those of secular treatment regimes" (p. 594).

In Hong Kong, the development of the religious approach in drug rehabilitation is said to have preceded even government action in drug treatment (Woo, 1983). The religious approach began as isolated efforts made by individual missionaries in the 1950s through to the 1970s. These efforts have since crystallized into several residential treatment centres run on Christian philosophy, with St. Stephen's Society being the largest in terms of its residential capacity. These centres were run on a voluntary basis until very recently, when in 1995, the then Hong Kong Government initiated a series of evaluative researches on the services offered by these organizations (Narcotics Division, 1995). The project was completed in

December 1997, and government subvention was granted to four eligible agencies from March 1998 (Action Committee Against Narcotics, 1998). Such an official endorsement of rehabilitative work of a religious nature should alert professional workers to the potential role religion can play in people's lives.

That there is a strong relationship between religious/spiritual commitment (e.g., church going) and the avoidance of alcohol and drugs is well established in the literature. Larson, Sherrill, and Lyons (1992) found patients who became involved with a religious community after alcohol treatment had lower relapse rates than those who did not. Ridgway (1972) and Bennett and Rigby (1991) found an improvement in mental health status in terms of the reduction of anxiety or depression, and an increase in self-acceptance and self-esteem in people undergoing rehabilitation in centres run on Christian philosophy.

Thus, there is evidence that a religious approach to drug treatment can be effective, though little has been written about the nature of these religious programmes. In Jilek's (1994) very impressive survey of non-western traditional healing methods for alcohol and drug abuse, he has provided descriptions of therapeutic approaches based on a variety of religious/spiritual traditions found in Asia, North, Central and South America, and in Southern Africa, such as Thai and Japanese Buddhist traditions, Islamic traditions for Malays and Arabs, Chinese medicine and Taoist traditions, the folk ceremonials like the Sun Dance in North America or Peruvian shamanic healing in South America, and Afro-Christian cults in South Africa. Of interest here are his descriptions of church groups led by charismatic prophet-healers. These churches not only prohibit the use of alcohol and drugs, they are also ready to rehabilitate repentant drug users. The rehabilitation process involves confession by the person who then goes through purification rites symbolizing the elimination of all evils in the form of ritual vomiting and body cleansing. Some churches have separated spiritual therapy from body therapy, the former consisting of purification by holy water, songs and prayers, or baptism, and the latter consisting of detoxification by drinking exactly dosed liquids like tea, lake water, salt solution, milk, coffee or oil over a specified period, and then by body stimulation.

A follow-up study of these programmes which was conducted in Malawi, South Africa by Peltzer (1987) found the average time of alcohol abstinence to be 2.8 years for one church programme; in another, five out of eleven men remained abstinent and became regular church-goers after six months of treatment. Another programme, which did not offer body therapy, was found to be less successful, as only one out of five men remained abstinent after six months.

While admitting that there have been very few investigations yielding hard scientific evidence on the traditional healing of addiction, Jilek (1994) nevertheless concluded by saying:

> In the rehabilitation and prevention of chemical substance dependence, therapeutic modalities based on indigenous cultural and religious traditions have been found to be generally as successful, and in some instances more successful, than "official" treatment and rehabilitation programs, as attested by many authors. (p. 246)

Jilek (1994) indeed also admitted that claims of effectiveness for scientifically based western interventions in the addiction field are similarly not as firmly grounded on experimental evidence as one would like them to be, as the evaluation of treatment effectiveness has been shown to be very complicated. How has the social work profession, as a provider of what Jilek referred as western interventions, been responding to the problem of addiction?

# CHAPTER 3

# Social Work and Drug Addiction

A review concerning mainly North American social work literature suggests that the social work profession was initially minimally involved in addiction work (Corrigan, 1979; Googins, 1984), however recent voices have argued for greater involvement in this area, since the profession is increasingly seen to have an unique role in drug prevention and treatment (Magura, 1994). The North American scene is taken as providing a background for discussion here because historically, the development of social work education in Hong Kong has been strongly influenced by traditions in the West (Ng & Kvan, 1998).

## Social Workers as Drug Workers

According to Googins (1984), social workers' negative attitudes towards drug abusers, their ignorance and misinformation about drugs, and their pessimism concerning therapeutic success have contributed to their avoidance of drug-related problems in clients. Also, perhaps the fact that, historically, addiction policy and practice have been dominated by the disease model, the "relatively uncritical acceptance" of this model has been seen to contribute to the reluctance of the profession to acknowledge addiction work as appropriate for social work intervention (Alaszewski & Harrison, 1992, p. 337). As a consequence, theory development regarding addiction within the social work field has not been impressive.

Since Googins' (1984) plea for overcoming the professional barriers that have prevented social workers from responding to drug abusing clients in the 1980s, recognition of the need for special training in addiction work has been voiced. (Griffin, 1991; King & Lorenson, 1989; Rhodes & Johnson, 1996).

While the ineffectiveness of the traditional forms of social casework or psychotherapy (largely based on the psychoanalytic approach) in addiction treatment has been recognized (Citron, 1978; King & Lorenson, 1989), treatment ideologies and models best suited for addiction work have been debated. For example, proponents of the disease model can be found in the works of King and Lorenson (1989) and Manoleas (1992), whereas opponents of the model have suggested alternatives such as the learning, the psychosocial, or the ecological models, with each emphasizing the relative importance of the environment or the interaction between the drug abuser and the environment as conducive to addiction (Barber, 1994, 1995a; 1995b; King & Lorenson, 1989; Roffman, 1992). Sweezy (1991), on the other hand, rejected the effectiveness of all models of treatment, and argued instead for legalization of drug use.

That diverse views are found in theoreticians' and practitioners' endorsement of addiction and treatment models is not surprising. Easthope's (1993) analysis of publications in *The International Journal of the Addictions*, a major academic journal in the drug field, has already demonstrated that there is little agreement in the perceived causes of drug use. Amid these debates, the ecological model for treatment appears to gain most support, as it is seen to embrace social work's dual emphasis on the person and the environment (Boehm, 1958). For example, Rhodes and Johnson (1996) see the ecological model, which seeks to understand transactions between the person and the environment, to offer a more robust model for describing the addictive process. This model is considered to give a more comprehensive view of human behaviour than the disease model.

While the ecological model is regarded as being applicable to addiction work in the social work field, there is, however, little development in terms of more specific theory building with regard to understanding addictive behaviour. Most debates so far have centred on the ideology of care (Burke & Clapp, 1997). Although there may be a link between the aetiology of a disorder and its treatment, this need not be so, since spurious correlation of events can occur between a presumed cause and an effective treatment of a disorder (Skog, 1992). Furthermore, the status of the ecological model as a generic perspective for social work has been fiercely attacked, as being too vague to be of any clinical use, by Wakefield (1996a, 1996b), who argued instead the need for domain-specific theories. Heeding his call for specialized knowledge would be most timely, if social work were to make a significant impact on addiction work. Magura (1994) listed the various contributions that social work can make. These include direct services to clients, evaluation and accountability of programmes, research on practice issues, and development of new treatment models.

Given that the social work profession in the North American context has had a slow start in addiction work, what is the situation in Hong Kong?

## Social Work and Drug Addiction in Hong Kong

Historically, Hong Kong has handled its drug problem mainly from a law enforcement point of view, by targeting drug trafficking back in the 1950s. Attempts to rehabilitate drug abusers came much later, and are still, by and large, medically oriented, leaving the approach of socially rehabilitating those afflicted undeveloped until the last decade when the number of drug-involved youth began to climb (Narcotics Division, 1997b). Furthermore, treatment for opiate abusers has been dominant because heroin still remains the predominant drug of abuse in Hong Kong. There are three major forms of treatment for heroin-addiction, namely, a) compulsory treatment for offenders in institutions operated by the Correctional Services Department; b) voluntary residential treatment provided by non-government agencies; and c) an out-patient voluntary methadone programme provided by the Department of Health in 21 methadone clinics, the largest treatment programme for heroin-addicted individuals.

While a gradual increase in young people under the age of 21 abusing psychotropic drugs has been observed since the 1980s (Narcotics Division, 1992), specialized services for this group have been extremely limited. For a long time, the only service available to these youngsters was the setting up of the PS33-Centre for Psychotropic Substance Abusers by the Hong Kong Christian Service in 1988 (Cheung, 1994). It was not until 1995, when the then Governor of Hong Kong called the first Summit Meeting on Drugs, that the Government initiated more action. In that year, the first Substance Abuse Clinic, under the auspices of the Hospital Authority, was set up to provide medical and psychiatric treatment of psychotropic drug abusers. Between that time and the present day a total of six clinics have been opened. In the same year, the Against Substance Abuse Scheme was implemented by the Social Welfare Department to provide therapeutic support to experimental and occasional users with no symptoms of physical dependence. This scheme was manned by teams of specially trained social workers. Recent developments include the subvention of several out-patient drug counselling centres and residential centres for young substance abusers run by NGOs (Narcotics Division, 2002a).

As seen from this brief survey on the development of drug treatment services in Hong Kong, the Government's direct commitment to these services appears to be heavily medically oriented, given the methadone programme to be the largest in terms of capacity, and given the more recent development of Substance Abuse Clinics also to be placed in the hands of medical personnel. Such a development is probably in line with how the problem of drug abuse is seen from the official viewpoint. The label "drug abuse" is used in official publications with the following definition:

> For the purpose of reporting, drug abuse is defined as the taking of drugs which harms or threatens to harm the physical, mental or social well-being of an individual, in doses above or for periods beyond those normally regarded as therapeutic. (Narcotics Division, 2002b, p. 2)

Springing from this medical orientation that drug abuse is regarded as a deviation from the therapeutic use of drugs, a drug abuser is likely to be seen as a victim of a biological or disease process which causes such a deviation of drug use, as such, the situation is to be contained by preventing withdrawal symptoms, or by reducing the demand for drugs through medical and psychiatric care. This medical stance further limits treatment goals to that of detoxification and abstinence, treating the drug abuser in isolation from the context of his/her total life. Under such circumstances, the deficiency of social work input into drug rehabilitation, until very recently, is understandable. Perhaps the beginning of a real break-through in facing the drug problem came in the 1995 First Summit Meeting on Drugs and the Second Summit Meeting held a year later. A series of action plans and proposals grew out of the two meetings (Narcotics Division, 1997c), after which the involvement of social workers in drug treatment and rehabilitation has become more apparent.

As of February 1997, with the release of the first ever published *Three-year Plan on Drug Treatment and Rehabilitation Services in Hong Kong (1997–1999)* (Narcotics Division, 1997d), the role of social work in drug rehabilitation has been affirmed. This document recommended the employment of "qualified professional social workers" (p. 21) to help strengthen the social rehabilitation and counselling services offered by non-government organizations to drug abusers. Apart from being employed in the Against Substance Abuse Scheme in the Social Welfare Department, social workers are now also in demand to provide social work support for substance abuse clinics run by the Hospital Authority, in order that "continuous social rehabilitation services are available for clients after medical treatment" (p. 34). As psychosocial support is now being seen as contributing to relapse prevention (p. 35), "professional social workers" are also seen as having an important role to play in helping former drug abusers (pp. 44–45).

Given such a belated recognition of the relevance of social work in drug rehabilitation, the role the profession plays in addiction work will be best positioned following a re-conceptualization of drug abuse from one of medical concern to that of a psychosocial and cognitive stance.

## The Social Work Role

Waldorf's (1983) study on heroin abusers who achieved remission on their own, and others who succeeded via treatment, found that the factors identified with cure represent the basic building blocks in human functioning, such as improvement in intimate relationships (e.g. marriage), changes in social networks, increased work opportunities, health concerns, and global factors like maturation and identity issues. If these factors are seen to relate to the aims and purposes of drug rehabilitation, then it rightfully belongs to the realm of social work, a profession that primarily aims to restore people's capacity for social functioning (Zastrow, 1999).

Evidence for the efficacy of social work involvement in addiction work is also available in recent research. In a follow-up study of former clients in a treatment centre run by a non-government organization (SARDA, 1998), findings indicated that compared with drop-outs, there is a substantial increase in the percentage of clients remaining drug free at case closure if they had completed the whole rehabilitation programme. Further, the protective factors against relapse are found to be those related to social functioning and social support, such as employment and support from family, friends, and also from formal support services such as job referral, medical, housing and welfare services. In a study of another non-government organization, Hong Kong Christian Service — PS33 clients (Lai, 1997), social workers have been rated as being more helpful, and the service they rendered as more satisfactory, than that of medical doctors. Some clients also came off drugs without medication but with the help of the services provided by social workers. In both agencies, these services included counselling and aftercare in the form of casework support, relapse prevention and referrals for financial, housing, and other welfare benefits, all of which are essential in the social rehabilitation of drug abusers.

The evolvement of an interdisciplinary model of addiction work would be a big challenge for the social work profession. Apart from direct services to clients and the development of new treatment models, evaluative research and the accountability of programmes are also important. Therefore the potential contribution of social work to drug rehabilitation must be recognized by the profession itself and the challenge taken up, with drug abuse seen in the totality of the context of a client's life.

## Re-conceptualization of Drug Abuse

Returning to Magura's (1994) plea for social work involvement in addiction work, a sound theoretical foundation would be needed to guide research and services. So far, Barber's (1995a) recent effort in developing a social work practice model for addiction seems to be the most systematic attempt. He based his social work practice model for addiction on Prochaska and DiClemente's (1983, 1992) trans-theoretical model of change which sees the treatment of addiction in five stages: a) pre-contemplation, when the person is resistant to change; b) contemplation, when the person thinks about the pros and cons of change; c) preparation to change, when intention to change is consolidated; d) action stage, when modification of behaviour takes place, and e) maintenance, when the changed behaviour is maintained. Having criticized Prochaska and DiClemente's model as being "a descriptive model of change, not a theory of addiction" (p. 46), Barber (1995a) went on to expand it beyond the individual level of contact with the drug user, appealing to the ecological perspective in addressing interventive efforts made at the microsystem, mesosystem, exosystem and macrosystem, since he saw Prochaska and DiClemente as having failed "to grasp the inescapably social context within which all individuals live and move and have their being" (p. 44), a perspective that is more akin to social work. Barber's (1995a) adaptation of the model, therefore, is primarily one of reaching towards an "understanding and modification of the social factors involved in client problems" (p. 40).

As Barber (1995a) so rightly points out, Prochaska and DiClemente's (1983, 1992) model is not a theory of addiction as it does not deal directly with the problem of drug abuse in the context of the drug user's life. To understand what impact social environment can have on an individual who takes drugs must necessitate seeing it from the vantage point of the individual concerned. This requires understanding how the person appraises the pleasure and displeasure he/she finds within the social context in which he/

she lives, his/her drug of choice being part of that context. The cognitive perspective on addiction, being domain-specific in its discourse and emphasizing the role of addictive beliefs for the drug abuser, therefore, serves this very purpose. It allows an insider's perspective on drug-taking behaviour by examining the meaning of a drug to its user as central in explaining addiction, i.e. stressing the drug abuser's active appraisal of events, without which any attempt to intervene into his/her problem could well be seen as irrelevant.

Adopting a cognitive perspective to addiction in this study is therefore compatible with the nature of social work practice. Not only is it compatible with the ecological perspective held so dearly by many social work practitioners, it also amends its anomaly as seen by Wakefield (1996a, 1996b), that "such a view could undermine the quality of professional education by leading to an emphasis on generic frameworks and a de-emphasis on substantive domain-specific theories" (p. 28).

By placing the role of belief as central in understanding human actions, the cognitive perspective on addiction also paves the way for an understanding of the role of religion in drug rehabilitation by examining the impact of acquiring religious belief (religious conversion) on the rehabilitation of chronic drug abusers.

# CHAPTER 4

# Religion in Everyday Life

In the social science literature, it is generally accepted that the concept of religion must be understood as multidimensional (Schumaker, 1992). Together with the related concept of spirituality, the two are often used both interchangeably (Canda, 1988, 1989) and separately (Prest & Keller, 1993).

## Defining Religion

One of the first social work writers to define religion was Spencer (1956), who regarded a religious person as one who believes in "the affirmative nature of the Universe and man's duty to do something in addition to advancing his own ends; a belief which furnishes some degree of comfort and strength to the individual" (p. 19). Later, Faver (1986), in her discussion on religion and social work research, adopted James Fowler's (1981) concept of faith as the essence of religion. Following Fowler (1981), Faver (1986) took *faith* to comprise three components: "the values around which our lives are centered; the images of power that we trust to sustain us, and the master stories that we rely on as explanations of the world and as fundamental truth" (p. 22). *Religion* then refers to various expressions of people's faith. Similarly, Joseph (1987), in discussing the religious and spiritual aspects of clinical practice in social work, also distinguished between faith and religion, with faith being regarded as "an internal system of beliefs and values which relates one to the transcendent or ultimate reality and orients one's life and behaviour accordingly" (p. 14), and religion being "the external expression of one's faith, comprising beliefs, ethical codes, and worship which unite one to a moral community" (p. 14).

While emphasizing the institutional and communal aspects in the expression of faith in religion, Joseph (1987) further distinguished *spirituality* from religion and referred to spirituality as:

> ... the underlying dimension of consciousness which strives for meaning, union with the universe, and with all things; it extends to the experience of the transcendent or a power beyond us. For believers, it includes one's relationship with and experience of God. (p. 14)

Spirituality is also seen by Canda (1988) as, the "human quest for personal meaning and mutually fulfilling relationships among people, the nonhuman environment, and, for some, God" (p. 243). Miller and Martin (1988) have further proposed a working definition for spirituality as "the acknowledgement of a transcendent being, power, or reality greater than ourselves" (p. 14). This may or may not involve organized religion. Prest and Keller (1993) perhaps summarized it best by describing spirituality as the "multifaceted relationship or connection between human and metaphysical systems" (p. 138).

The distinction between religion and spirituality is usually made with reference to an association with the institutional aspects of organized systems of beliefs and practices of religion, tying it to proselytizing, while spirituality refers to the inner feelings and experiences of a higher power (Bullis, 1996). They both refer to a higher power, whether it is conceptualized within formal religious systems or not, or whether such power be seen as God. Both concepts point to what Lewis (1984) referred to as a central belief in an "invisible, personal, and living Spirit" (p. 451). Religious and spiritual experiences are manifested or mediated through rituals and other forms of communication such as beliefs, myths, metaphors, texts, emotions and behaviour.

The present study adopts the concept of religion as it highlights the institutional and communal aspects of the practice of faith. These are embodied in the structure of the drug rehabilitation programme that the participants of the study have undertaken, but there is no dismissal of the more intra-individually oriented concept of spirituality. The central thesis is to regard the religious or spiritual perspective as giving order and meaning to life as it evolves from a relationship between the human and the divine (Lovinger, 1984). As Fromm (1950) put it, "I understand by religion any system of thought and action shared by a group which gives the individual a frame of orientation and an object of devotion" (p. 21).

Aside from seeing religion as providing order and meaning to life, this investigation has also opted to follow Flournoy's (1903) "Principle of the Exclusion of the Transcendent" in studying the impact of the religious dimension on people's lives, in that no theological position is taken regarding the existence of the transcendent. Rather, the active viewpoint of the believers provide data for study in terms of the beliefs arising from their religious faith and how these may affect the individual in his/her daily life (Paden, 1992). To social work practitioners, whether religion contributes to the mental health of the believers would be a relevant question to ask.

## Religion and Mental Health

Earlier reviews on the relationship between religion and mental health have been inconclusive. For example, while Argyle and Beit-Hallahmi (1975/ 1958) found religious orthodoxy was associated with better overall adjustment, as religious participation offered support, companionship, and a sense of identity to the participants, Dittes (1969) associated religion with personal inadequacy, intellectual inadequacy, hyper-suggestibility, maladaptive defences, and pathology and deficiency. Sanua (1969) did not find a relationship between religiousness and mental health. Stark (1971), on the other hand, claimed a negative relationship between psychopathology and religious commitment. Lea's review (1982) of two decades of research offered the following conclusions: a) religiosity is detrimental to adjustment for students, but positive to adjustment for adults, especially the elderly; b) religiosity is not related to either social deviancy or moral behaviour; c) "healthy" religion encourages social responsibility and relatedness to a being greater than oneself, however defined; and d) "unhealthy" religion involves a preoccupation with guilt-generating concerns (e.g. sin, evil), and rigidity in sexual and emotional functioning. However, Batson and Ventis (1982) found that the relationship between religion and mental health alters according to one's definition of mental health. A positive relationship appeared when it was defined in the traditional sense as an absence of psychological symptoms, but religion was associated with impaired psychological functioning when mental health was defined with reference to personal competence, self-actualization, and flexibility. Their review also explored religion in terms of intrinsic, extrinsic, and quest orientations, yielding a negative relationship to mental health for the extrinsic orientation. Payne, Bergin, Bielema and Jenkins (1992) also found extrinsic religion as an impediment in areas of psychological adjustment and social conduct whereas intrinsic religion is a generally positive force in these domains.

It was Allport and Ross (1967) who first distinguished between intrinsic (good) and extrinsic (bad) religiousness, or in William James' (1902) term the religion of *healthy-mindedness* versus the religion of the *sick soul*. While Bergin (1991) found no correlation between religion and mental illness, he considered such a null relationship could be due to a summation of both positive and negative correlations, depending on whether "good" or "bad" religiousness was measured. However, overall, he still saw the average effects of religion as generally positive, a view shared by L. B. Brown (1994) in seeing religions to offer preventive and therapeutic resources, most obviously among the poor, homeless, bereaved, and for those who are physically or mentally ill.

The lack of consensus regarding the impact of religion on mental health has led researchers to realize that religion cannot be seen as a homogenous, unidimensional construct. More recent studies using refined measures are yielding positive relationships between religion and mental health (Koenig, 1998; Schumaker, 1992). For example, religious involvement is found to relate to reduced anxiety and depression (Karp, 1996; Koenig, Ford, George, Balzer & Meador, 1993; Koenig, Hays, George & Blaser, 1997). Koenig, McCullough and Larson's (2001) review on religion and health indicated that religion is positively correlated with thirteen mental health outcomes, such as better well-being, hope and optimism, purpose in life, greater marital stability, less anxiety, fewer suicides, less delinquency and crime, and less alcohol and drug abuse.

Perhaps, as described by Spilka and Werme (1971), religion serves many functions. It can be seen as a means of expressing emotional disturbance, as a haven from stress, as a source of stress, as a means of social acceptance and conformity, or as a means of growth and fulfilment. Specific to drug use, the situation is less controversial.

## Religion and Drug Use

Since the 1970s, a body of literature has emerged focusing on the relationship between religiousness and drug use (Gorsuch, 1995). Gorsuch and Butler's (1976) review first concluded that there was a negative association between religiousness and drug use. Subsequent research has indicated that this relationship holds over various demographic subgroups and regardless of how religion and drug use are measured, as in church attendance, religious salience, frequency of devotional behaviour like prayer or bible-reading as religious measures, and alcohol, marijuana, tobacco, and illicit drug use like heroin, cocaine, or amphetamine as drug use measures (Benson, 1992; Donahue, 1987; Spilka, Hood, & Gorsuch, 1985). However, while such a relationship is found to be highly persistent, it also tends to be rather modest (Benson, 1990; Brook, Whiteman, Gordon, & Brook 1984; Donahue, 1987; Hundleby, 1987) which some researchers attribute to relatively low rates of drug use (Dudley, Mutch & Cruise, 1987).

When religious variables are taken together with other social and psychological variables, religion is found to predict drug use better than some of these variables but not others. Generally, religion tends to predict better than personality variables, e.g., self-esteem, locus of control, and purpose in life, but not as well as forms of constraints such as parental standards, or environmental reinforcement such as peer use or tolerance of deviance (Benson, 1990; Benson, Wood, Johnson, Eklin, & Mills, 1983; Benson, Yeager, Wood, Guerra & Manno, 1986; Hadaway, Elifson & Petersen, 1984; Hundleby, 1987; Jessor and Jessor, 1977). Similarly, Clayton (1992) found that being nonreligious was consistently seen as a risk factor for substance abuse. Gorsuch's (1995) survey found all religious groups to have fewer alcohol abusers than were found within the nonreligious population. In addition, religious groups with more anti-alcohol norms had fewer abusers.

Religion's inhibiting effect on drug use has been explained by the social control function it serves, in that religious institutions maintain social order by discouraging deviance, and by instilling personal restraint through norms and values. Burkett and White (1974) showed that a particular set of religious beliefs, such as drug use being regarded as a sin, was negatively related to alcohol and marijuana use. Bahr and Hawks (1995) see bonding to religious organizations as providing people with conventional activities and an anti-drug use network. In particular, it offers the following deterrent effects on drug use: a) attachment to a church and its congregation which endorses non-drug use; b) involvement in religious activities means less time or opportunities for experimentation with drugs; c) religious commitment provides meaning to life, making drug use less attractive; and d) the anti-drug norms promulgated by the church reinforces personal beliefs against drug use.

How explicitly different religious groups express sanctions against drug use is also found to have varying inhibiting effects on drug use. Judaism is found to be most conservative, with Protestantism in between, and Catholicism as most liberal in tolerating drug use (Perkins, 1985). However, such effects can be modified as people become socialized to other value orientations that endorse drug use. Religion has the most inhibiting effect when there is also social consensus against drug use, and is least effective when it is but one dissenting voice amongst others that encourage drug use (Hadaway, Elifson, & Petersen, 1984; Nelsen & Rooney, 1982). However, in so far as religion promotes positive mental health, this may insulate a person from pressures to experiment with drugs through providing meaning in life, support in times of stress, a healthy friendship network and recreational activities.

While the relationship between religion and drug use seems to be well-established, Benson (1992) observed that most research concentrates on investigating the role of religion in preventing the onset of use, while little is known about the role of religion in the various stages of drug use, i.e., in preventing people moving from experimental use to regular use, or to addiction. He suggested that research on changes in drug use patterns as related to changes in religiousness would be particularly useful. Further, he saw concentration on the social control function of religion in preventing drug use as limiting. He pointed to the need to understand how religion promotes personal resources (pro-social values, social competence etc.) and social resources (social support, family harmony etc.) which then function to prevent drug use. Finally, he raised the question of the need to understand how spiritual growth and development can affect lifestyle and behavioural choices, drug use being one of them. In so far as religion is seen as effecting lifestyle changes, examining the role of religion in therapy would help to highlight how religion may bring about therapeutic changes in people seeking help.

## Religion and Therapy

Historically, social scientists' views of religion have not been friendly. Except for the early fathers like William James (1902) who spoke favourably of people's religious experiences, in the mental health arena, religion has been pathologized by Freud and Ellis, and ignored by Skinner. Freud dismissed religion as a "universal neurosis" which spared us "the task of forming a personal neurosis" (Freud, 1964 [1927], p. 77). When behaviourism became popular in the 1950s, Skinner (1953) considered religion as just another variable of social conditioning, as not much could be made out of religious beliefs since behaviourism did not account for the inner world of individuals in terms of their values and beliefs (Sperry, 1988).

In more recent years, Ellis (1980) regarded religion as a threat to mental health: "The elegant therapeutic solution to emotional problems is quite unreligious … The less religious they [clients] are, the more emotionally healthy they will tend to be" (p. 637).

Even within the religious community, intensive religious experiences may be considered as pathological, as noted by S. Grof (1985): "If a member of a typical congregation were to have a profound religious experience, its member would very likely send him or her to a psychiatrist for medical treatment" (p. 335).

While William James (1902) spoke positively of religious experience, he did not deal with the role of religion in therapy. It was Carl Jung (1972) who saw the development of the client's religious attitudes as central to therapy. To him, religion is "an attitude peculiar to a consciousness which has been altered by the experience of the numinous" (p. 6), numinous being a transformative experience that gives a person a new sense of orientation and purpose. Jung's foundation work later led to pastoral counselling (Wicks, Parsons & Capps, 1985).

That social scientists have been blind to the healing powers of religion is regrettable, if one were to take note that religion is healing. *Religio*, the Latin word which gives rise to the English word *religion*, means to bind together; the Latin word *salvatio* from which the English word *salvation* comes, means being made whole; or the Greek verb *sozein*, and its derivative, *soteria*, corresponding to the English words *save* and *salvation* all have the root meaning of being alive and well in every aspect of one's being (Harpur, 1994). That religion is healing is an idea not confined to the Christian faith, as Harpur (1994) reminds us. For example, for Sakyamuni Buddha, the realization of escape from illusion is considered as the ultimate salvation. In the Hebrew religion, God tells Moses, "for I the LORD am your healer" (Exodus, 15:26, Revised English Bible, 1989). In Christianity, stories about Jesus as healer run through the four Gospels. Jesus' first public act of healing is described in Mark 1:23, where Jesus healed a man possessed by an unclean spirit. Shamanic healing, of course, has been regarded as "the most ancient of humankind's religious, medical, and psychological disciplines" (Walsh, 1990, p. 3). The roots of healing are thus inherent in many religious systems.

Despite the initial dismissal of the healing powers offered by religious faiths, some practitioners have argued for the relevance of religion in psychotherapeutic work. G. A. Miller (1992) argued that the clients' concerns are often conveyed within the meaning they give to their lives and actions, and a religious framework can play a central role for some clients; further, both therapy work and religion are concerned with people's lives and the healing of human suffering. While therapists search continually for effective therapies (Bergin & Garfield, 2002), religious rituals and practices can also act as powerful mechanisms to invoke calm when used in times of stress. In the Christian tradition, the sacraments of reconciliation, the Eucharist and the Anointing also provide a means of healing. Indian yoga and Buddhist meditation exercises can be used for the control of stress and anxiety (Joseph, 1998).

The integration of religion in therapy, however, is not without difficulties. Clement and Warren (1973) first raised some of the problems involved, such as the lack of dialogue between the two disciplines, the use of different conceptual languages leading to communication difficulties between the two parties, mutual under-valuation, and the fact that even those showing an interest in integration may not be well-versed in both fields. There are viewpoints on both sides that argue for segregation as well. The Orthodox view as exemplified by Mowrer (1961) sees mental problems as guilt from sin, hence counselling should be provided by the church; the Atheistic view as typified by Ellis (1966) sees people as making logical mistakes, and no guilt is involved, therefore it is irrelevant whether God exists or not; Rogers' (1951) Neutralist view refrains from religious arguments; and Oden's (1966) Moderate view advises against therapists imposing their religious orientations onto clients. Each of these four views acknowledges a separation of religion from therapy. Further, Meadow (1986) even spoke explicitly of the dangers of including religion in therapy for fear that therapists may force their limited knowledge of religion onto their clients, as religious beliefs may colour one's views on mental health.

Meadow's (1986) concern is perhaps unwarranted as it has now been firmly established that values are constantly at play in therapy, and that clinicians all hold certain values and attempt to develop them in their clients (Bergin, 1980; Bergin, 1985; Bergin, 1991; London, 1986). The issue is one of how to use values to therapeutic advantage without violating the client's autonomy (Thompson, 1990), because when the therapist attempts to enhance a client's functioning, decisions have to be made as to what constitutes positive behaviour and life goals, and these are based frequently on implicit values held by both therapist and client. The more explicit the valuation process is and the more informed the client, the more effective the collaboration between therapist and client is. Richards (1989) found that Mormon clients seemed more trusting of counsellors who disclosed a belief in God. In so far as therapists will encounter clients with professed religious backgrounds, religion must play a role in the therapeutic process.

Therapy and religion meet when both have been seen to offer a cure of souls (McNeill, 1965; Szasz, 1978). Seward Hiltner, the founder of pastoral psychology, has been cited as saying that psychoanalysis and religion have in common an "accent on truth and honest self awareness" (Wallace, 1990, p. 200), thus highlighting a fundamental compatibility between therapy and religion. Others have noted the similarity between the concept of acceptance in therapy and the concept of God's grace (Mowrer, 1961; Tillich, 1963); still others see both the therapist and God as serving as a benevolent and accepting transference figure (Pattison, 1969). Bianchi (1989) elaborated on the comparability between religion and therapy in terms of the client-therapist encounter as follows: a) both the therapist and the minister act as soul shepherds to their clients; b) transference from client to therapist resembles an act of faith; c) the exploration of problems is a kind of confession, through confession, insight, and forgiveness, the client is healed; and d) communion is achieved between therapist and client, with both making sacrifices, the former in the form of dedicated listening, and the latter in the offering of vulnerabilities.

Based on Fowler's (1981) work on the development of faith, Bianchi (1989) also drew a parallel between spiritual growth and psychological maturing that ultimately focused on community life and involvement with the eco-system. In so far as religion and therapy offer guidance to human development, R. H. Cox's (1973) volume on religious systems and therapy is ample evidence for the collaboration of the two disciplines in the quest for answers to the problems of human existence. Bergin (1991) highlighted three major contributions to therapy arising from a religious perspective, in that religion offers a conception of human nature, a moral frame of reference, and a set of techniques that can be therapeutic, like the use of prayers which brings peace, or scripture study that offers group support. Taggart (1994), a clinical social worker, argued fervently for the relevance of spirituality in therapeutic practice on the grounds that we all make assumptions (have beliefs) about reality, and for some people these are cast in religious terms. Such beliefs provide a powerful hidden agenda that colour a person's life. Until we understand what someone believes, we cannot understand what that person thinks, feels, and does. Therefore, it is imperative that we should explore the client's religious beliefs, just as we would any other beliefs. By *religious beliefs*, Taggart refers to belief systems which impute "a definition of universal meaning to human life, usually, *but not always*, implying some sort of deity" (italics in the original, p. 33). Further, she sees religious belief systems, as well as all other belief systems, as serving two distinct purposes: defining what is real and what is good. In other words, from definitions of reality come moral awareness, giving direction and purpose to life.

In Klass' (1992) ten-year ethnographic study of a religious self-help group for parents who had lost a child, he mapped out the experiential and social dimensions of religion particularly in the area of generating solace in bereaved parents. The group was an effective aid in the resolution of parental grief by means such as sharing the grief experience through identification within the group, an identity that included an inner representation of the lost child who was remembered by ritualizing the memory in a yearly holiday candlelight memorial service. He urged the clergy to develop solace-supporting liturgy, and asked mental health professionals to re-examine their models of grief by noting the healing aspects within people's religious faith.

In working with religious clients, Lewis and Lewis' (1985) study found that religious clients were rated by therapists as requiring significantly fewer therapy sessions than their nonreligious counterparts, independent of whether the therapist was religious or not. Propst (1980) reported the superiority of religious over nonreligious imagery in treating mildly depressed religious clients. Gartner, Larson, and Allen's (1991) review on religion and mental health also indicated that participation in religious activities and religiously based psychotherapeutic interventions, tended to be followed by improvement in psychological functioning.

Thus, a religious perspective offers additional therapeutic techniques that arise out of religious practices such as prayer, and rituals that are already a part of the believer's daily routine, therefore tapping into "natural" resources available for healing instead of imposing the learning of whatever alien practices a therapist might deem necessary. Most recently, George, Larsons, Koenig and McCulloch (2000) summarized that the role of religion in healing included: a) health promotion, given that the body has spiritual significance apart from its material significance; b) enhancement of social support through social bonding outside of the family; and c) provision of a sense of coherence and meaning. But more importantly, as Bergin (1991) has pointed out, a religious perspective makes explicit the moral framework under which discourses, decisions and actions are to take place between therapist and client. So how far is the social work profession sensitive to the healing powers of religion?

## Religion and Social Work Practice

Historically, the concept of social welfare has its roots in religious charitable activity (Leiby, 1977; Marty, 1980). Yet the social work literature has ignored the impact of religion on practice until recent years. Marty (1980) gave several reasons for this shying away from religion within social work and other social sciences, the most influential of which would be the belief that the rational scientific approach to understanding the world is essential to social work, particularly in its earlier struggle to become scientific (Heineman, 1981; Imre, 1982). Since religion is regarded as the antithesis to science, it would be irrelevant to social work. Other reasons are that since religion is a value-laden enterprise, it may be incompatible with social work values such as client self-determination or non-judgementalism; or since religion is concerned with the spiritual, that this will lead to a neglect of basic human and social needs.

The dominance of positivistic science, and the assumption that natural science methods of research are the only methods appropriate for a true science (Brennan, 1982; Toulmin & Leary, 1985) would make religion a most unlikely candidate for research, as science traditionally favoured a strictly objective, value-free description of behaviour that ultimately excludes freedom of will, purpose, morality, value, and other subjective phenomena that are vital in religious practices.

By the 1970s, however, tension between the social sciences and religion began to ease as a result of the eroding of the positivistic view of science, with Kuhn (1962/1970), the historian and philosopher of science, being the first to draw social scientists' attention to the importance of contemporary *historicist* trends in the philosophy of science. This refers to the acknowledgment of non-empirical factors that shape scientific enterprise, including cultural and historical factors, values, worldviews, and language systems. Jones (1988) held the view that "… contemporary understandings of the nature of scientific knowing and methods, by their explicit incorporation of non-empirical influences in their understanding of science, open the possibility that religious beliefs and commitments may have a valid role in the scientific process" (p. 142). Such a swing within the behavioural sciences away from the dominant, objective behaviourist doctrine also resulted in what has been called the cognitive revolution (Matson, 1971), in that a new outlook, a new way of understanding the world emerged, including the full range of people's inner experiences as legitimate for research. The cognitive revolution altered the fundamental concepts within the human sciences to become less atomistic, less mechanistic, and more subjectivist, contextual, and humanistic. This paradigm shift, according to Sperry (1988), has integrated the physical with the mental, the objective with the subjective, fact with value, and positivistic thought with phenomenology, thus greatly enhancing the possibility for integration of the social sciences in the study of religion, since now they both acknowledge the importance of the inner world of the individual.

In the past two decades, attention to the relevance of religion in social work has been increasing. D. R. Cox (1983) found that a majority of religious immigrants preferred welfare workers of the same religious and ethnic background. In working with Puerto Ricans with mental disorders, Berthold (1989) raised the need to consider the two spiritist traditions among Puerto Ricans — Mesa Blanca and Santeria, which centre on a belief in reincarnation and on the worship of saints respectively, since about one-third of all adult Puerto Ricans psychiatric patients would consult spiritists rather than seek psychiatric treatment. In his work with rural populations, Meystedt (1984) acknowledged the prominent role religion played in treatment since religion is a dominant feature in rural life. Religious beliefs influence how one experiences the role of women, family, and the community, and the Church can also serve as a support system for its congregation. In devising a health care programme for the elderly, Wilson, (1992) discovered that it was most effective for the programme to be embedded in the black church when working with rural black elderly women in North Carolina.

In relation to specific issues such as women and sexuality, Rhodes (1987) traced an historical overview of the role of women in society, and found that religion has a powerful influence on behaviour relating to fertility and infertility, whereas Bullis and Harrigan (1992) examined several religious denominational policy statements on sexual issues, which necessitated attention to the religious and spiritual traditions of the clients in clinical practice.

In working with the elderly, Koenig, George, and Siegler (1988) found that religious coping behaviour was used by 45% of their sample of 100 older people in responding to stressful life changes. Abramowitz (1993) found prayer ritual to have a therapeutic value when included in a daily programme for mentally impaired elderly Jewish clients in Israel. In the incidence of death of an elderly parent, Scharlack and Fuller (1994) found religion to be one of the helpful coping resources for a group of adults, and this was particularly true for daughters rather than for sons.

In the area of interventive approaches, Breton (1989) found that liberation theology in Latin America was able to provide ideas for social group workers to engage the poor and the oppressed, whereas Prest and Keller (1993) integrated spirituality into family therapy by using myths and metaphors. Nakhaima (1994) found a family's church or religious community can become a healing resource but that its potential has been overlooked so far.

Religion is also seen to have the potential to shape the development of the social work profession, as religious traditions can have significant implications for the conduct of social work research and knowledge-building, by influencing the ways in which research questions are asked, what research methods to use, and how the findings are interpreted (Faver, 1986). Caplis (1983) urged the inclusion of theological and philosophical principles in social work theory, and Siporin (1986) considered that religious values help renew social work values which in turn could increase the effectiveness of the profession.

While the spiritual and religious dimension is implicated in micro-practice, the impact of religion on macro-practice has also been noted. Horsburgh (1988) provided an example of how the Christian faith has influenced the development of social welfare in Australia, relating religion to social policy. Netting, Thibault, and Ellor (1990) examined organized religion as a driving force within the welfare state and religious organization as human service providers, and discussed religious content for incorporation into courses in policy, organization, administration, and community practice. In social work education, educators have advocated the inclusion of religious content. Joseph's (1988) survey of 61 clinical social workers indicated that 46% considered it important to attend to religion in their practice, with 36% believing that a greater emphasis should be placed on religion in graduate education, but with only 16% rating religion as "very important" in their own education. Sheridan, Bullis, Adcock, Berlin, and Miller (1992), who studied 328 randomly selected clinicians including social workers, psychologists, and counsellors, found that although as a whole, they valued the religious and spiritual dimension in their own lives and also dealt with it in practice, 79% of them reported that religious and spiritual issues were not included in their training and education. Sheridan, Wilmer, and Atcheson's (1994) survey revealed 82.5% of their 280 full-time social work educators supported the inclusion of the topic of religion and spirituality in the social work curriculum, albeit primarily as an elective. Concerns were also raised with regard to how it should be taught. Canda (1989) suggested the use of a comparative approach to examine religion as a universal aspect of human culture, religious diversity, and the usefulness of religious beliefs and practices. He also pleaded inter-religious tolerance and appreciation and advocated fervently for the inclusion of the spiritual dimension into social work practice (Canda & Furman, 1999; Canda & Smith, 2001).

Religion then appears to be an aspect of culture that positively affects both individual and collective behaviour, and social work professionals now acknowledge such an impact. However, caution should also be raised regarding the negative influence of religion on behaviour. Wikler (1986) found that orthodox Jews tended to refrain from using mental health services because of the stigma the Jewish community attached to seeking treatment, as some associated the need for treatment with insanity. York (1987) studied families with critically ill infants in the neonatal intensive care unit, and found some families used a harmful form of religious denial — a belief in miracle, to deal with treatment decisions, thus withholding treatment from their infants. McShane (1993) investigated female survivors of satanic sexual abuse and presented a domination-legitimisation-resistance paradigm for understanding the issues involved. Earlier, Wheeler, Wood, and Hatch (1988) devised assessment and intervention guidelines for working with adolescents involved in Satanism.

But how does one begin to understand the impact of religion on human development? The phenomenon of religious conversion provides such a starting point.

## Christian Religious Conversion

### Conversion and the Meaning of Change

The study of religious conversion in the social sciences began with Stanley Hall. In 1881, he suggested that adolescence was the typical age for conversion. He regarded conversion as "a natural, normal, universal, and necessary process at the stage when life pivots over the autocentric to a heterocentric basis" (quoted in Beck, 1965, p. 47). By this Hall meant a redirection of life involving basic changes from egotism to altruism.

Edwin Starbuck (1915) and William James (1902) each contributed to the study of conversion by looking at its cause and experience respectively, with Starbuck seeing conversion as "a process of struggling away from sin rather than of striving toward righteousness" (p. 64), so that there would be sudden changes of character "from evil to goodness, from sinfulness to righteousness, and from indifference to spiritual insight and activity" (p. 21). William James (1902), on the other hand, focused on religious experience in his many case studies. Conversion is "to be converted, to be regenerated, to receive grace, to experience religion, to gain assurance ... and consciously right, superior, and happy in consequence of its firmer hold upon religious realities" (James, 1961, p. 157). Conversion thus becomes a *lived experience*, stressing the unification of the self. Though James (1902) emphasized the sudden crisis of conversion, he allowed for gradual change as well. He also pointed to the symbolic nature of conversion, in that for the convert, "holiness is woven into all his powers, principles, and practices. The sincere Christian is quite a new fabric, from the foundation to the topstone. He is a new man, a new creature" (1961, p. 185).

Other researchers focused on various aspects of conversion, such as conversion as a process with intellectual, moral, or social contents (Thouless, 1971), as an integration or reintegration process where a person is made whole (Grensted, 1930; Wieman, 1926), as religious awakening in the form of a radical or emotional change from irreligion to religion (Clark, 1929), or as achieving insight into one's true relation to God and other people (Oman, 1925). These earlier studies of conversion bring about three main concerns: the nature of the conversion process as sudden or gradual, as a turning point or change of direction, and as a new birth into a relationship with God, also conversion is seen as healthy, normal, and leading to maturity. However, religious conversion has also been seen as regressive and pathological.

Beginning with Freud (1959) who saw conversion as a reaction process resulting from Oedipal jealousy and anger, leading to a sudden turn to faith for fear of the omnipotence of God, others linked conversion to psychopathology. Boisen (1936) saw conversion as an alternative to schizophrenia or schizoid states in the resolution of personal problems arising from inner conflict and disharmony. Both involved severe emotional upheavals but conversion represented a successful outcome through a reorganization of oneself, resulting in a re-evaluation of values. Salzman (1954) allowed for a regressive or pathological kind of conversion resulting from pressing personal and interpersonal difficulties, apart from the progressive or maturational kind of conversion. Christensen (1963) gave an even more negative view of conversion, regarding it as an "acute hallucinatory episode occurring within the framework of religious belief ..." (p. 207). Sargent (1957), in correlating conversion with the process of thought-reform and brain-washing, noted the use of psychological conditioning through the generation of intense anxiety or strong emotions such as fear, anger, hate, and guilt to disorganize the person in order that new beliefs and action could be established.

In their review of the literature in the 1970s, Scroggs and Douglas (1977) concluded that conversions are crisis experiences and problem solving processes that involve emotional turmoil, which then leads to cognitive changes that help stabilize personality. Summarizing the position of contemporary theorists, they saw religious conversion, brainwashing, and therapy as fundamentally identical or similar processes, as all three activities involved confession and the use of structured organizational approaches such as suggestion, surrender, and the use of new vocabularies.

Despite the observation that conversion may be correlated with negative affects, especially in the pre-conversion stage, the effect of a conversion experience is more often seen as positive. Wieman (1926) and Grensted (1930) whose views were later echoed by Strunk (1962) equated religious conversion experience with that of actualization, a process that stabilized and motivated people. Later, Paloutzian (1981) specifically identified a higher measure of perceived purpose in life in converts, while Chamberlain and Zika (1992) found meaning in life to be strongly associated with psychological well-being. Meaning in life is found to mediate the relationship between religiosity and well-being, although religion is not the only source of meaning in life, but may become increasingly important with age (Reker & Guppy, 1988).

In Christian practices, conversion is highlighted by confession and repentance. Moore (1989) noted that in the evangelical movement conversion is emphasized as the goal of religious education which brings about "a radical change in one's life orientation, or a turning point leading to a new state of being and a new posture in the world" (p. 29). The key to the understanding of such a change is the self-integration of the conversion experience, with religion providing an ideological framework that offers an experiential knowledge of the deity from which feelings and emotions develop.

Studies of religious conversion therefore suggest that conversion is a dynamic, multifaceted process of change manifested through alteration in people's thoughts, feelings, and actions. Gillespie (1991) has provided a useful summary on conversion: "Conversion is a thorough-going turnaround, with a reorientation to the meaning of life." (p. 28) Conversion results in unity of direction and provides an answer to life's questions through the knowledge or discovery of a divine will. Changes in lifestyle and allegiance, and a state of subjective well-being usually follow conversion.

### Conversion and Identity

Religious conversion leads to new beliefs and values that may be understood through changes in self-identity. Kurewa (1980) described Christian conversion as follows:

> Conversion means turning to Christ and identifying with him; it also means community solidarity around Christ. In other words conversion to Christ means that a new convert takes his or her place with other members of the community around Jesus Christ. (p. 164)

Working within tradition, Mol (1976) saw conversion as a major source of stability and strength that provides roles and social mores that shape one's personal identity. Identity is then "anchored in a transcendent order symbolized in concepts and myths" (pp. 59–60). That identity is rooted within the context in which life is lived is a thesis shared by other theorists. In socio-psychological terms, identity is usually seen as the product of interaction with others in social settings. Erikson's (1950, 1968) psychosocial theory of identity formation remains the most influential in the study of identity. He sees identity as self-continuity and sees identification with something beyond oneself as acquiring the essential characteristics of the group to which one belongs. For Wheelis (1958), the group provides stability for the individual in a world of change. In interacting with others, identity is created out of living in congruity with one's values — values that are lived by one's own group. For Strauss (1959), identity is derived from judgement of others, hence from one's relationship with others. Through the judgements and appraisals of others, and by our own judging of ourselves, we mirror the identity expected of us. Religion then, may play a major role in establishing identity through its organized and structured institutionalized practices. A religious sect can provide models for social encounters, and a person's identity is validated by the group by going through various structured stages. These turning points in one's growth within an institutional structure help to establish identity.

The relationship between religion and identity is well summarized by Gillespie (1991) who sees all conversion experiences as identity-related, though not all identity experiences are religious conversions, for the following reasons: a) both conversion and identity experiences lead to important changes in one's life; b) in both cases, the resultant changed frame of reference has ethical implications for changes in behaviour; and c) both experiences involve changes in core values which affect personal attitudes and feelings.

Given that religious conversions are reported to have profound transformative powers on believers, an investigation of the impact of Christian conversion on chronic heroin-addicted persons offers valuable insights into drug rehabilitation. In taking the cognitive perspective of addiction, religious beliefs may be taken as one important dimension in influencing a person's behaviour, particularly in the post-conversion stage, in that religion serves as a cognitive mediator in understanding a person's behaviour. Such an understanding is achieved by using Kelly's Personal Construct Theory.

# CHAPTER 5

# Belief and Change: Personal Construct Theory

When a person drinks in a party because he thinks it will help him be funny and sociable, his drinking follows on from the belief he has about the effects of drinking. When a man shoots himself up with heroin, thinking it will give him tremendous sexual prowess to entertain women in bed, he has a belief about what heroin can do for him.

## Beliefs and Therapeutic Change

In everyday usage, the word *belief* can have different meanings. It can convey religious beliefs or moral attitudes such as, "I believe in God", "I believe in the freedom of speech", or it can mean the acceptance of someone's statement: "I believe he is telling the truth". It can express what we take to be true: "I believe Nancy is a social worker". It can also indicate predictions of future events: "I believe your mother-in-law is coming for dinner, so prepare for battle!" All these usages refer to a set of assumptions people make about what is taken to be true. Fraser and Gaskell (1990) regarded belief to mean "views of the world or of some socially significant aspect of the world", or just "'views' for short" (p. 3). Using premises for beliefs, Bateson (1972) offered a definition in greater detail:

> What is important is a body of habitual assumptions or premises implicit in the relationship between man and environment, and these premises may be true or false … premises which govern adaptation (or maladaptation) to the human and physical environment. In George Kelly's vocabulary, these are the rules by which an individual "construes" his experience. (p. 314)

By construal, Kelly (1955) meant our act of interpreting experiences from which we form rules to guide our future actions. The ability to create personal meanings in response to the world and to other people, but always with reference to a set of internal meanings, have been seen as the essential quality of living organisms, as Maturana and Varela (1980) put it: "Living as a process, is a process of cognition. This statement is true for all organisms with or without a nervous system" (p. 8).

In therapy, a fundamental question is how people's beliefs are seen to contribute to their problems. Most forms of therapy involve challenging, either directly or indirectly, the assumptions that people hold about their problems and about themselves, and these views often serve to maintain their painful conditions. This idea is not new. In his discussion of therapy in traditional Chinese medicine, Wu (1982) gave the following example:

> A woman accidentally swallowed worms at a meal and thus became ill. A famed doctor diagnosed the cause of her illness as being merely "suspicion", and prescribed emetic/laxative medicine. The doctor ordered the nurse to tell the woman that small worms were discovered in her vomit. When the patient heard this, she felt peace at heart and became well. (p. 294)

Here the woman was given a particular authoritative view about an event, as a consequence her behaviour changed. In European history, the view that "people are disturbed not by things, but by the view which they take of them" has been credited to the Phrygian stoic philosopher Epictetus [ca. A. D. 55–ca. 135] (Arnkoff and Glass, 1993, p. 658). In Western medicine, the placebo effect exemplifies the role of belief in healing, the most common example of such an effect, which is given by Benson and Stark (1996), is that the mere calling for a doctor's appointment can help relieve symptoms of an illness prior to medical intervention. Placebo effects refer to "the healing effects of the arousal of hope" (Frank, 1978, p. 33). Benson and Stark (1996) renamed it as "remembered wellness" which they see as "activated by the individual's unique set of beliefs". These "belief-engendered effects" (pp. 28–29) can be most effectively elicited when the following three conditions are present: a) belief and expectancy on the part of the patient; b) belief and expectancy on the part of the caregiver; and c) belief and expectancies generated by the relationship between the patient and the caregiver (p. 32). Belief alone has been found to cure nausea and vomiting in pregnancy, chest pain, headache, back and abdominal pain, impotence, weight loss etc., or to have a substantial impact on even a serious illness like cancer (Frank, 1978).

In therapy, Cushman (1993) acknowledged that mesmerism, made popular in the mid and late 19th Century, and marking the beginning of American therapy, regarded emotional illness as being caused by improper, negative thoughts, whereas mental health was a matter of thinking the right thoughts. In other words, an early form of cognitivism has been employed to explain disturbed behaviour. Mind cure in the form of hypnosis, telepathy, spiritual advice, instruction in religious texts, and group experiences were used as remedies, and moral exhortation was the centre of treatment strategy through the second half of the 19th Century (Fuller, 1982).

Despite the medicalization of mental problems that began slowly in the 19th Century, and which was later fuelled by Freud in the early 20th Century, and the rise of behaviourism in the post war years, the emphasis on cognition in therapy remained strong. Albert Ellis' formulation of rational-emotive therapy in the mid-1950s was seen to have brought about the beginning of modern cognitive therapy (Arnkoff and Glass, 1993). Cognitive therapy aims to change a client's *assumptive world*, and the therapeutic process always brings about some modification of values, expectations and images, in other words, a cognitive change (Frank, 1961).

Published in 1955, Kelly's (1955) Personal Construct Theory entails a form of therapy that helps clients to change their beliefs about themselves and others through developing and testing what he calls role constructions. This leads to an understanding of the religious rehabilitation of drug-addicted persons through studying changes in their role constructions upon religious conversion.

## Personal Construct Theory

Kelly's (1955) model of man is that of Man-the-Scientist, the actor, and active construer of events. Each one of us has many implicit beliefs about many things, such as smoking, sleeping, loving, and eating breakfast. All these beliefs, which are expressed in what Kelly called bipolar constructs, are ways of distinguishing similarities and differences, for example, seeing someone as kind rather than cruel, or an event as pleasant or painful. These constructs express our values, intentions and beliefs, and together form a personal construct system. This system provides networks of meaning through which we experience the world by anticipating the future based on past experiences.

Constructs need to evolve continually in order for us to adapt to environmental changes. This leads to Kelly's (1955) philosophical doctrine of *Constructive Alternativism*, which states: "We assume that all of our present interpretations of the universe are subject to revision or replacement" (p. 15). While objective reality does exist, people see it in different ways, and there is no such thing as an interpretation-free view of the world. Further, all our present perceptions are open to reinterpretations: "We take the stand that there are always some alternative constructions available to choose among in dealing with the world. No one needs to paint himself into a corner; no one needs to be completely hemmed in by circumstances; no one needs to be the victim of his biography" (Kelly, 1955, p. 15). Thus, we all attempt to control events by actively representing them within our inter- pretation, and our actions are fundamentally oriented towards the future and anticipatory in nature. Our actions change as we revise our ideas about events. Much like scientists revising their hypotheses in scientific inquiries, we revise our personal constructs based on experience.

### *Personal Construct*

A personal construct is an idea or thought that a person uses to construe or interpret, explain, or predict his or her experiences. It may be very general, like "life is getting more stressful", or very specific, such as "my teacher is very helpful". Constructs are also bipolar, as they represent our discrimina- tory view of events. The *emergent pole* of a construct denotes similarities between two events while the *implicit pole* indicates how they differ. A construct is thus our way of distinguishing similarities from differences when we affirm and negate something simultaneously. Therefore, when I say social work is a challenging subject, I am not saying it is challenging as distinct from being difficult. What I am saying is that for me it is a challenging subject and not a boring one. Constructs also have a range of convenience, in that they apply to only a particular set of events beyond which they will have little relevance. For example, the construct "hard working versus lazy" would be meaningful in describing a person's work attitude, but not his marital status.

While constructs need to evolve continually to adapt to environmental changes, they also provide us with a sense of continuity and predictability, since we predict the future by expecting the replication of past events. For example, when I return to my office after a brief holiday, I expect my colleagues to behave in much the same way as when I last saw them. Constructs therefore provide a bridge and continuity between the past, the present, and the future.

Constructs are formed into a system that gives each person a personal construct system composed of hierarchically linked sets of bipolar constructs. Through our personal construct system, we are able to predict and control our dealings with the world. If a construct leads to an accurate prediction of an event, we are likely to retain the construct. Conversely, if a prediction is disconfirmed, the construct is likely to be revised or discarded. The validity of a construct is tested in terms of its predictive efficiency. In Kelly's (1955) view, we go about our daily business guided by our constructs. The essence of life is seen as a form of process or movement. For Kelly (1955), the concept of motivation is therefore redundant and unnecessary.

The central tenets of Kelly's (1955) theory are stated in the form of a fundamental postulate and eleven corollaries.

*Fundamental postulate*: a person's processes are psychologically channelized by the ways in which he anticipates events. (p. 32)

The phrase "person's processes" suggests that human beings are dynamic and in motion, and the term "channelized" means behaviour is relatively stable across time and situations. The word "ways" is synonymous with *constructs*, while the pronoun "he" highlights the individuality of the construer. Like a scientist, we predict reality by the anticipation of events through the unique template of our constructs.

As details of the eleven postulates can be found in Kelly's (1955) original writing, only two of them, which are of immediate and direct relevance to the present study, will be elaborated on here. The others will be given as the need arises in subsequent discussions. The relevant two are the Commonality and Sociality corollaries.

*Commonality corollary*: to the extent that one person employs a construction of experience that is similar to that employed by another, his psychological processes are similar to those of the other person (p. 63).

Commonality is said to apply to a group of people when they use the same constructs within a similarly organized construct system to interpret events. For example, in a family, being thin might be interpreted as "healthy", "elegant" and "beautiful", implying that one should be selective in what one eats in order not to grow fat. People are not similar because they have experienced the same set of life events or because they behave similarly, but because the events have approximately the same psychological meaning for them.

*Sociality corollary*: to the extent that one person construes the construction processes of another, he may play a role in a social process involving the other person. (p. 66)

This corollary means that for two people to interact effectively they do not have to be similar in their construing but they do have some constructs that tell them how the other sees things, i.e. some degree of empathy. For example, a mother and a daughter will have different concerns, yet they can have constructs about each other that enable them to interact meaningfully. The mother might construe her daughter as interested in fun and games and will yield to her request to stay out late. The daughter in turn might construe her mother as concerned about her safety and so refrain from coming home late. To interact meaningfully with another requires that a person try to construe at least some part of the construct system held by the other. Harmonious social interaction requires one person to place himself or herself in the shoes of another, so that he or she is better able to understand and predict the other's behaviour.

Playing a role in relation to another person does not necessarily mean agreeing with the person, but as indicated by the commonality corollary, it is easier to understand the other person if we share similar views, though this is not essential for effective role-playing. Here Kelly's use of "role" is different from the use of the term in sociological role theory. For a sociologist, a role is a unit of the social structure which people occupy, e.g., teacher, president, mother. A role in Kelly's system is taken as "a psychological process based upon the role player's construction of aspects of the construction systems of those with whom he attempts to join in a social enterprise" (p. 97). The emphasis is on the role player. The person who is in a role relationship "plays out his part in the light of his understanding of the attitudes of his associates, even though his understanding may be minimal, fragmentary, or misguided" (p. 98). Role playing, for Kelly is thus social, because it requires the testing of constructs against the consequences of other people's reactions to the construer.

While Kelly's theory has been seen as highly intra-individual, the commonality and sociality corollaries can be regarded as providing a bridge between the individual and the wider social context through references to social relationships.

To recapitulate, in Kelly's view, while scientists formulate theoretical constructs to describe and explain events, we too behave like scientists in that we formulate personal constructs which are ideas or thoughts that people use to construe or interpret, explain or predict their experiences. Constructs also evolve continually to adapt to environmental changes. We can be free from the domination of our past by reconstruing reality. The principle of

Constructive Alternativism paves the way for movement and change, since a *redefinition* or *reconstruction* of events would lead to a different world-view and different actions.

Although the area to which Personal Construct Theory has been applied is extremely wide-ranging (Neimeyer, Baker, & Neimeyer, 1990; Neimeyer & Neimeyer, 2002), the applied field of interest most relevant here is that of therapy. In Kelly's terms, therapy is carried out through exploring personal construct systems, using the various techniques he devised along with Personal Construct Theory, such as the grid method and self-characterization. During the process of reconstruction, new beliefs will emerge, which in turn will lead to new behaviour in the client. The grid method is described below.

## *The Grid Method*

The repertory grid technique (Beail, 1985; Fransella & Bannister, 1977) or what was originally called the Role Construct Repertory Test is a method for exploring personal construct systems, that is, giving an understanding of a person's worldview as expressed in his/her own words. Basically this takes the form of a structured interview, yet it is a flexible scheme for examining a person's constructs about any aspect of a person's experience: people, relationships, situations, occupations, facets of oneself etc. For example, if we want to examine how someone sees his or her family members and other significant persons, friends and colleagues, we compile a role list of those people who serve as *elements*. The respondent is asked to give the names of people who correspond to these roles. Elements may also be supplied by the researcher to a client. Three elements are then selected either randomly or systematically, for example, my father, sister, boss, and the person is asked how two of these are seen as similar to each other and different from the third. The similarities and differences so elicited form the bipolar constructs, as a series of triadic comparisons of the elements are made. Finally the person is asked how each element is judged on each of the constructs, using either ranking or rating, to be presented in a grid form, as in Table 5-1.

After the completion of a grid, the rankings or ratings may be subjected to statistical analyses to give numerical measures of associations between constructs and elements. Computer programmes have been developed to aid in such analyses either on an individual or group basis (Slater, 1977). The programme called INGRID, devised by Slater (1972), which performs

**Table 5-1  An Example of a Repertory Grid**

| | Self | Mother | Father | Wife | Sibling | Boss | |
|---|---|---|---|---|---|---|---|
| Elements | | | | | | | |
| Construct (Emergent pole) | | | | | | | Construct (Implicit pole) |
| Helpful | 4* | 1 | 3 | 2 | 3 | 5 | Selfish |
| Insecure | 2 | 2 | 2 | 1 | 4 | 5 | Confident |
| Smart | 3 | 2 | 4 | 1 | 2 | 1 | Stupid |

\* Numbers represent hypothetical ratings on a 5-point scale for each element on each construct

a principal component analysis of an individual grid, is the most widely used. It gives a variety of measures in terms of inter-correlations between elements and elements, and between elements and constructs. Many grid indices have subsequently been developed to express these relationships (Beail, 1985; Button, 1985; Fransella & Bannister, 1977; Slater, 1976; Winter, 1992). One in particular, Norris and Makhlouf-Norris' (1976) self-identity system gives measurements of how a person sees himself or herself. It presents essentially subjective data in a standardized and quantitative manner that facilitates cross comparisons between individuals. This will serve as one index of change for the present study. Technical details of all the measurements derived from the grid analyses are given in Appendix I for readers interested in using these in their own work.

Briefly, Norris and Makhlouf-Norris (1976) see a self-identity system as comprising at least three important components: the *Actual Self*, the *Social Self*, and the *Ideal Self*. The inter-relationships amongst these three aspects of self with reference to significant others give four indices to describe the identity status of a person: a) *Self Convergence* means similarity between the Actual Self and the Ideal Self and there is no wish for change for the person; b) *Actual Self Isolation* means the Actual Self is isolated and has little basis for social interaction; c) *Self Alienation* occurs when the Actual Self and the Ideal Self are completely dissimilar; and d) *Social Alienation* is when the person is represented as unlike all other people. Using these measures, changes in self-identity as a result of therapy can be mapped, or these changes can be used to indicate the mental status of people with psychological disorders. For example, self alienation has been found in young offenders (Stanley, 1985), and in depressed, anxious, and obsessive clients (Norris & Makhlouf-Norris, 1976).

The grid method thus provides researchers with a variety of indices for measuring individual and group differences, or for measuring change from an insider's perspective, as a person sees and experiences events. Such a perspective provides an important counter-balance to the outsider's perspective that has been prevalent in social science research. Furthermore, apart from statistical analyses, the grid data are also amenable to qualitative analyses, for example, in reflecting changes in the construct labels as a function of the therapy process (Button, 1985), or in revealing personal changes in a case study approach (J. A. Smith, 1995).

Application of the grid method in many areas of practice and research has been well documented, for example, in measuring therapeutic changes in clinical and educational settings, along with the development of personal construct theory itself (Beail, 1985; Button, 1985; Fransella & Thomas, 1988; Neimeyer & Neimeyer, 1990, 2002; Winter, 1992). Mair and Crisp (1968) see the grid method as having the four essential requirements of a clinical tool: a) it can focus on an individual's particular problems; b) it assesses and explores an individual's psychological functioning; c) it focuses on both unique and common meanings for an individual's behaviour in terms of thoughts, feelings and actions; and d) it measures psychological changes. Bennett and Rigby (1991) see the value of the grid method in its oblique nature, in that unlike questionnaires where the questions asked may often be obvious to the respondents, the grid method is more global, making it difficult for them to fake results in order to give socially desirable responses. Houston and Adshead (1993) also noted that the grid can be tailored to highly individualized situations and does not constrain responses in the way a questionnaire might, hence it is much less open to distorted responding.

In Hong Kong, the use of the grid, so far, has been very limited. A few attempts have been made to use it to investigate perceptual experiences such as the perception of films, pornography, music, food, and language needs (Blowers & McCoy, 1986; Blowers, 1991; Blowers & Bacon-Shone, 1994; Kvan, 1989; and Lee & Ng, 1989). Even fewer attempts have been made to use the grid in clinical settings (Lau, 1994; McCoy & Kvan, 1979). Finally, Salili (1994) explored the concept of achievement in students. Hence, local use of the grid is still a largely unexplored area.

Apart from the grid, Kelly had also derived two other techniques from his theory in aid of therapy. These are the techniques of self-characterization and fixed-role therapy.

## Self-characterization

By inviting clients to say something about themselves, self-characterization serves as a personal assessment tool. Here, Kelly was making a point about how sceptical professionals could be of their clients, as if they were all deceiving in nature, hence the use of a lie scale or social desirability scale in questionnaires. Instead, Kelly said, "If you do not know what is wrong with a person, ask him; he may tell you." (1955, pp. 322–323). This very simple approach consists of requesting that clients write their own character sketch:

> I want you to write a character sketch of Harry Brown, just as if he were the principal character in a play. Write it as it might be written by a friend who knew him very *intimately* and very *sympathetically*, perhaps better than anyone ever really could know him. Be sure to write it in the third person. For example, start out by saying, "Harry Brown is ...". (Italics in the original, p. 323)

The purpose of writing the sketch is to encourage clients to assess themselves in a non-threatening manner. The aim is to discover how clients see their immediate world, and how they relate to it. The character so produced also serves as the first step towards implementing fixed-role therapy to be used when therapists require some impetus to move their clients forward.

## Fixed-role Therapy

Fixed-role therapy aims at personal exploration and experimentation. The client is first asked to write a self-characterization. Then the therapist draws up a fixed role sketch that is a portrait of a person who is psychologically at ninety degrees to the self-characterization. Afterwards this is checked with the client, who can make changes to the sketch until it is plausible, likable, and acceptable; the client is then asked to play this role, to act as if he/she were that person for about three weeks. This fixed role is a hypothetical one for the client to experiment with. During the process, the therapist and client discuss the interpretation of the fixed role, and consider the experiences the client is having. At the end of this role enactment, it is hoped that the client will have experienced behaviour from other people that he/she will not have been able to elicit as his/her usual self. Thus, clients are led into a self-examination that might lead to a reconstruing of themselves. This is the essence of personal construct therapy — a reconstruction of reality.

### Therapy and Change

The view that people have the capacity to make creative changes is central to Kelly's theory. Therapy for him is seen like the relationship between a research student and his/her supervisor. Both are engaged together in an exploration of the unknown. Clients and therapists are trying to make sense of what is happening within the therapeutic encounter, each having their own set of hypotheses about what is going on. The therapist and the client need to come to a shared agreement about what the purpose of the therapy is, and this involves a negotiation between the two parties, rather than the therapist being seen as having the "correct" view. Here Kelly's Sociality Corollary applies, as it points to the therapist construing the construction process of the client, gaining understanding and empathy from seeing things from the client's perspective, and helping the client to reconstruct his/her view of reality through exploring personal belief systems, thereby allowing new beliefs to emerge, which in turn lead to new behaviour in the client.

Based on the general idea of decision-making on the basis of past experience, Kelly's Personal Construct Theory provides the framework and the precision needed for understanding beliefs in terms of personal constructs, examining the way people construe experience in order to anticipate the future by using the grid method, which technically gives a map of a person's construct system. Further, his philosophical position of Constructive Alternativism points to the inevitability of change that is central to drug rehabilitation. Personal Construct Theory has been applied to the study of drug addiction.

## Personal Construct Theory and Drug Addiction

Kelly (1955) first made reference to the organization Alcoholics Anonymous as serving a valuable function to alcoholics by providing a new role for the individual, and suggested that Personal Construct Theory can contribute "to the psychological understanding of certain forms of alcoholism" (p. 527), but he did not specify how such an understanding could be achieved. Researchers have since studied drug users, using Personal Construct Theory and the grid method in a variety of ways, though the research literature relating the theory to drug addiction is still limited.

In exploring structural disorders in construing, heroin users were found to display less logical inconsistency in their construct relationships than ex-users, suggesting greater differentiation of construing in ex-users who were undergoing a process of cognitive reorganization in relation to their drug use (Goggins, 1988). Penrod, Epting, and Wadden (1981) found lower differentiation in construing to be associated with a repressive perceptual style that differentiated heroin and barbiturate users from amphetamine users.

For self-construal, Dawes (1985) and Viney, Westbrook, and Preston (1985) postulated that drug addiction would result in a person developing a construct subsystem of a drugged self which would carry more implications for action than the non-drugged self subsystem, though Goggins (1988) failed to confirm this. The understanding of drug users' construct system, however, may be complicated by their tendency to dissociate themselves from their symptoms. (Hoy, 1973, 1977; McCartney & O'Donnell, 1981), as high self convergence and self alienation have been found in drug addicted persons (Norris and Makhlouf-Norris, 1976; Stojnov, 1990). An increase in self-esteem, but no change in the construing of the Ideal Self, has been found by Bennett, Rigby, and Owers (1990) in residents at a Christian drug rehabilitation centre. These clients' identification with drug users decreased, and their identification with Christianity increased, as did similarity to their mother. Increased identification with others is considered to indicate the effectiveness of therapy since self-other differentiation is one of the most stable of grid measures in people who are not receiving therapy (Adams-Webber, 1989).

The above array of studies points to the potential contribution of Personal Construct Theory to the study of drug addiction. What then is the research implication of Personal Construct Theory for drug rehabilitation? Personal Construct Theory can offer a theoretical framework for investigating the changes that occur in the form of *cognitive reorganization* in relation to drug use in people undergoing drug rehabilitation. Based on the existing literature reviewed, the study of self-construals has produced fruitful information about drug-addicted persons. As Mair (1977) suggested, we all possess a *community of selves* that is a set of subsystems about ourselves. For people undergoing drug rehabilitation through religious conversion, changes in their perception of the various aspects of self and their relationship to other people may throw light on their rehabilitative experience.

Further, in Christian practices, conversion is highlighted by confession and repentance, according to the teachings of Jesus. In his discussion on the relationship between sin and psychotherapy, Kelly (1969a) interpreted confession and repentance in terms of his theory as *observing incidents* and *formulating constructions*. To him, the aim of therapy is to help the client "to reconstrue his role, experiment with it, and keep it open to continuing revision" (p. 187). The task is to develop and test role constructions. Here Kelly's Personal Construct Theory leads to an understanding of religious conversion through studying changes in role constructions, or transformation in identity. Further, the grid method can provide the structure and the precision needed, in the form of the repertory grid, for analysing beliefs and examining beliefs systematically in the form of the ways in which people construe experience in order to anticipate the future. This procedure provides both idiographic as well as nomothetic, quantifiable data. Kelly, a clinician at heart, made provision in his theory and methodology to allow for the quality of private experience to unfold, as the grid basically taps an insider's perspective of the world, yet grid data can also be treated quantitatively for group comparisons, giving flexibility in methodology that is in synchrony with postpositivist thinking. Before the specific design and methodology of the present study is discussed in the next chapter, research issues are highlighted for those interested in the philosophical background of research.

# CHAPTER 6

# Research Issues and Study Design

All research expresses some position about effective ways of developing knowledge, a *research paradigm* that states the basic worldview that guides the investigator in their choice of theory and methodology. Logical positivism as a foundation for knowledge has long dominated social sciences research. However, with the advent of the cognitive revolution since the 1970s, bringing about the realization that humans do behave differently from tables and chairs (which involve physical properties alone), alternative paradigms have become more acceptable in the scientific community, giving life to other research methods that pay due respect to people as social beings.

## Logical Positivism

Logical positivists are naïve realists who regard knowledge as objectively derived and verified through empirical sense data and mathematical techniques (Guba, 1990). Prediction, control and objectivity are seen as primary goals in scientific inquires. Theory and observation are seen as clearly differentiated, but bridged by Bridgman's (1927) doctrine of operationalism. Truth about an external reality can then be established through the formulations of laws (theories) that can explain and predict events, and the business of science is the justification of theories. These ontological and epistemological assumptions lead to the endorsement of predominantly quantitative methodologies, with an emphasis on the use of experimental designs and statistical methods in hypothesis testing as yielding knowledge in the form of causal explanations for the events observed (Anastas, 1999).

Logical positivism flourished in the first few decades of the twentieth century. However, strong opposition has emerged against the dominance of the positivistic paradigm, most vigorously in psychology in the 1970s, and later joined by social work, when in the early eighties, Heineman (1981) led the debate with the following remark: "in a misguided attempt to be scientific, social work has adopted an outmoded, overly restrictive paradigm of research" (p. 371).

Heineman (1981) and other critics (e.g., Harré & Secord, 1972; Lincoln & Guba, 2000) raised issues regarding the myth of the independence of theory from facts, the decontextualization of research caused by moving subjects into laboratories or experimental settings, thus rendering the exclusion of meaning and purpose from human behaviour and diminishing the generalizability of the study, the limits of operationalism and reductionism, the asymmetry of prediction and explanation, and the exclusion of discovery in inquiry. In their views, the complexity of real social life is reduced to highly irrelevant and naive units of behaviour, such as reaction time and eye blinks in the experimental situation. The experiment, according to them, is a study of strangers whose behaviours are highly ritualized.

The predominant use of statistical methods for hypothesis testing was criticized by Maltz (1994) who pointed out some of the problems such as researchers' ritualistic reliance on statistical significance even when the assumptions on which statistical significance tests are based (random sampling) are often not met, as in the case when convenience samples are used; or they mistakenly try to use a larger N to look for support for their theories, when Bakan (1968) had long argued convincingly that a sufficiently large number of observations would lead inevitably to the rejection of the null hypothesis. Further, practitioners may also have difficulty applying to their individual cases the results of research based on aggregate or grouped data. As Wood (1990) pointed out, clients are each "'a universe of one', who may or may not be like the clients who responded to the experimental intervention" (p. 377). Pieper (1985) also lamented researchers' blind adherence to statistical rules, which may yield results that are statistically significant but that may lack substantive significance.

Empirical methods also dehumanize clients in an attempt to control or manipulate. The use of control groups, where interventions may be withdrawn, or deception and subtle coercion may be used, may lead to the dehumanization of the very people social workers seek to help (Imre, 1982, 1984). Finally, if randomization is not possible in experiments, the positivist's claim of establishing causal relationships between events would be flawed.

Clarke and Byrne (1993) advanced the argument that causal explanation is irrelevant to understanding human behaviour. They argued first that, human acts, which are fully voluntary, involving intention, thought, reason and emotion, are different in nature from the actions of inanimate objects and mere bodily movements. The power of human intelligence is being discarded when the experimental design is used to control for human bias in inference and in observation. Secondly, as reasons, purposes and intentions are vital in human acts which are voluntary, there is a need to address motives, purposes and desires to understand the inner significance of the act to the actor. Also, beliefs are central to reasons, motives, and intentions. The actor's beliefs about the context of the act give the intention or reason embodied in the act. For example, the act of a man giving a rose to a woman acquires different meanings, depending on what the man believes the rose signifies — a declaration of love? Or a last farewell? In addition, beliefs and intention provide both the description and the explanation of human acts, since to describe an act fully is to discover the actor's intentions and beliefs within the act, to ask "Why was the act done?" To answer this question is to account for the act. So when we discover the inner significance of an act, we both discover what the act is and account for it at the same time. Therefore the description and the explanation of a human act cannot be separated. Finally, explaining, describing and interpreting are equivalent in the explanation of human acts. Here, Clarke and Byrne (1993) first make a distinction between explaining, and describing and interpreting as follows: In English, *to explain* allows three types of explanation — to make known in detail by giving a full description, to make intelligible by interpreting or paraphrasing, and to account for, such as citing causes. However, not all descriptions and interpretations are explanations in the sense that the *why* question is not answered. For example, explaining a government policy on housing may consist of giving a full description of what the policy entails in practical terms, but one may still ask the question "Why is there such a policy?" Explanations are then relative to the context of enquiry and the nature of that context will determine the nature of the explanation sought and offered. A scientific explanation in the positivistic sense asks for law-like generalizations and the uncovering of hidden causal mechanisms behind events. In terms of explaining human acts, this involves giving reasons to account for the act, because it shows why it was done; it also makes the act known in detail in giving a fuller description of it, and finally it makes the act intelligible because it sets out the meaning of what is done. Explanation through reasons, then, works by citing particular circumstances in terms of beliefs, reasons and intentions that are contextually connected to the act to be explained. It does not move away from the thing to be explained, as in the case of the citing of general laws or searching for some hidden causal mechanism. The contextualization of meaning thus makes the act of explaining equivalent to describing and interpreting. This brings us finally to Clarke and Byrne's (1993) conclusion, that scientific paradigms are inapplicable to the explanation of human acts, since the citing of beliefs, reasons, and intentions must be contextualized, knowledge of covering laws or causal mechanisms are not required for explaining them. Causes and reasons are different things. "A cause is an object, event or state of affairs; a reason is something expressed in a proposition or embodied in a belief" (Clarke & Byrne, 1993, p. 45).

To summarize the case against logical positivism, as a research paradigm for understanding human behaviour, for Clarke and Byrne (1993), explanations are relative to the context of inquiry; therefore, asking for law-like generalizations in the positivistic sense is inapplicable in explaining human actions. For Heineman (1981) and other critics, positivistic inquiry is fundamentally flawed because, apart from confining itself to the study of the observable, the data gatherers may influence that which they observe and the interpretation of the phenomena. Ample evidence suggests that researchers' expectations, client apprehension, and other *demand characteristics* of the research context may distort data (Orne, 1969; Rosenthal & Rosnow, 1969). Apart from relying on the study of artificial settings (in the case of experiments), positivistic-empiricists also find it difficult to operationalize abstract concepts encountered in social work, such as ego strength, self-esteem and homeostasis, and frequently have trouble documenting causal relationships among variables. True experimentation, including random assignments to experimental and control groups, and pretests and posttests, are rare in social work, either because a sufficient number of research subjects are not available or because the withholding of intervention from some clients would be unethical. Furthermore, some important research questions simply cannot be subjected to experimentation. For example, one cannot randomly assign children to abusive and non-abusive settings to investigate the effects of abuse. The positivistic paradigm is therefore restrictive in its research scope when applied to the study of human behaviour. However, in the face of such frontal attacks on positivism, there is no lack of defence for positivistic inquiry.

## In Defence of Positivistic Science

Admittedly, researchers are not unaware of the limitations of positivist research, but often they combat these by appealing to a more vigorous use of statistics and design methodology. For example, Cronbach (1975) looked for "higher order" interactions such as motivation, attitudes, and meanings that might arise from uncontrolled conditions that could bias observed effects (p. 124). To solve design problems, a control group may comprise clients on waiting lists, since ethical considerations preclude the use of controls. For statistical purposes, Salmon (1971) suggested that they could be evaluated by the criterion of statistical relevance, meaning a certain factor is statistically relevant to the occurrence of an event when it makes a difference to the probability of that occurrence, as statistical probability, however high, will not necessarily turn a prediction into an explanation. For example, if a man takes his wife's birth control pills, he will not become pregnant, is a highly probable, but a non-explanatory prediction. For nonparametric statistics, or their equivalents, Edgington (1966) suggested that the statistical test can provide evidence in relation to an argument, but not as the basis for generalization which should be made on non-statistical, rational grounds. Further, Cronbach (1975) advised that any generalization should be treated as a working hypothesis, and not a conclusion. Heeding the above cautions, positivistic inquiry still has its merits in that empirical measurement offers the opportunity to monitor and evaluate clinical practice systematically, or test practice-relevant hypotheses. It offers a possibility, though not a guarantee, of consistency, reliability, and replications that may be difficult to achieve with non-empirical inquiry (Fischer, 1993). Quantitative approaches can provide useful survey data. They can also assess the incidence, epidemiology and boundaries of problems under investigation, for example, a comparison of the incidence of social problems such as poverty or child abuse in sub-groups, or sets of factors can be selected for further consideration. Ultimately such research data may contribute to policy planning, the framing of legislation, the planning of services or monitoring the implementation of change (Fraser, Taylor, Jackson, & O'Jack, 1991), as much of social work practice takes place in organizational and institutional settings, accountability, particularly in terms of performance evaluations, have become a part of organizational life (Ruckdeschel & Balassone, 1994).

Therefore, while admitting to the limits of any research approach, the canons of empirical research can still be seen as providing useful guidelines to observe the world, rule out spurious, confounding, and alternative explanations for observed phenomena, and help provide the clearest possible answers about the best available way to help the clients and consumers of social work services.

In adopting Kelly's (1955) model of man-the-scientist as the theoretical thrust, the present study places the attempt to understand people as paramount. While acknowledging the many pitfalls of positivistic science, and the fact that many of its philosophical assumptions have been challenged, particularly those underlying the use of quantitative and statistical approaches, these challenges, however, do not deny the usefulness of such approaches, but rather challenge the idea that any useful research must conform to these methodological constraints. Some kinds of questions may be better answered by a certain methodology than others. As Terwee (1990) has pointed out, there is a difference between logical-positivistic philosophy as entailing an empirical-analytical worldview that claims reality cannot be understood in any other way but that of positivist inquiry, and that of the empirical-analytical method as one of the possible methods of research. The adoption of the positivist worldview is not necessary for scientific inquiry. Indeed, proponents of an empirical orientation described as postpositivism argue for many ways of knowing the world.

## Postpositivism

Postpositivism accommodates the criticisms against positivism and redresses its inadequacies, but maintains prediction and control as its aim (Guba, 1990; Lincoln & Guba, 2000). Postpositivists assume the position of critical realism in place of naive realism, admitting that while a real world exists, it is impossible to know it directly given human sensory imperfections, and the inevitable interpretation of an experience means assigning meaning to the experience from a particular viewpoint, so that only a modified and approximated objectivity can be achieved by subjecting the findings of an inquiry to the "critical tradition", that is, the existing scholarly tradition of the field, or the "critical community" of peer review, acknowledging that competing theories may exist concurrently.

Methodologically, meaning-making necessitates multiple constructions of reality, as people are inevitably differently situated, e.g., due to sex, socioeconomic class, or ethnicity. As no construction of reality reflects reality as it is, they all constitute acts of interpretation (Gergen, 1988). Interpretations are not just the result of a person's dialogue with the world, but also that of dialogues between people. This social construction of multiple realities entails critical multiplism (Cook, 1985), or a form of triangulation (Denzin, 1970), meaning the findings of an inquiry are based on as many sources of data as possible. As objectivity can never be obtained, reliance on many different sources reduces the likelihood that distorted interpretations will be made.

Furthermore, research is carried out in more natural settings to counteract the context-stripping of positivistic inquiry; the heavy reliance on quantitative, statistical and mathematical methods are balanced by the use of qualitative methods, such as ethnographic, phenomenological, or case study methods, to enhance depth and richness in understanding a phenomenon within context. The combined use of quantitative and qualitative methods, however, has been vigorously debated in the social sciences literature.

## The Paradigm Debate

Traditionally a gap is seen to exist between quantitative and qualitative research, each endorsing different philosophies and methodologies regarding the production of knowledge and the research process. Quantitative methods are employed in positivistic inquiries, and are said to yield objective measures using standardized instruments, resulting in data that is supposed to be reliable, generalizable, and population-oriented, giving an outsider's perspective of the phenomenon under investigation, and which can lead to the verification of theories through the hypothetical-deductive process. Qualitative research is seen to be subjective, giving an insider's perspective that is valid for a particular case but ungeneralizable. It is more process-oriented and suited to the discovery of ideas rather than theory building (Lincoln and Guba 1985; Patton, 1988).

In the heyday of positivistic thinking, quantitative research methodology was seen as "scientific" as it was seen to explain the world through a cause and effect scheme within which the social scientist could quantify phenomena in order to predict future events. As qualitative research does not attempt to manipulate the research setting, it can only be regarded as exploratory in order to pave the way for a proper scientific study. Given the fundamental differences in what counts as data, issues of validity, reliability, and causality in the two research paradigms, there are those who maintain that quantitative and qualitative methodology cannot be combined in the same research (Bednarz, 1985; Buchanan, 1992). Reamer (1993) has provided a lucid summary of the debate, drawing the conclusion that while the limitations of positivistic inquiry are acknowledged, the value of qualitative inquiry is also recognized, and "the most viable model of social work research must contain a number of key elements, including a variety of qualitative and quantitative methodologies and multiple data sources" (p. 144). Further, Tebes and Kraemer (1991) argued for the integration of qualitative approaches into quantitative designs, acknowledging that "quantitative knowing depends on qualitative knowing because scientific knowledge based on applications of the scientific method ultimately must conform to common-sense understanding" (p. 740). Others have taken a pragmatic view that it is possible to subscribe to the philosophy of one paradigm, yet also employ the methods of the other, because each method has its strengths that can be used to compensate for the limitations of the other. Still others consider that the issue is no longer about whether to use quantitative or qualitative methods, but rather about how they can be combined to produce more effective strategies because human behaviour is so complex a phenomenon that it requires the application of multiple methodologies in order to be understood properly. (Steckler, Mcleroy, Goodman, Bird, & McCormick, 1992). Perhaps the most convincing argument has been provided by those who argue that the epistemological gulf between quantitative and qualitative research is but a myth (Brannen, 1992; Hammersley, 1992; Datta, 1994). The breaking down of the epistemological gap between quantitative and qualitative research has led to vigorous discussions on the use of mixed methodology, whether it will lead to the integration of data sets which are consistent with each other, thus enhancing validity, or whether the two sets of data will be complementary to each other without the need for consistency (Brannen, 1992). However, Bryman (1992) suggested that researchers should not arbitrarily put their confidence in either set of data, but should treat inconsistent findings as suggestive of new lines of enquiry. For Brannen (1992), when discrepancies arise in the results from different methods, these contradictions ought to be dealt with in the interpretation of the data and in accounting for the linkages between methods, data and theory, while Tashakkori & Teddlie (1998, 2003) discussed strategies for combined approaches, declaring the paradigm war as over, and that a pragmatic view should be adopted, making use of "what works", accepting that there are many ways of knowing.

When the natural scientists use their own beliefs to construct a theoretical understanding about their subject matter, the concepts they use belong to the discipline they bring to bear on the things they study. However students of human behaviour must, if they are explaining human acts, uncover the beliefs of the people they are studying, for people's beliefs are the source for understanding and explaining their actions. This in turn means that the concepts the researchers use must not simply belong to their own discipline, but must reflect as well the concepts of the people they study. This is where Kelly's Personal Construct Theory is most relevant.

## Study Design

Placing Kelly's (1955) Personal Construct Theory against a postpositivist background, the study endorses critical multiplism, that there are many ways of knowing through the use of multiple sources of data. In this case, both quantitative and qualitative measures are used to investigate different aspects of the rehabilitative experience of heroin addicted persons.

## The Research Questions

This study begins by examining the psychological changes that occur in drug addicted persons who undergo the various stages of a religious drug rehabilitation programme in the form of religious conversion. To capture these changes, a series of questions is asked in relation to the research participants' religious conversion experience:

1. What is the participants' history of drug taking like?
2. How is the process of religious conversion to be understood?
3. What are the changes observed upon religious conversion?
4. What is the role of religion in drug rehabilitation as perceived by the participants?

## Research Design

### Venue

St. Stephen's Society (hereafter called the Society for short) runs a year long voluntary residential programme for chronic heroin addicted men. The programme has four stages, the first being non-residential.

   Stage 1. *The Prayer Meeting.* Active drug abusing persons come for prayer meetings held in town twice a week, for several weeks, during which Christian beliefs and practices are introduced with Jesus emphasized as a personal saviour. Prayer, confession, repentance, personal testimony, hymn singing and worship are the main activities. Those who are punctual and active in participation are selected to enter Stage Two.

Stage 2. *The New Boys Home*, far removed from the city, offers a residential stay from four to six months, with the first ten days being a period for detoxification without medication. A so-called "new" boy will be unconditionally attended to, in all daily routines, by helpers who are either former heroin-addicted persons or volunteers, some of whom are foreigners from other countries who have come with a mission to serve the needy. Prayers are offered to counteract withdrawal pains. After detoxification, the new boy will enter communal living together with other residents called "brothers". As brothers, they will learn to serve each other and other new boys. The daily routine includes spiritual studies, counselling, recreation, and work activities in running the Home. Residents are considered ready to be transferred to a half-way house located back in town when they show self-discipline and behave according to Jesus' teachings.

Stage 3. *Hang Fook Camp*. The brothers enter a half-way house situated in the city area for three to six months. They learn simple vocational skills in addition to regular bible study and worship meetings. The task of rebuilding family life is emphasized through regular home-leaves. Missionary training is offered to those considered suitable through joining the *Help Mobile Team* which is a three-month training programme also open to members of the public. The trainees learn to serve the needy in the streets of Hong Kong.

Stage 4. *Peer Leaders*. Recovered individuals may choose to return to their family, seek open employment, or stay with the Society, serving as volunteer helpers. Over the years, a core group of peer leaders has remained to serve in the Society.

### Participants

There are two samples. The first is a *cross-sectional* one and consists of 86 participants from the four stages of rehabilitation as follows: Group A = 26 (Stage 1), Group B = 20 (Stage 2), Group C = 19 (Stage 3), and Group D = 21 (Stage 4). For Group A, only active drug abusing persons from their second week of attending the prayer meetings were randomly selected by the leaders of the meeting and referred to the author. Group B participants were brothers who had been in the New Boys Home for at least one month, a time during which conversion was reported to occur most frequently. All members from the Help Mobile Team (operating from September 1996 to

December 1996) formed Group C. Almost all peer leaders (over 85% of those serving in the program) who could be released from active duty to attend interviews formed Group D. Participation in the study was entirely voluntary.

A second sample is a longitudinal one and consists of 11 out of the 26 participants from Group A. These 11 participants have been followed through from their Prayer Meeting Stage (Stage 1) and interviewed a second time when they reached Stage Two.

## *Measures*

The participants were interviewed individually. They were given three mental health measures to gauge psychological changes, an individual grid to reflect beliefs (constructs) regarding self and others, and a series of semi-structured questions that probed their addiction experience and their conversion process.

## Mental health measures

Three standardized self-report measures were given to each participant individually. For those who showed difficulty in reading the written materials, all the items were read to them by the author.

### *1) The Chinese Beck Depression Inventory (C-BDI).*

This is a commonly used 21-item self-report measure of the severity of depressive symptoms (Beck, Ward, Mendelson, Mock, & Erbaugh (1961). The Chinese BDI has been translated and has been reported to have acceptable reliability and validity (Chan & Tsoi, 1984; Shek, 1990).

### *2) The Chinese Hopelessness Scale (C-HOPE).*

This scale was first introduced by Beck, Weissman, Lester and Trexler (1974) to quantify the degree of pessimism in an individual. A Chinese translation has been done by Shek (1993) and found to have acceptable reliability and validity.

### *3) The Chinese Purpose in Life Questionnaire (C-PIL)*

This measure was designed to quantify existential meaning in life as perceived by an individual (Crumbaugh, 1968). The Chinese version has been translated, and the high reliability and validity of the Chinese PIL has been reported (Shek, 1986, 1988).

## Grid measures

The self-identification method (Kelly, 1955) was used to elicit twelve constructs from each participant, using twelve supplied elements. These were: Actual Self, Ideal Self, Social Self (other people's conception of the person), Drug Self (prior to joining the programme), Jesus, Helper (recovered persons now serving in the programme), Brother (fellow residents in the programme), Mother or surrogate, Father or surrogate, Sibling or surrogate, Spouse or Girl Friend, and a Religious Person. The grid was completed by using a 6-point scale for the rating of elements. The INGRID programme was used for data analysis (Slater, 1972). Norris and Makhlouf-Norris' (1976) convention of using distance between pairs of elements as an indicator for understanding the inter-relationships amongst elements was adopted. In particular, their four indices of self-identity, namely Self convergence, Actual self isolation, Self alienation, and Social alienation were also used.

## Semi-structured interview

To capture the participants' drug experience and their experience of being in the programme as they wished to tell them, guided open-ended questions were asked. Three areas were probed: the conversion experience, the relationship between conversion and drug rehabilitation, and their drug career. This part of the interview was tape-recorded with the consent of the participants.

## *Procedures*

A multi-method ethnographic approach was used. Three months before data collection, the author entered the research sites to identify informants and arrange contact with the participants. Data collection took seven months. Observations were made of the programme activities during each stage. The individual interviews with the participants began with each participant taking the three mental health scales. The grid was then administered, with the conversation flowing into the semi-structured interview. Each contact lasted three hours on average, with lunch or tea breaks in between. Some Group A participants, being still active drug users, were not able to concentrate for such lengthy periods, therefore, their interviews were an hour shorter. All interviews took place either at Hang Fook Camp or the New Boys Home.

For data analysis, both the mental health measures and the grid data are used for individual profiling and group comparisons to probe changes in mental health status and the perception of self and others as a function of undergoing the various stages of drug rehabilitation. The interview data is content analysed to obtain a description of the participants' conversion experience and their drug career.

As this study accepts multiple sources of data which are seen as complementary to each other, each source tapping information on different but related aspects of the participants' functioning, the group data can be regarded as providing templates for change, within which individual variations may be understood. Further, a negotiation of the outsider perspective (standardized scale measures) and the insider perspective (the grid data and the individual phenomenological reporting of experience) provides the most useful information on the participants' rehabilitative experience. The next chapter presents the findings of the study.

# CHAPTER 7

# Those Were the Days

Who are these people who called themselves "heroin coffins"? A description of the research participants' drug career path prepares the background for an understanding of their rehabilitative experience.

According to demographic data, no significant differences in terms of individual characteristics are found across the four groups of participants. As a homogenous group, their mean age is 38 years old. They have an average of six years of primary schooling, being the middle child in a larger than average household (the mean number of siblings is 4.7), given the average household size of 3.2 for Hong Kong at the time of study (Hong Kong Government, 1996). Most are single, a few are divorced or living with their girl friends. On average they have abused heroin for 18 years. Hence, their addiction to heroin is chronic. Further, 35% of them are repeaters of the programme, in that they have dropped out and re-entered the programme twice or three times in a few cases. The interview data on their history of drug use indicates that their drug career path may be roughly divided into three phases: a) initiation; b) becoming a regular user; and c) being a "heroin coffin" when the person has locked himself into a revolving door of arrest, detoxification, relapse, incarceration, release, and re-addiction.

## Initiation

Before coming into contact with drugs, 80% of the participants claim to have been involved in triad-related activities like gang fights and drug trafficking. Some also tampered with soft drugs while still at school. While the average age of first contact with drugs is 18 years, most participants got initiated into drug use soon after they dropped out of the school system around the age of fifteen. Table 7-1 gives in frequency of responses the reported reasons for first contact with drugs:

**Table 7-1  Reasons for First Contact with Drugs**

| Reasons | Total (N=86) | % | Group A (N=26) | Group B (N=20) | Group C (N=19) | Group D (N=21) |
|---|---|---|---|---|---|---|
| Fun | 57 | 66 | 18 | 14 | 16 | 9 |
| Curiosity | 47 | 55 | 15 | 12 | 12 | 8 |
| Identity | 13 | 15 | 2 | 2 | 3 | 6 |
| Boredom | 7 | 8 | 1 | 1 | 1 | 4 |
| Medicine | 6 | 7 | 4 | 0 | 1 | 1 |
| Trauma | 6 | 7 | 1 | 1 | 0 | 4 |

The first contact with drugs usually occurs in social situations such as hanging out with friends for fun, in the work place or in a gang in which a friend who is already on drugs offers the first smoke. The reason given for responding to the invitation is inevitably that of having fun in the company of peers. Curiosity about what it feels like to take drugs ranks second. Then some pinpointed the need to gain peer acceptance or identify with leaders in a gang: "似大哥", (like a big brother). Three were selling drugs before they actually used them. Interestingly, five were introduced to heroin in order to kill boredom while in prison or in a detention centre. A few claimed heroin helped them through some physical ailment such as toothache, or an emotional trauma, like being jilted by a girl friend, or suffering heavy gambling losses.

Beginning heroin use is therefore not a solitary activity, as the role of others already on drugs is crucial for introducing a novice into the drug culture (Becker, 1953). The fact that all novices reported their first use of heroin as an unpleasant experience that involved nausea and vomiting speaks to the intensely social aspect of the situation. After the initial unpleasantness which all were able to overcome, the typical description of the experience that follows is one of euphoria, known as "烏吓烏吓" (the letter and number following all the quotations identify the speaker and his stage of rehabilitation):

> 有種感覺飄飄然，好似麻醉咗你D神經咁，個腦差唔多空白，之後好似好 enjoy個感覺，感覺好得意。 (A23)
>
> A kind of flighty feeling, like having your senses drugged, your mind is almost

blank, after that there seems to be a very enjoyable feeling, a very interesting feeling.

開頭時間快過，即係好似無憂無慮，無煩惱，輕飄飄，用唔完之精力。 (A16)

At first time passes quickly, which is like there is no worry at all, no trouble, flighty, endless energy.

食咗你個心係空的，腦係空白，無野，個人兩邊盪下飄下，尤其是係當燈光打落離，個人輕飄飄，好high，無人煩倒我，理倒我。 (B15)

Having taken it your heart feels like empty, your mind blank, nothing there. You sway from side to side, especially when light shines on you, you feel light, very high, no one can trouble me, bother me.

High D，食左成日無野想，烏吓烏吓，人好似飄飄然，好似醉左。 (C10)

Feels high, having taken it there is no need to think all day long. Dreamy, flighty, as if drunk.

嘔之後好似唔使諗野，時間好快過，可能你烏吓烏吓又幾個鐘頭，同埋你覺得好輕鬆，你唔需要諗野，好似話你所有野都唔駛理，唔駛負責任，你係你自己世界裏面，想點樣諗野都得，諗好多野又得，唔諗都得。 (D21)

After having vomited, you don't have to think, time passes quickly, may be as you get dreamy, several hours would have been gone, and then you feel relaxed, you don't have to think, like you don't have to be bothered about anything, no need to bear responsibility, you are in your own world, think as you wish, you can think a lot, or not think at all.

From the transcriptions, it appears that the strong analgesic properties of heroin are able to relieve tension, giving the user a feeling of superb tranquillity, and a feeling of being trouble free and being master of one's fate rather than a victim. But the most frequent psychological effects are that of time passing quickly and a care-free state of bliss. Some of these effects in fact contribute to the continual use of heroin.

## Becoming a User

Uninterrupted use of heroin leads to physical dependence within weeks. Not all participants were able to identify when they found themselves addicted to heroin, because for most, taking heroin begins casually, though a few continue daily after the first dose. The reported time lag from the first dose to becoming dependent, that is with noticeable withdrawal symptoms, ranges from a month or two to three years, while heavy users take only a week to ten days. Usually the participants are not aware of their physical dependence until they find themselves in situations where they are cut off from supply, such as going on a long trip or being imprisoned. Such a low awareness also prompted some of them to say that they never thought they would become addicted. Table 7-2 gives the reported reasons for the continual use of heroin in frequency of responses.

**Table 7-2  Reasons for Continual Use of Drugs**

| Reasons | Total | % | Group A (N=26) | Group B (N=20) | Group C (N=19) | Group D (N=21) |
|---|---|---|---|---|---|---|
| Escape reality | 58 | 67 | 14 | 16 | 12 | 16 |
| Heroin high | 12 | 14 | 4 | 2 | 1 | 5 |
| Boredom | 11 | 13 | 3 | 4 | 1 | 3 |
| Identity | 11 | 13 | 2 | 3 | 1 | 5 |
| Sexual power | 10 | 12 | 4 | 1 | 2 | 3 |
| Energy | 7 | 8 | 1 | 2 | 2 | 2 |
| Catharsis | 5 | 6 | 3 | 1 | 1 | 0 |

As indicated in Table 7-2, the dominant reason for continuing drug use is that heroin is seen as helping the participants escape reality. The following extracts explain what this means:

好似麻醉自己，時間快過，有好多野唔敢面對，好煩。(A10)
Feel as if I am drugged, time passes quickly, there are a lot of things I would not dare face, very troubled.

麻醉自己，最直接係麻醉自己，好多人都係接受唔倒現實，諗住連記憶都唔使諗，唔想諗佢……醒咗覺得空虛。(B18)
Drugged myself, the most direct way is to drug myself, a lot of people cannot accept reality. Don't even have to think about memories, don't want to think about them … when I wake up I feel very empty.

你個腦諗咁多野好煩，可以個刻真係帶你離開D煩野，但其實都係好短暫，所以當你食咗過得一兩日，又煩啦，你始終都煩，又食，其實只係腦裏面個種感覺，令你暫時無咁多野諗。(C7)
It's very troublesome to have to think so much, for that moment it can remove you from all that trouble, but in fact it is very temporary, therefore, after you have taken it, a day or two later, there is trouble again, ultimately you are troubled, then you take it again, in fact it is only a feeling in your head, so that temporarily you don't have to think so much.

你唔想諗野，你食，你咩都唔使諗，遇倒壓力，遇倒問題，或者悶之時間，若果食，你唔使諗野，你未可以烏吓烏吓咁做人，發生咩事都唔知。(D8)

You don't want to think, you take it, you don't have to think of anything, on meeting stress, meeting problems, or perhaps when bored, if you take it, you don't have to think, then you can go through life dazed, whatever happens, you don't have to know.

Escaping reality apparently refers to heroin-intake helping its users face life problems, as it sends them into a state where they do not need to think or do anything. Time flies and disappears along with their problems. Such an experience, coupled with the subjective "high", gives them a very comfortable state of bliss and satisfaction, but the high feeling is not emphasized as the most important factor for continual use of heroin. By the time the participants came for help, almost all reported no high feeling. Instead, the main reason for heroin use by then was to prevent withdrawal symptoms that they found intolerable. However in the mid-stage of the participants' drug career (Table 7-2), apart from being an aid to escape reality, heroin is also seen to have other effects such as relief from boredom, the provision of an identity within a peer group, the enhancement of sexual power and physical energy, and the facilitation of emotional catharsis.

It should be noted that while almost all the participants began taking heroin in a social situation, usually in the company of friends, as they moved on in their drug careers, they inevitably ended up taking drugs alone. According to them, this was due to their gradually taking on a social identity to which they adhered the labels of "heroin coffin", or "dope fiend" (道友), and which isolated them from ordinary social interactions.

## The Social Identity of the Dope Fiend

After habituation to heroin, physical dependence sets in, and this is when compulsion begins. For participants, the first form of drug taking is that of smoking, then comes "chasing the dragon" (snorting from a tin foil), and finally injection. Towards the "rock-bottom" stage, which is just before the user is pushed by some crisis such as being caught by police, or pressure from family to come forward for treatment, poly-drug abuse is frequent (a combination of heroin with psychotropic drugs or methadone). In order to combat their increasing demand for drugs, many become incarcerated for petty crimes, possession of, or trafficking in, heroin.

## *Lifestyle*

Supporting a drug habit requires hard cash. Given the fact that the participants are either school drop-outs or have limited schooling, there is little opportunity for them to have legitimate, meaningful and gainful employment. Further, drug abuse makes it difficult for them to adhere to a regular work routine. A few participants explained their lack of motivation in seeking regular employment by saying that they felt it would be foolish to spend hard-earned money on dope; they preferred to engage in dubious activities which could bring them quick cash, like running extortion rackets or gambling dens, drug trafficking, burglary, or robbery. Most participants were involved in these crime-related activities. Asking for, or cheating money from family or friends is also frequent. The kind of so-called decent employment, which some of them have tried mostly for short periods, includes casual work in restaurants, bars, construction sites, factories, and delivery services. Less than a quarter claimed to have held some form of skilled employment such as being a driver or a hair dresser, or servicing air-conditioners. Some of the participants even claimed that they could control their drug habit and that they did not appear to be a typical dope fiend to others.

It is apparent that only very few active drug users manage to lead a stable and legitimate working life. Worse still, most of them have also been involved in arrests and convictions.

## *Incarceration*

After prolonged addiction, drug abusers become entrenched in a morbid pattern of wanting little but the next fix, and when they cannot afford it they steal, rob, or hustle, in their parlance, "行古惑", which means "any activity that utilizes guile or deceit to gain money" (Waldorf, 1973, p. 50), thus landing many of them in jail. A further consequence is isolation and alienation, because when everyone is trying to exploit everyone else, the result is that everybody becomes suspicious of, and guards against, each other. So while the introduction to drugs begins in a social situation, chronic drug abusers invariably become isolated at the end stage of their drug career. The grid data using Norris and Makhlouf-Norris' (1976) Self-identity System illustrates this sense of isolation and alienation, as shown in Table 7-3, giving in frequency of responses and percentages the four identity statuses.

According to Table 7-3, Group A participants, who are all active chronic heroin users, have the lowest percentage in Self Convergence, but the highest

**Table 7-3 The Self-identity System**

|  | Group A (N=26) | Group B (N=20) | Group C (N=19) | Group D (N=21) |
|---|---|---|---|---|
| Self Convergence | 6 | 12 | 16 | 20 |
|  | 23% | 60% | 84% | 95% |
| Actual Self Isolation | 12 | 5 | 0 | 0 |
|  | 46% | 25% | 0% | 0% |
| Self Alienation | 8 | 0 | 1 | 0 |
|  | 31% | 0% | 5% | 0% |
| Social Alienation | 6 | 3 | 0 | 0 |
|  | 23% | 15% | 0% | 0% |

percentages in Actual Self Isolation, Self Alienation, and Social Alienation. The last three scores, however, decline with progress in rehabilitation, whereas alternatively, an increase in Self Convergence is seen. This suggests that the participants move away from isolation and alienation and see themselves in an increasingly positive light as a function of drug rehabilitation. The initial low Self Convergence score, however, is contrary to overseas observations where active drug abusers have been found to dissociate themselves from their own negative stereotype of being a drug abuser, hence an indicator of poor motivation for change (Norris & Makhlouf-Norris, 1976; Stojnov, 1990). This initial low Self Convergence perhaps suggests high motivation for change for the participants at Stage One. In fact, before entering the Society's programme, most participants have tried to quit heroin on their own.

## Quitting Drugs

Most participants have been involved in numerous attempts to quit, but inevitably without success. These attempts may include a combination of forced drug withdrawal through imprisonment or admission to other forms of voluntary treatment centres in Hong Kong, including methadone centres. Locking oneself at home or going to Mainland China are also two very popular means. However relapse is the usual outcome, with the period of abstinence lasting no more than a week to ten days. They reported that release from prison brought on an almost immediate desire, and action, to return to drugs, as they were forced to quit heroin through imprisonment. Prior to their release from prison, they usually got involved in drug talk, about what the market would be like, and where to go for high quality heroin etc., so that most were already prepared to return to drugs upon being released from prison. Many of them also failed to complete other forms of voluntary drug treatment

It is of interest to note that a few participants remarked that if the first attempt at quitting proves too comfortable, particularly when medication is used to ease withdrawal symptoms, they then find it easy to go back to using heroin as they now know of an easy way to quit.

Of all the participants, only seven claimed that they had no desire to quit heroin prior to their contact with the Society. The motives cited for quitting, however, are circumstantial ones, e.g. pressure from family members, or financial difficulty, or that they might attend methadone clinics to give themselves some breathing space. Some might quit for a short time in order to allow their body to re-experience the "high", which is typically absent after habituation to heroin. A handful also mentioned that the quality of heroin has deteriorated in recent years, so that it does not produce the same euphoric effect as when they first started doing drugs.

## *Relapse*

Despite the fact that many of the participants have tried to quit, all failed repeatedly. Table 7-4 gives in frequency of responses the reasons for relapse.

It indicates that returning to old associates triggers craving. Old friends and acquaintances are usually quick to offer the abstainer a fix, either to

### Table 7-4  Reasons for Relapse

| Reasons | Total (N=86) | % | Group A (N=26) | Group B (N=20) | Group C (N=19) | Group D (N=21) |
|---|---|---|---|---|---|---|
| Return to old associates | 40 | 47% | 10 | 10 | 11 | 9 |
| Kill boredom | 18 | 21% | 8 | 4 | 4 | 2 |
| Bad moods | 18 | 21% | 7 | 6 | 3 | 2 |
| Psychological dependence | 18 | 21% | 4 | 5 | 5 | 4 |
| Troubled by problems | 14 | 16% | 5 | 4 | 3 | 2 |
| Low status in society | 11 | 13% | 3 | 5 | 1 | 2 |
| Fear of withdrawal | 4 | 5% | 2 | 1 | 1 | 0 |
| High feeling | 2 | 2% | 1 | 0 | 1 | 0 |

keep each other company or to demonstrate friendship, and most abstainers find it difficult to refuse, as their circle of friends is limited.

Killing boredom, along with emotional turmoil and the awareness of a psychological dependence on drugs are the next set of reasons given for relapse.

Since chronic heroin abusers usually have no regular employment, they maintain a rather irregular daily routine, such as sleeping through the day and waking in the late afternoon. Such an unstructured daily pattern leaves them with plenty of leisure time, and one of the problems they find is that they do not know how to deal with "leisure". Getting a fix, besides giving them euphoria, also helps pass the time, as the most characteristic feature the participants have described with reference to the euphoric state has been that of time passing quickly. The analgesic properties of heroin also help to remove tension and anxiety, thus it serves to counter bad moods brought on for a variety of reasons. The habitual use of heroin also creates psychological dependence, what the participants called "心癮". A Stage 2 participant explains what this means:

> 自己個種傾向，食過始終有個陰影響度……總之有人鎖住就咩，但出番離有
> 自由就傾向去食番……十個著咗九個為尋求個種刺激，心癮最難頂。（Q：
> 咩叫做心癮？）自己慾望，短暫時間之感覺舒服，刺激，一種感覺用錢可以
> 即時買番離。(B16)
>
> There is this tendency in me, having taken it there is always this shadowy reminder … It's better to be locked up, but once I get free there is this tendency to take it again … nine out of ten persons go after that kind of stimulation, psychological dependence is most difficult to bear. (What is psychological dependence?) My own desire, temporarily feeling comfortable, stimulated, a kind of feeling that money can buy instantly.

That heroin offers the user instant relief, is taken by some as a panacea when they are plagued by life problems, such as being fired, quarrelling with others, or being nagged at. Whatever bad moods they might have resulting from stress would be alleviated by a fix, giving them a temporary sense of relief. The uplifting of negative moods also brings relief to those who feel lost and purposeless, and who are not making it in society. As a Stage 1 participant puts it:

> 做人無乜目標，即係好似食咗又係咁，唔食又係咁，完全無目標。(A16)
>
> Life has not much of a purpose. That is, whether I take it (heroin) or not, it does not make any difference, absolutely no purpose at all.

Or a Stage 2 participant:

> 接受唔倒現實，唔咁心打回原形，已經有過，想搵返，覺得橫掂都係咁 (指
> 食白粉)，覺得要有番要好耐時間，甚至無可能。(B18)
>
> Can't accept reality, not contented to be back to where I first started. What I
> have had, I want to get it back. It doesn't matter one way or the other (meaning
> taking heroin), I feel that it will take a long time to get back what I want, may
> be it is not even possible.

It should be noted that the above reasons for relapse are largely psychological in nature. Those related to the chemical properties of the drug are largely underplayed, as only a few cited the fear of withdrawal or the need for the "high" as reasons for relapse. This indicates the relevance and importance of the interpretative aspect of the drug experience, as opposed to the medical concept of addiction that is based primarily on the impact of the chemical properties of the drug on the user.

## Identity of the Chronic Heroin Abuser

Given the importance of the psychological overlay of the drug experience, chronic drug use leads to changes in the lifestyles of the drug users, as evidenced by their life experiences chronicled above. Prolonged drug use so overwhelms the users that they must hustle on a continual basis to support their insatiable drug needs. With hustling come arrests, conviction, imprisonment, abstinence, release, and relapse, as drugs and the necessary activities to get them become the only focus for life, an end in itself.

The dope fiend becomes increasingly isolated, as each is alone in his effort to seek out drugs daily. In the business of stealing, selling and taking drugs, there is little honour left, with each person trying to use, or take advantage of, the other. They are also increasingly alienated from society as they are repeatedly defined as criminals. The exploitation of others also results in a sense of guilt or remorse in many of them, and repeated failure in trying to quit drugs results in the erosion of self-confidence, and a very poor self-image. Hence, towards the end stage of the drug career, most chronic abusers find themselves alone with their addiction, without family or friends. The only reason for their addiction at this point is that heroin is taken to prevent withdrawal symptoms, which they find intolerable. There is no more euphoric high, and nothing satisfies them. A Stage 1 participant has this to say:

以前玩就享受，而家就唔享受，而係比佢控制住自己，而家一定需要，係唔
食就辛苦。(A8)

I enjoyed it before, now I don't enjoy it, now I am being controlled by it, now
I must have it, if I don't take it, I suffer.

A Stage 2 participant describes his negative identity resulting from
other people's perception of him:

身不由己。你叫我地唔食，同正常人一齊溝通唔倒，我地覺得人唔接受我
地，一出食番，自己會失望同提唔起自信心，人地睇死你，自己試過太多次
失望過，無咗信心。(B17)

Can't help it. You ask me not to take it, can't communicate with other
normal people, we find other people don't accept us, we relapse immediately
on release, will get disappointed and lack self-confidence, other people think
you are hopeless, I have been disappointed many times, thus losing my self-
confidence.

A Stage 3 participant talks about the desperate situation regarding his
drug taking:

無曬感覺食到，打埋藥。最慘唔可以唔食，但又無得食。有係度，食唔倒，
無辦法食。加藥打，唔可以打肌肉，打根，我又無根，睇住係度，你話慘唔
慘？(C9)

There is no more feeling; I inject myself with other drugs too. The most tragic
thing is I can't do without it, but then there is none available. When it is
available, I can't take it. There is no way I can take it. When I combine it with
other drugs, I can't inject them through the muscles, I need to inject them
through the veins, but then I have no more veins to shoot up, I see it (heroin)
there; don't you think it is tragic?

A Stage 4 participant, on retrospect, gives a most dramatic description
of his end stage:

為頂癮，無 feeling，死又無膽，完全去麻醉自己，放棄咗自己，好似死人，
無思想，只係諗住食白粉，過埋今日，無明天……逃避好多野，係垃圾堆，
等於自己好似 D 垃圾，無晒感覺。(D9)

To fend off withdrawal symptoms, there is no feeling, I don't have the guts to
die, drugged myself completely, abandon myself, just like a dead person, no
thoughts, just thinking of the next fix, going through the day, no tomorrow …
escaping from a lot of things, (sleeping) in a rubbish dump, just like I am
rubbish, no feeling at all.

The following description from a Stage 1 participant sums up the process of addiction succinctly:

初初high feeling，再食頂癮，白粉吸引到咁上下，無乜feeling，後尾典癮係辛苦先需要之嘛……生活只專注係典癮，頂癮，賺錢食白粉，其他乜都唔理。(A16)

Initially it's the high feeling, then it's a matter of stopping withdrawal distress, the attraction of heroin then falls off, then not much feeling, at the end it is taken when withdrawal pains come … the whole lifestyle is geared towards suffering withdrawal pains, preventing withdrawal pains, getting money for heroin, nothing else matters.

It is worth noting that the description of the drug career path given by the present sample of chronic heroin abusers largely corroborates observations found elsewhere. For example, Chein, Gerard, Lee, & Rosenfeld's (1964) four stages of drug use (experimentation, occasional use, habitual use, and efforts to break the habit) are equally applicable to the present sample. The same is true of Waldorf's (1973) description of the drug career of his New York sample of heroin users, or Hanson, Beschner, Walters, and Bovell's (1985) study of untreated black ghetto heroin users in several American cities. Stewart's (1987) detailed description of her own and other heroin abusers' drug experience is a parallel version, that is very telling of the hassles involved in becoming addicted. There are of course minor differences such as the age of first contact with drugs or the method of first use, between the Hong Kong sample and the overseas samples. Chein et al.'s (1964) group was slightly younger (sixteen) when they first had contact with drugs, and they snorted heroin as opposed to smoking it, as in the present sample, or shooting it, as in Hanson et al.'s (1985) sample. The drift into a drug career, however, is remarkably similar: contact with the drug subculture, then curiosity and elevated social status as motivating forces, the heroin "high", then the hustling. Likewise, the effects of heroin, as gauged in the descriptions of the psychological states undergone by the abusers, are also very similar: the euphoria, the habituation, and the withdrawal pain. To give an example, Stewart (1987) gave the following description of her friend Jimmy's "heroin high" which is very similar to that of one Stage 1 participant (A16) that was reported earlier on:

… When I'm on it I feel totally relaxed and I feel nice. My problems all go away till I've got no gear again. It's like being sedated but still being able to do things easily. It's not a hassle. It's a dead nice buzz. (Stewart, 1987, p. 15)

Stewart (1987) called such a state "being on the nod" (a semi-waking stage induced by taking opiates (p. 14) which is very close in meaning to the term used by our participants, that of "烏吓烏吓", which is derived from the act of one's head nodding periodically as one becomes dazed by the drug. Medically, *nodding* refers to a "twilight state in between alertness and sleep, during which the individual is quiescent but arousable" (Thomason and Dilts, 1991, p. 108).

So when do drug abusers come forth to seek help? How did the participants come into contact with St. Stephen's Society? Is salvation possible?

# CHAPTER 8

# Born Again

St. Stephen's Society was formally registered as a charitable organization in 1981, but charity work had already begun in 1966 with the coming of the founder, Miss Jackie Pullinger (1980) to Hong Kong. The Society's charitable services are known through their outreach work to prisons and on the streets of Hong Kong. As the founder of the Society states:

> I was not aiming for addicts but looking for the poor in spirit and body. It so happened that most of those who knew they were wretched and poor also happened to be drug addicts — they were the ones who responded to Jesus. Helping them to get off drugs was the inevitable next step. (Pullinger, 1989, p. 33)

The emphasis here is first and foremost salvation and rebirth. Yet the concerns of the heroin abusers themselves can be quite a different matter in the beginning. The participants usually come forward for help when they meet with some form of crisis, for example, being caught for drug offences, or being pressurized by family members. What happens to them on entering the programme? How does religious conversion occur? The participants' narratives reveal interesting experiences for students of social sciences to grapple with.

## The Conversion Process

### *Believing in Jesus (Stage One)*

Most participants are introduced to the Society through either one of the following means: through former friends who have gone through the programme, referred by probation officers from the Social Welfare Department in Hong Kong, or through the Society's outreach work in methadone centres, prisons, or on the streets of Hong Kong.

At the Prayer Meeting, all new comers are asked to accept Jesus as their personal saviour and have their sins pardoned. What does it mean to them when they inevitably say "yes" to the question "Do you believe in Jesus?" Table 8-1 gives their reasons in frequency of responses. For Groups B, C, and D, the question was asked in retrospect.

**Table 8-1  Believing in Jesus at the Prayer Meeting Stage\***

| Meaning | Total (N=86) | % | Group A (N=26) | Group B (N=20) | Group C (N=19) | Group D (N=21) |
|---|---|---|---|---|---|---|
| Obtain help from Jesus | 23 | 35% | 6 | 5 | 6 | 6 |
| Hope, purpose | 19 | 22% | 16 | 2 | 0 | 1 |
| To get rid of drugs | 15 | 17% | 1 | 4 | 8 | 2 |
| Desire for change | 14 | 16% | 7 | 3 | 3 | 1 |
| An attempt to believe | 14 | 16% | 2 | 4 | 0 | 8 |
| Compliance | 14 | 16% | 2 | 5 | 4 | 3 |
| Use Jesus to solve court case | 11 | 13% | 0 | 4 | 3 | 4 |
| Unclear | 8 | 9% | 2 | 1 | 1 | 4 |

\* Each participant has given more than one answer.

Table 8-1 indicates that Jesus is seen as a source of help and hope, and provides a purpose for action together with a corresponding desire to kick the drug habit. Such a desire is echoed by the declaration of an intention to at least try believing in Jesus. Some profess more pragmatic views, such as treating their verbal commitment to believing in Jesus as simply a condition for attending the meetings, or as they plainly put it, to use Jesus to escape jail for drug offences. Six in Group A explicitly qualified their answer "yes" by saying they really did not believe in Jesus. Further, none in Group B and C admitted to being converted at the Prayer Meeting Stage. There were six in Group D, though, who considered themselves as having been converted prior to, or during, the Prayer Meeting Stage.

Different concerns are apparent across the groups. The expressed concerns for Group A centre mainly on seeing Jesus as a source of hope and providing a purpose for action. Then a desire for change is coupled with the belief that Jesus helps those who believe in Him. As noted earlier, seeing Jesus as offering help is emphasized in all groups, but Group A tends to de-emphasize the more practical issues of their drug habit and court involvement, whereas these issues are more explicit for the other three groups.

Therefore, it appears that conversion rarely takes place at the Prayer Meeting Stage. At best, there is an indication of a desire to believe and to change. The act of joining the Society's programme, though, signifies hope and the acceptance that help is available. When does conversion take place?

## *Time of Conversion*

The analysis of the conversion process is confined to Groups B, C, and D, a total of 60 participants. Conversion does not necessarily take place during their first admission to the Society. Out of these 60 participants, 43% are repeaters (B=10, C=11, D=5). The most frequent time for the participants to drop out of the programme is at Stage 2, ranging from one month to five months of residence. A few left before the end of a month's stay. Table 8-2 gives the reported time of conversion for the participants in frequency of responses.

### Table 8-2  Time of Conversion

| Time of Conversion | Total (N=60) | % | Group B (N=20) | Group C (N=19) | Group D (N=21) |
|---|---|---|---|---|---|
| No conversion | 1 | 2% | 1 | 0 | 0 |
| Another Christian Organization | 3 | 5% | 2 | 0 | 1 |
| Prayer Meeting stage | 6 | 10% | 0 | 0 | 6 |
| In Home 1–3 weeks | 13 | 22% | 4 | 2 | 7 |
| In Home 1–2 months | 22 | 37% | 8 | 10 | 4 |
| In Home >3 months | 4 | 7% | 1 | 2 | 1 |
| Second admission | 6 | 10% | 3 | 3 | 0 |
| Third admission | 5 | 8% | 1 | 2 | 2 |

For 11 out of the 26 repeaters, conversion occurred in subsequent admissions. However, when conversion does occur, it is predominantly experienced at Stage 2, even for repeaters. This accounts for 50 out of 60 participants. The only participant who still reports no conversion experience at the time of interview has been in the New Boys Home for eleven weeks. For all groups though, conversion is most frequent during the first and second month in the New Boys Home.

Out of the 26 repeaters, 14 claimed to have been converted during their first admission, but only two completed the rehabilitation programme on first admission, with the rest leaving within one to five months stay at the Home. Apparently conversion can still take place without the participants finishing the programme. For the other twelve, one claimed he was converted in another Christian organization for drug rehabilitation and the rest during subsequent admissions.

That conversion takes place most frequently in the New Boys Home can be seen to relate to the experiential basis for conversion.

### *Basis for Conversion*

When the participants are asked to account for why they come to believe in Jesus, they cited events and experiences that they had encountered mostly in the New Boys Home. Table 8-3 gives their reasons in frequency of responses.

**Table 8-3  Basis for Conversion**

| Basis for Conversion | Total (N=60) | % | Group B (N=20) | Group C (N=19) | Group D (N=21) |
|---|---|---|---|---|---|
| Jesus' love | 30 | 50% | 7 | 9 | 14 |
| Personal testimony | 28 | 47% | 10 | 8 | 10 |
| Unusual events (miracles) | 24 | 40% | 9 | 5 | 10 |
| Reading Bible | 13 | 22% | 4 | 7 | 2 |
| Physical well-being | 11 | 18% | 5 | 1 | 5 |
| Messages from God/Jesus | 8 | 13% | 4 | 2 | 2 |
| Changed self | 8 | 13% | 1 | 3 | 4 |

Except for two participants who were converted at the occurrence of one single critical event, all others cited multiple reasons to justify their belief in Jesus. One Stage 2 brother was led to believe in the power of Jesus after he was caught dangerously between sharp boulders while swimming one day during recreational time, but then came away unhurt. One Stage 4 participant became convinced of Jesus' intervention after he prayed for his son's safety. The boy underwent surgery and was healed. The occurrence of unusual events, or what the participants call miracles, is in fact the third most frequently cited reasons for conversion. Some typical examples would be prayers being answered, particularly regarding the outcome of court hearings, in that the participants were spared prison terms and recommended for probation or attendance of the Society's programme. These were seen as a very lenient way of paying for their offences. The healing of physical illness after prayers was also experienced in a small number of cases, for example, a Stage 3 participant reported the incident of his being cured of an infection contracted, he believed, while swimming. Physical well-being during the withdrawal stage (first ten days) in the Home is also a significant factor for conversion, in that of all 60 participants, 50 (B=18, C=13, D=19) recalled their experience of the first ten days as memorable. In particular, they reported less physical distress during drug withdrawal, or that the period of suffering was shortened when compared to other forms of quitting the drug. Ten participants regarded the fact that during this period they could fall asleep peacefully after being prayed for as one reason for believing in Jesus.

The most overwhelming phenomenon arising from the ten-day withdrawal period is in fact the experiencing of what the participants labelled as Jesus' love, which was the most frequently cited reason leading to conversion. This is the result of the round-the-clock continuous care and concern that is shown to the new boys. The rationale given is that the kind of non-stop care they receive is beyond any experience they have ever had. This form of care is so overpowering as it is seen as being humanly impossible if it were not inspired by Jesus' love. Hence, the total and unconditional care and concern given to the new boys is taken as an expression of Jesus' love through the actions of the brothers and helpers. Some descriptions of their experiences are:

耶穌之愛在兄弟姊妹當中，藉著佢地比倒我關心同愛。 (B7)
Jesus' love in the midst of brothers and sisters, through them I am cared for and loved.

感受倒佢地關心我，神比佢地關心我，感受倒神去使用佢地。 (C10)
Feel that they care for me, God let them care for me. I can feel that God makes use of them.

有咁多弟兄姊妹關心你，去服侍你，同埋覺得耶穌係佢地個度。 (D5)
So many brothers and sisters caring for you, to serve you, and feeling Jesus is within them.

Another equally significant justification for the belief in Jesus is the witnessing of successful role models in reformed individuals, many of whom have now become helpers in the Society. The fact that the participants are surrounded by people who have been rehabilitated, is taken as a significant evidential force for their belief in Jesus:

見耶穌改變ＸＸＸ，見倒佢行為，見證，信耶穌，如果唔見改變，我唔信。
(B14)

Seeing Jesus changing XXX, seeing his behaviour, his testimony, I believe in Jesus, if I had not seen him changed, I wouldn't have believed it.

見倒朋友信耶穌之後得救，見証倒比我睇佢真係會改變倒你。 (C6)
Having seen a friend being saved after believing in Jesus, this allows me to see that He can really change you.

睇倒人地之關心，同埋見倒人真係改變咗，同以前完全唔同，咁我先至信耶穌。 (D20)
Having seen other people's concern, and also seeing that people really have changed, so unlike what they were before, then I believe in Jesus.

For a number of participants, their own personal transformation is also a source of evidence for believing in Jesus, because in the past they have many failed attempts at quitting drugs. The fact that they can now change by following Jesus is taken as a form of miracle:

變倒我一半，都可以叫做神蹟。 (B20)
Having changed me half way is already a miracle.

我唔食係世界已經係好大見証。 (C11)
That I have stopped taking drugs is already one enormous piece of testimony.

聖經裏面講神蹟醫治，我確信我已經係神蹟裏面一部份。 (D1)
The Bible talks about miracle cure, I firmly believe that I am already part of a miracle.

The two remaining categories of the basis for conversion are the experience of having received messages from God/Jesus in the form of pictures, images, dreams, or words spoken by other people, and the reading of the Bible. Since Bible study forms a regular part of the daily routine in the Home, the participants have learned to accept the Bible as containing God's word. In some cases, God's word is also experienced as being conveyed through dreams, pictures and spontaneous utterances, their own or those of others, during worship sessions.

To summarize, the three major reasons for conversion are: a) the experiencing of the continuous care and concern by the participants during their withdrawal stage, or what they called Jesus' love, which also explains the finding that most conversions take place in the New Boys Home; b) the witnessing of successful transformation in others; and c) the experiencing of extraordinary events which are regarded by the participants as miracles.

Upon conversion, the meaning of believing in Jesus changes, from one expressing extrinsic motives such as seeing Jesus as a form of help or using Him to solve problems, to one that makes reference to the psychological interior of the individual, as seen in Table 8-4 which gives the meaning of conversion in frequency of responses.

### *Meaning of Conversion*

#### Table 8-4 Meaning of Conversion

| Meaning of Conversion | Total (N=60) | % | Group B (N=20) | Group C (N=19) | Group D (N=21) |
|---|---|---|---|---|---|
| Change (new life, hope) | 28 | 47% | 10 | 8 | 10 |
| Emotional security | 22 | 37% | 9 | 5 | 8 |
| Dependence on God/Jesus | 21 | 35% | 7 | 7 | 7 |
| Moral guide | 13 | 22% | 4 | 6 | 3 |
| Jesus satisfies and helps | 13 | 22% | 7 | 1 | 5 |
| Jesus as model | 10 | 17% | 5 | 4 | 1 |

Seeing conversion as bringing about change dominates the formulation of the meaning of conversion for the participants in all three stages. Such a change includes having a new life or a new direction, which also brings hope and peace to the individual, as expressed by the following participants:

> 耶穌鼓勵我做人面對每一樣問題都識得去面對，改變倒我，比我一個新生命，思想成熟，有盼望，有平安。 (B3)
> Jesus encourages me to face every problem, changes me, gives me a new life, mature thinking, there is hope, there is peace.

> 信耶穌係話改變倒人之心，其次方向，目標，改變咗你之睇法，改變咗你對人對事之心態。 (C7)
> Believing in Jesus means changing a person's heart, then the direction, purpose, changing the way you look at things, changing your attitude towards people and things.

> 我自己睇倒神係自己生命裏面之改變，對我之祝福。 (D19)
> I can see how God has changed me in my life, his blessings on me.

A second important concept in conversion is that of the healing done by Jesus, called the great doctor, and that the person who is healed obtains love, security, strength, confidence, peace and happiness, collectively labelled as emotional security:

要倚靠神的話語同祈禱，求神將我軟弱變成剛強，耶穌係世界上最好的醫生。 (B14)

Need to rely on God's words and prayers, ask God to turn me from weak to strong, Jesus is the world's best doctor.

信咗耶穌之後，以前的野釋放咗，我唔知點解，話醫治好，乜都好。 (C11)

After believing in Jesus, everything in the past got relieved, don't know why, call it healing, or whatever.

耶穌係真理，生命，要人靈魂得救。 (D4)

Jesus is truth, life, saving people's souls.

As God/Jesus means bringing about change through healing, a total dependence on him is also emphasized to ensure correct behaviour:

要倚靠神；人性軟弱，無時無刻要祈禱，一離棄咗神，就見倒弟兄跌倒。 (B13)

Need to depend on God; human nature is weak, need to pray constantly, once God is abandoned, one sees the brothers falling.

識得咩野都求神，咩都去祈禱，等神決定，等神回答，等神去話比我聽點做呀。 (C3)

Learn to ask God for everything, pray for everything, let God decide, wait for God to reply, wait for God to tell me what to do.

要信靠耶穌，唔係靠我自己；每一樣野都在神之手。 (D15)

Need to depend on Jesus, not to depend on myself; everything is in God's hands.

The dependence on God/Jesus in turn means taking God/Jesus as a moral guide:

佢帶你行番一條正路，唔比你再沉淪。 (B8)

He leads you back to a correct path, will not let you be corrupt again.

神好似我地爸爸，佢每日指點我地，用聖經，佢自己說話，咩野可以做，咩野唔可以做。 (C6)

God is like our father, every day He guides us, using the Bible, His words, telling us what can be done, what cannot be done.

耶穌好真實帶住你，一路一路幫緊你，不斷同你溝通，比緊一的答案，教緊你點樣做。 (D6)

Jesus is really leading you all the way, communicating with you constantly, giving you answers, and telling you what to do.

Apart from serving as a moral guide, Jesus is also seen as helpful and able to fill a believer with satisfaction:

相信耶穌幫倒我，改變我地，改變以往自己的行為，思想，係神裏面好舒服。(B7)
I believe Jesus can help me, change me, change my past behaviour and thoughts, I feel very comfortable in God.

跟隨耶穌，感覺神係我身邊保護我。(C5)
Follow Jesus, feeling that God is beside me protecting me.

耶穌係個靈，有希望，有愛，需要佢每日滿足我。(D2)
Jesus is a spirit, with hope, with love. I need Him to fill me up daily.

Finally, Jesus is also a model to emulate:

耶穌係我地之榜樣，學耶穌去愛。(B4)
Jesus is our model, learn to love like Jesus.

學習過程都係想去關心，去搵愛心，付出愛心。(C10)
Through the learning process, I learn to care, search for a loving heart, giving out love.

一個真理之教導。(D1)
The teaching of truth.

Seen across groups, i.e., across different stages of rehabilitation, one obvious difference in the conceptualization of conversion appears to be a decreasing emphasis on Jesus as a moral guide and a model for learning. This seems to be in line with the different demands expected in the various stages of the rehabilitation process. As Group B and C participants are at the stages where all are expected to learn and perfect their ways with the help of Jesus, their emphasis on Jesus as help and model is high. By the time the converts have become helpers themselves, such a need diminishes (Group D). But for all three groups, believing in Jesus primarily means a new life, the gaining of emotional security, and a dependence on Jesus.

Upon conversion, believers also report religious experiences that they find meaningful. Table 8-5 gives the various types of experience reported in terms of frequency of responses.

### Religious Experience

The most frequently reported experience by the participants is the comfort

### Table 8-5  Types of Religious Experience

| Religious Experience | Total (N=60) | % | Group B (N=20) | Group C (N=19) | Group D (N=21) |
|---|---|---|---|---|---|
| Prayer (joy and comfort) | 25 | 42% | 11 | 8 | 6 |
| Worship (peace, release) | 13 | 22% | 4 | 7 | 2 |
| Pictures, words | 11 | 18% | 4 | 2 | 5 |
| Physical manifestations | 8 | 13% | 2 | 3 | 3 |

and joy they feel after praying. This is particularly so in the drug withdrawal stage where prayers offered by helpers would bring sleep to the person. As the participants begin to pray on their own, the calm and joy experienced earlier becomes a regular after-effect. Similar feelings of peace and relief also occur in worship sessions. Some feedback about the experience of prayer and worship sessions are given below:

祈禱後有舒適感覺，問題有人解決。(B2)
After praying there is a comfortable feeling, the problem will be solved by someone.

係敬拜時將唔開心D野，唔快樂D野，將憂愁D野完全放低，完全交比神，係好輕鬆，同埋係有任何問題都好，你向神禱告，神一定應許你。(C14)
During worship, you unburden all the sad things, unhappy things, all the worries completely onto God, it feels light and relaxed, also for whatever problem, you pray to God, God definitely will grant you your wish.

祈禱係一種溝通，你聽倒佢同你講野，係心理上去祈禱將你心裏D野講出離會舒服D。(D6)
Praying is a form of communication, you can hear Him (Jesus) talking to you, psychologically that is you speak out what is inside you, and then you will feel more comfortable.

For some individuals, messages from God can be received in the form of being touched by the Holy Spirit in two ways: first, pictures, images, or words may appear to a person during worship, or words spoken by another person are felt to fit in with one's situation and provide answers to one's query. Sometimes while a person is reading the Bible, a special passage might occur that is seen to give insight into the person's current predicament, as when a Stage 2 participant was struggling over whether he should leave the programme after three months in the Home, he found a message in the Bible which he phrased as: "賺倒全世界，賠咗條命，何必呢？" ("Having won the whole world over, you lose your life, what's the point?" The original verse is in St. Mark 8:36 — "What does anyone gain by winning the whole world at the cost of his life?")

The second form of communication from God, but a less common manifestation, is that of body movements experienced by the participants either during prayer or worship. These may be in the form of shivering, hand tremors, body shaking, or a feeling of dizziness, or could be as dramatic as dropping onto the floor, as this participant recalled during the time he was being prayed for in his withdrawal period:

> 突然間好似有 D 野打落我度，呼一聲我成個人坐咗係地下。而家知係聖靈充滿我。(D19)
>
> Suddenly something seemed to be hitting me, 'bang' and there I sat on the floor. Now I know this is the Holy Spirit filling me up.

In the participants' own words, to be born again is to have a new life and new hope. They acquire love, strength, security and confidence through being healed by Jesus on whom they depend for guidance. Religious experiences like praying, worship, and receiving messages from Jesus bring peace, comfort, and joy. Apart from the verbal accounts, findings from the mental health measures and the grid data give two other perspectives on the post conversion status of the participants.

# CHAPTER 9

# Post-conversion Bliss

To be born again brings joy and happiness and more. Post conversion changes in mental health are reflected through a comparative study of the four groups of participants in terms of their mental health measures, as shown in Table 9-1.

Reliability analyses show that the three instruments employed are reliable for the present sample, (C-BDI Cronbach's alpha = .91, C-HOPE

**Table 9-1 Differences between Groups on Measures of Depression, Hopelessness and Purpose in Life**

| Scales | Total | Group A | Group B | Group C | Group D | F Ratio | Duncan post hoc |
|--------|-------|---------|---------|---------|---------|---------|-----------------|
|        | (N=86) | (N=26) | (N=20) | (N=19) | (N=21) |         | P < .05 |
| C-BDI Score | 16.14 | 30.35 | 12.9 | 11.16 | 6.14 | 56.39 p < .0001 | A > B A > C A > D B > D C > D |
| C-Hope Score | 50.15 | 59.31 | 49.85 | 51.37 | 38.00 | 8.84 p < .0001 | A > B A > D B > D C > D |
| C-PIL Score | 96.42 | 62.92 | 105.25 | 102.05 | 124.38 | 59.19 p < .0001 | A < B A < C A < D B < D C < D |

= .87, C-PIL = .94). These figures compare favourably with those previously reported on the psychometric properties of these instruments (Shek, 1986, 1990, 1993). Regarding the differences between the four groups in terms of indicators of mental health, several one-way analyses of variance with post-hoc comparisons using the Duncan Multiple Range test were performed. Results show that the C-BDI scores and the C-HOPE scores decrease whereas the C-PIL scores increase across groups. Comparisons of group mean scores using the F test reveal significant differences between groups. Subsequent post hoc comparisons using the Duncan Multiple Range Test show significant reduction in depression and hopelessness and an increase in purpose in life as a function of the stages of rehabilitation, but no significant difference is found between Group B and Group C.

Adopting both overseas and local normative data on the C-BDI (Bennett and Rigby, 1991; Bumberry, Oliver, & McClure, 1978; Chan & Tsoi, 1984; Shek, 1991), Group A participants who are active drug abusers would be regarded as clinically diagnosable as suffering from severe depression, Groups B and C can be said to be mildly depressed, while Group D is free from depressive symptoms. Similarly for the C-HOPE, Group D emerges as the least pessimistic, with Group A participants seeing themselves as the most hopeless of all four groups, and Group B and Group C fall within the normative range. The C-PIL indicates Group D as having unusually high purpose in life, surpassing both local and overseas indices on the same scale, while Group B and Group C participants are again approaching normative measures, and Group A participants see themselves as significantly poorer in quality of life (Crumbaugh, 1968; Shek, 1986). In short, as rehabilitation progresses, there is a lifting of depression and hopelessness, with a corresponding increase in purpose in life. Also in all three measurements, Group D turned out to be in top form, being free from depression and its associated hopeless feelings, as well as perceiving themselves as having meaning and purpose in life. Compared with overseas observations, Paloutzian's (1981) finding of a higher measure of purpose in life in converts is also found here. Specific to drug abusers, Ridway's (1972) study also found that as his subjects moved through a religious rehabilitation programme, they came to reject the drug culture as they found new goals and purpose in life, having gained self-acceptance and the acceptance of others, and an accepting God. Bennett and Rigby's (1991) study on female drug misusers undergoing a year-long drug rehabilitation centre run on a Christian philosophy also found an increase in self-esteem and reduction in depression within the first three months of residence.

Post-conversion changes then, are clearly significantly positive in the once chronic heroin abusers. Further, the longer the converts stay within the Society and remain committed to its cause, the better their mental condition. The changes that occur in the participants, as reflected in their changing perception of their own identity and their relationship with other people, exemplify the characteristics found in conversion experience by many, which is summed up succinctly by Gillespie (1991), who remarked that "conversion is a thorough-going turn-around, with a reorientation to the meaning of life" (p. 28). The very high post-conversion PIL scores attest to such a re-orientation to a new found meaning in life.

Apart from the mental health measures, the grid data throw further light on the changes observed in the participants in terms of their perception of self and others, and their worldview in personal construct terms.

## Changes in Self Organization

Three grid measures are derived from the INGRID programme to reflect changes in how the participants see themselves in relation to others, in other words, how their constructs about self and other people change as a function of their rehabilitative experience. These measures are the cognitive complexity index, analysis of element distances, and analysis of constructs. The technical details of these grid measures are explained in Appendix I.

From the participants' personal accounts, it has been found that the most dominant effect of heroin on the participants is to spare them from the need to think as they drift into oblivion, riding on the "heroin high". Thus, it will be of interest to examine their thinking style, that is, whether they see the world in a very simple or complex manner. This can be expressed by looking at the cognitive complexity index (the higher the index, the less complex the person's thinking). The indices are 79%, 72%, 80% and 76% for Groups A, B, C, and D respectively. These are extremely high indices when compared to findings from other studies. As a comparison, Smith and Evans' (1980) study of male alcoholics and social drinkers gave an index of 53.74%, whereas Ashworth, Blackburn, and McPherson (1982) found an index of 43.9% for their alcoholic group. Therefore, although a strict comparison of these studies is complicated by variations in the grid procedures used, the present sample of participants can be considered to have very low cognitive complexity, meaning they see things in very simplistic terms, using very few constructs to describe many things.

As conversion is said to bring about an identity change in the convert, an analysis of the relationship between the participants' self elements with reference to other elements shed light on changes in how the participants see themselves and others as a function of their rehabilitative stages. Table 9-2 gives the relationship between the Actual Self and other elements, in particular, the Drug Self, which represents the participant when he was still actively taking drugs.

**Table 9-2  Distances and Standard Deviations between Actual Self and Other Elements**

|  | Group A N=26 | Group B N=20 | Group C N=19 | Group D N=21 | F Ratio Df=3,82 | Duncan post hoc |
|---|---|---|---|---|---|---|
| E2 Ideal Self | 1.08(.38) | 0.71(.31) | 0.46(.35) | 0.39(.25) | 21.81** | A>B>C,D |
| E3 Social Self | 0.65(.31) | 0.54(.29) | 0.39(.17) | 0.42(.21) | 4.85* | A>C,D |
| E4 Drug Self | 0.69(.43) | 1.51(.38) | 1.50(.31) | 1.59(.22) | 35.22** | A<B,C,D |
| E5 Jesus | 1.37(.27) | 0.94(.36) | 0.57(.40) | 0.54(.35) | 30.01** | A>B>C,D |
| E6 Helper | 1.18(.27) | 0.74(.21) | 0.49(.40) | 0.47(.22) | 32.24** | A>B>C,D |
| E7 Brother | 0.64(.31) | 0.59(.32) | 1.31(.35) | 1.40(.23) | 42.26** | A,B<C,D |
| E12 Religious Person | 1.26(.31) | 0.75(.25) | 0.49(.26) | 0.54(.20) | 43.6 ** | A>B>C,D |
| E8-E11 Relatives (MO, FA, SIB, SP) | 1.17(.25) | 0.77(.21) | 0.78(.24) | 0.87(.22) | 16.15** | A>B,C,D |

Note:  The values represent group means; those in parentheses are standard deviations.
   MO = mother; FA = father; SIB = sibling; SP = spouse.
   $* p < .005.$   $** p < .0001.$

Technically, adopting Norris and Makhlouf-Norris' (1976) convention of using an element distance close to zero to denote similarity, two for dissimilarity, and one as indifferent, Table 9-2 indicates that differences in element distances are most significant between Groups A and B when the participants' status changes from that of an active drug abuser to that of a Christian. For Group A, the Actual Self is seen as similar to Social Self, Drug Self and Brother, dissimilar to Jesus and Religious Person, and indifferent to Ideal Self, Helper and Relatives. For Group B, the Actual Self is seen as most dissimilar from the Drug Self. Seen across groups, this relationship remains unchanged through Groups C and D. Another significant change after conversion is the continued coming together of the Actual Self with all other elements, except for Brother, for Groups B, C, and D, that is, the Actual Self is seen as progressively closer to the Ideal

Self, Social Self, Jesus, Helper, and Religious Person and Relatives. For Brother, as Group B participants interpreted Brother as one of their own kind, i.e., converts in the New Boys Home, it is therefore seen as close to the Actual Self, whereas for Groups C and D, Brother signifies the drug-using persons whom they serve in the rehabilitation programme, hence Brother is seen as similar to the Drug Self.

The most salient changes in self organization, from the pre-conversion to the post-conversion status then are the dissociation of the Drug Self from the Actual Self after conversion, and its convergence with all other elements except the Drug Self and Brother. In other words, a very negative identity (Drug Self) is shed, and a positive one is adopted upon conversion, that of a Christian, a Jesus follower. These observations lend support to the literature on identity change consequent upon conversion discussed in Chapter 4. These changes can be further understood through an examination of the relationship between constructs and elements.

Using Landfield's (1971) classification scheme, 16 categories have been generated out of 408 constructs, out of which five categories are seen as the most salient, showing clear indications of being used differentially by the four groups of participants. The categories so obtained are *social interaction* (e.g., distant/loving each other), *self-sufficiency* (e.g., no confidence/with confidence), *morality* (e.g., lying/pious), *tenderness* (e.g., cruel/docile), and *involvement* (e.g., couldn't care less/helping others). Table 9-3 shows the construct categories in relation to four self elements. As the difference between Group C and Group D is minimal, they have been combined as one group. Non-parametric statistical analyses are used for comparisons of group means.

Table 9-3 indicates that compared across groups, the Actual Self and the Social Self have the lowest rating, i.e., are seen most negatively, in all categories for Group A. On the other hand, the Drug Self is seen uniformly as negative and the Ideal Self as positive. For Groups C and D, the Ideal Self nearly overlaps with Jesus, suggesting close identification between the two elements.

The significant changes that can be seen upon conversion occur most clearly in the case of the Actual Self and the Social Self. From the image of a person with low morality whether as seen by oneself or by others, who has little compassion or tender feelings, who is distant from other people, and lacking confidence, conversion brings about a moral person as seen both by oneself and by others, a person with tender feelings and concern for others, who is engaged with other people, as well as being confident and self-reliant.

**Table 9-3 Ratings of Elements by Constructs**

| | Group A Mean# | Mann-Whitney z A vs B | Group B Mean | Mann-Whitney z B vs C+D | Group C +D Mean | Mann-Whitney z A vs C+D |
|---|---|---|---|---|---|---|
| Actual Self | 2.08 | 6.78** | 4.49 | 4.81** | 5.37 | 9.21** |
| Social Interaction | 3.17 | 2.44* | 5.5 | 0.34 | 5.68 | 2.84** |
| Self Sufficiency | 1.64 | 1.78 | 3.43 | 1.76 | 5.11 | 4.18** |
| Morality | 1.85 | 4.36** | 4.6 | 3.08** | 5.5 | 5.18** |
| Tenderness | 2.29 | 3.33** | 4.5 | 2.56* | 5.36 | 3.74** |
| Involvement | 2.4 | 1.69 | 4.00 | 2.63** | 5.36 | 3.79** |
| Drug Self | 1.34 | 1.55 | 1.18 | 0.34 | 1.17 | 2.05* |
| Social Interaction | 1.83 | 2.06* | 1.13 | 0.09 | 1.11 | 2.20* |
| Self Sufficiency | 1.14 | 1.16 | 1.29 | 0.24 | 1.37 | 1.05 |
| Morality | 1.3 | 1.31 | 1.07 | 0.21 | 1.05 | 1.65 |
| Tenderness | 1.36 | 0.24 | 1.27 | 0.14 | 1.29 | 0.10 |
| Involvement | 1.4 | 1.60 | 1.00 | 0.47 | 1.08 | 2.24* |
| Social Self | 1.96 | 6.42** | 3.72 | 7.92** | 5.3 | 9.92** |
| Social Interaction | 2.33 | 1.79 | 3.88 | 1.89 | 5.22 | 3.02** |
| Self Sufficiency | 2.00 | 0.89 | 2.71 | 2.91** | 5.1 | 4.31** |
| Morality | 1.93 | 4.29** | 4.2 | 4.47** | 5.55 | 5.57** |
| Tenderness | 1.57 | 4.15** | 3.69 | 3.64** | 5.14 | 4.37** |
| Involvement | 2.3 | 1.63 | 3.6 | 3.14** | 5.36 | 3.74** |
| Ideal Self | 5.25 | 0.42 | 5.41 | 2.89** | 5.83 | 2.25* |
| Social Interaction | 3.83 | 2.66** | 5.88 | 0.09 | 5.89 | 2.80** |
| Self Sufficiency | 4.93 | 1.63 | 4.00 | 3.16** | 5.79 | 1.28 |
| Morality | 5.41 | 0.24 | 5.67 | 1.42 | 5.95 | 1.69 |
| Tenderness | 5.5 | 1.19 | 5.46 | 1.03 | 5.71 | 0.30 |
| Involvement | 5.8 | 0.18 | 5.6 | 0.20 | 5.8 | 0.00 |

Note: # This is a weighted mean against the total number of responses in each category
of constructs, as the number of responses differs for each of the categories.
A rating scale from one to six is used, with six denoting the most positive end of
the scale. The element of Jesus is rated as six in all cases.
* $p < .05$. ** $p < .01$.

Given the very impressive self transformation reported in the participants, how do they see the relationship between their Christian conversion and their drug rehabilitation experience?

## Conversion and Drug Rehabilitation

All participants have been asked what they see as the relationship between religious conversion and drug rehabilitation.

While most participants can elaborate on the relationship between believing in Jesus and kicking drugs, even those in Group A, for whom conversion has not yet taken place at the time of interview, a minority sees no relationship (A=7, B=2, C=2, D=0), whereas seven others (B=4, D=3) see conversion and drug rehabilitation as two different but related processes. Table 9-4 gives a breakdown of the frequency of responses for those who can formulate a relationship between conversion and drug rehabilitation in terms of what they see as important in helping them to kick their drug habit.

**Table 9-4  Conversion and Drug Rehabilitation**

| Conversion & Drug Rehabilitation | Total N=86 | % | Group A N=26 | Group B N=20 | Group C N=19 | Group D N=21 |
|---|---|---|---|---|---|---|
| Jesus' love & Comradeship | 33 | 38% | 9 | 10 | 7 | 7 |
| Emotional security | 33 | 38% | 12 | 5 | 7 | 9 |
| Internal changes | 17 | 20% | 2 | 4 | 4 | 7 |
| Moral guide | 8 | 9% | 6 | 2 | 0 | 0 |
| Jesus heals and satisfies | 5 | 6% | 0 | 0 | 2 | 3 |
| Unclear/don't know | 9 | 10% | 6 | 1 | 2 | 0 |
| Gospel as primary | 14 | 16% | 0 | 7 | 0 | 7 |

Except for nine people who cannot elaborate on the relationship between conversion and kicking the drug habit, all others see a multitude of relationships between the two. One of the most frequent emphases for the participants, with regard to what conversion does in helping them to kick their drug habit, is what they feel as love coming from Jesus, and the comradeship offered by the group of brothers and helpers, who bring them support and encouragement. Many also attribute the care and concern they receive from other people as given in the name of Jesus, with the exception of Group A. If one recalls that Jesus' love is the most frequently cited reason for conversion, and the experiencing of such love is primarily in the withdrawal stage, then the absence in Group A of this experience is logical, since the participants have not yet gone through drug withdrawal.

It is of equal significance that conversion is seen to provide confidence and strength, as well as direction and hope, which are collectively grouped under the label "emotional security" for brevity's sake, and which are all ego-enhancing qualities lacking in drug abusers. Next, conversion leads to changes occurring from within, which include the abandonment of a psychological dependence on drugs and changes in outlook on life and ways of thinking. Again, this emphasis on change is consistent with seeing conversion as bringing about change. Similarly, the provision of moral guidelines for behaviour here is consonant with seeing the meaning of conversion in the same light (Table 8-4). It appears that the characteristics of conversion are the same as helpful strategies for getting rid of the drug habit: the change, the giving of hope, new direction, love, care and concern, as well as the provision of new rules for behaviour. The healing aspect and the satisfaction derived from conversion are interestingly echoed here by five participants who regard their need for Jesus as replacing their former need for heroin:

> 戒毒好容易，但邊樣野先至可以滿足倒你？我地食白粉想求一個滿足但係一食完之後，feeling過左之後，你就會去再搵啦。但信耶穌唔使搵，個feeling係每一日都係度，每一日都咁新鮮，咁滿足。(D7)
> Kicking drugs is easy, but what can satisfy you? We take heroin because we want satisfaction, but once consumed, when the feeling is over, you have to search for it again. But there is no need for searching when you believe in Jesus. The feeling is there every day, every day it is so fresh, so fulfilling.

In other words, Jesus fills the emptiness left when the drug is no longer allowed into the body. Jesus takes the place of heroin for these participants.

Finally, 14 participants qualify their views regarding the consequences of conversion in kicking their drug habit by stating that the latter is but a step towards believing in Jesus. For them, conversion is the primary goal, not drug rehabilitation, although the drug abuser's need to be rid of drugs provides the pathway to Jesus. This, of course, is also the official view of the Society. A Group D participant represents this view:

> 戒毒不過係一個橋樑，福音行先，一個真理裡面之教導，藉著福音係你裡面戒毒……。
> Kicking drugs is but a bridge, the gospel comes first, which is the teaching of truth, the gospel within you gets rid of your drug habit. (D1)

While participants in Groups B, C, and D have been drug free for varying lengths of time, the question of whether heroin still presents a challenge has been put to them, so as to probe the level of conviction they have in remaining drug free, given the fact that at least for Group B, and to a lesser extent for Group C, they have been physically isolated from heroin.

# The Attraction of Heroin

**Table 9-5  The Attraction of Heroin**

| Degree of Attraction | Total (N=60) | % | Group B (N=20) | Group C (N=19) | Group D (N=21) |
|---|---|---|---|---|---|
| No attraction, Jesus with me | 31 | 52% | 3 | 7 | 21 |
| No attraction now, uncertain of future | 20 | 33% | 13 | 7 | 0 |
| Can't say no, uncertain of future | 9 | 15% | 4 | 5 | 0 |

As shown in Table 9-5, which gives the frequency of responses regarding the degree of attraction of heroin in the participants' lives, the attraction clearly diminishes as the participants continue with the rehabilitation programme. None in Group D regard heroin as attractive or relevant to them, and most mention Jesus as a protective factor in their resistance to heroin, in that the satisfaction given by Jesus surpasses that given by heroin in their former lives. Their views are as follows:

白粉你唔能夠滿足倒我，只有耶穌基督可以刺激倒我。 (D1)
Heroin you can't satisfy me, only Jesus Christ can stimulate me.

耶穌係個靈，有希望，有愛，需要佢每日滿足我。 (D2)
Jesus is a spirit, with hope, with love. I need him to fill me up daily.

求神, 同一班弟兄姊妹生活，平安，喜樂，比我地 D 足夠勝過呢 D (指白粉)。 (D4)
Ask God, living together with a group of brothers and sisters, peace, happiness, such satisfaction surpasses what it (meaning heroin) can give us.

白粉比你一時滿足，神比你時時滿足，信耶穌得到滿足，有平安，有喜樂。 (D10)
Heroin gives you temporary satisfaction, God gives you satisfaction all the time, you can obtain satisfaction by believing in Jesus, there is peace, and there is happiness.

Jesus as a protective factor also functions in other ways. First, contingent upon believing in Jesus, the participants appeal to prayers and other support by their peers to resist temptation. Second, obtaining a new direction and purpose in life, namely to serve God, provides meaningful activities to fill the space once occupied by heroin. Third, Jesus serves as a moral guide and promotes a person's ability to tell right from wrong. Taking heroin is unacceptable for a Christian.

Still, 48% of participants from Group B and Group C admitted to the possibility of their being tempted by heroin in future. Two in Group B even suggested that they might try heroin once they came out of the confines of the programme, though they would not indulge in it as before. The reasons given for the lack of confidence in oneself in resisting heroin in future are a) too many failures in the past results in a lack of self-confidence; b) for Group B participants, there is a need to test oneself by facing heroin squarely, since they are all isolated from the drug when in the Home; and c) there is a need to learn gradually to change one's way of life.

That heroin can still have attraction for Group B and Group C participants is understandable, judging from the experience of Group D, as some of them reported that it takes between two to five years after coming off heroin before they can be certain of themselves, but, as some remarked, they are certain as long as they are attached to Jesus and to the community of Christian brothers and sisters.

Given that the analysis of post conversion changes so far is based on a cross-sectional sample, a sub-sample of eleven participants out of the 26 in Group A were followed up when they moved on to Stage 2. The next chapter tells their stories.

# CHAPTER 10

# Individual Profiles

The cross-sectional data so far indicate that religious conversion brings about significant changes to a group of chronic heroin addicted persons. After conversion, they shed their former Drug Self who is one who lives in isolation and alienation, is clinically severely depressed, feels hopeless and has little purpose in life. Their new found identity as a Christian brother transforms them into happy and contented souls. The validity of these observations is supported by data from a longitudinal sample of eleven Stage One participants who have been followed through to their Stage Two experience.

This sub-sample of participants was interviewed in the New Boys Home about four months after their first interview. At the time of the second interview, their period of stay in the Home ranged from seven to twelve weeks. All regarded themselves as being converted on average after one month's stay in the Home.

As the changes found in the participants' mental health measures and the grid data from their pre-conversion to their post conversion state replicate, almost in their entirety, that of the cross-sectional sample, the profiles of two particular participants are given instead to illustrate their conversion experience and the use of the grid method as an investigative tool. These two participants are selected as their individual characteristics match closely the group profile: being middle-aged, coming from a large family and each having a long history of addiction. However, they differ in their conversion experience. One was appreciative of the positive effects his conversion experience had on him, while the other was still doubtful, though both claimed to have been converted. Since data from the INGRID programme allows for the plotting of a two dimensional diagram showing relationships between elements and constructs from an individual grid, (see Appendix I for details of the construction of the diagrams), two sets of diagrams are given to illustrate the pre-conversion and the post conversion status of the two participants whom we shall name King and Kong.

## The Story of King and Kong

Diagrams 10-1 and 10-2 show King's pre- and post- conversion statuses:

**Diagram 10-1  Plot of Elements in Construct Space for
King's Pre-conversion Status**

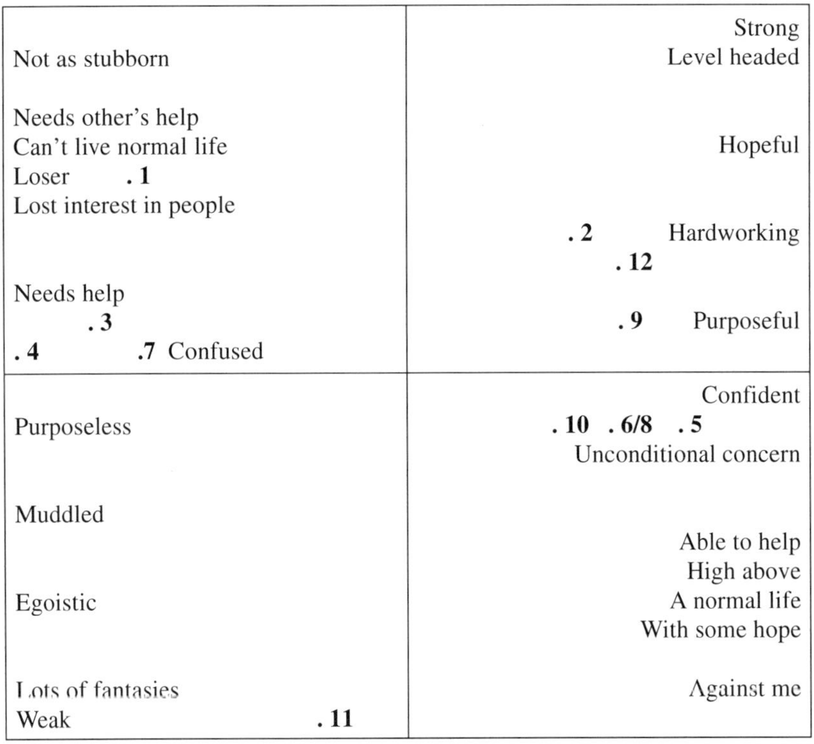

| | |
|---|---|
| Not as stubborn | Strong<br>Level headed |
| Needs other's help<br>Can't live normal life<br>Loser     . 1<br>Lost interest in people | Hopeful |
| | . 2        Hardworking<br>. 12 |
| Needs help<br>. 3<br>. 4          .7 Confused | . 9     Purposeful |
| Purposeless | Confident<br>. 10  . 6/8  . 5<br>Unconditional concern |
| Muddled | |
| Egoistic | Able to help<br>High above<br>A normal life<br>With some hope |
| Lots of fantasies<br>Weak                          . 11 | Against me |

Note:  For all diagrams the figures refer to the elements, the labels being the constructs

Elements list:
1= Actual Self; 2= Ideal Self; 3= Social Self; 4= Drug Self;
5= Jesus; 6= Helper; 7= Brother; 8= Mother/surrogate;
9= Father/surrogate; 10= Sibling/surrogate;
11= Wife/Girl friend; 12= Religious Person

**Diagram 10-2  Plot of Elements in Construct Space for
King's Post-conversion Status**

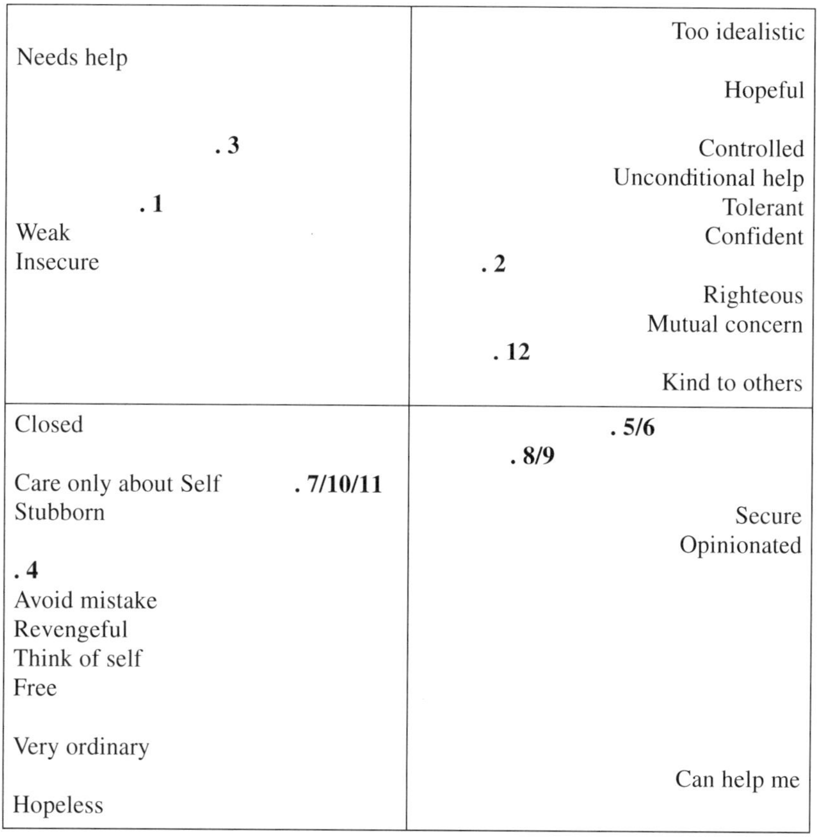

| | |
|---|---|
| Needs help<br><br><br>     . 3<br><br>   . 1<br>Weak<br>Insecure | Too idealistic<br><br>Hopeful<br><br>Controlled<br>Unconditional help<br>Tolerant<br>Confident<br><br>   . 2<br><br>Righteous<br>Mutual concern<br>   . 12<br><br>Kind to others |
| Closed<br><br>Care only about Self     . 7/10/11<br>Stubborn<br><br>. 4<br>Avoid mistake<br>Revengeful<br>Think of self<br>Free<br><br>Very ordinary<br><br>Hopeless |        . 5/6<br>   . 8/9<br><br><br>Secure<br>Opinionated<br><br><br><br><br><br>Can help me |

King, aged 44, had been a divorcee for over ten years and had been on heroin for 23 years. He was sent to attend the rehabilitation programme by his probation officer. Like many other participants in the study, he had previously been to a rehabilitation programme run by a non-government agency, had gone to Mainland China, and had tried methadone. However, he had made no attempt to quit drugs in the past ten years.

While he estimated his conversion to have happened around the seventh week in the Home, he had no meaningful prior contact with other religions beyond the fact that when he was little, his mother was a Catholic, in the sense that she could receive food supplements from church-run charities. He was living with her before he began the programme. Since his conversion, he felt much more peaceful and learned to pray to relieve himself when he felt stressed. He liked to stay in the Home as there was much less conflict, compared to the outside world. He also appreciated the opportunity to learn things, like how to be tolerant of the other brothers, how to co-operate with people, and how to be serious at work.

Looking at King's profiles (diagrams 10-1 and 10-2), it can be noted that before conversion, his perception of the various elements is very much like Group A's profile, in that the Actual Self, Social Self, and the Drug Self (and the Brother as well) are seen closer together, yet at the same time, the Actual Self can also be seen as isolated, as the Drug Self, Social Self, and Brother form a subgroup on their own, leaving the Actual Self which is described as needing other's help, can't live a normal life, a loser, and one with no interest in other people. Upon conversion, the most distinct change is for the Drug Self to become distanced and isolated. However, the Actual Self, while moving closer to the Social Self, is still far from the others, presumably because it is still seen as weak and insecure.

It is of interest to note that King's perception of his wife is also rather negative. First, she is isolated and seen as weak and full of fantasies. Then in the post-conversion stage, she is put next to the Brother and the sibling, who, together, were described as stubborn and selfish. The mother, on the other hand, is seen as very positive, being close to Jesus and the Helper, and described as confident, kind, and showing unconditional concern for others etc.

Perhaps one unusual observation at the post-conversion stage is the use of the construct *free* in relation to the Drug Self, amongst other rather negative ones — avoid mistakes, revengeful, selfish, ordinary, and hopeless. If King were in therapy, such unusual constellation of constructs would offer the opportunity to generate working hypotheses worth pursuing with him. The grid, of course, is designed for just such a purpose.

For the other participant, Kong, while he has been able to articulate some of his experiences of a religious nature, such as the effects of praying, he still remains doubtful of his religious commitment, though he considers himself as starting to believe in Jesus after over a month's stay in the Home, however, he claims he has not seen concrete signs of God's work on him yet. His profiles are given in Diagrams 10-3 and 10-4.

Kong, aged 36, and married, has been on heroin for 16 years. He had also tried numerous times to quit drugs and would not have thought of entering a religious programme, had he not been pushed by his probation officer.

Kong had thought of leaving the Home after his ten-day period, but was moved by the care and concern given by the helpers. Although he was

**Diagram 10-3  Kong's Pre-conversion Status**

| | |
|---|---|
| Easy to communicate with<br>Responsible<br><br>Care about family<br>Care for others<br>Active<br>Persuade others to be kind<br>　　　　　　. 5/6<br>　　　　　　. 7/12<br>　　　　　　　　. 2 | Help me<br>Poor relationships<br>No need for Jesus<br><br>Dissatisfied with reality<br>Not very hopeful<br><br>Look at the present |
| Look ahead　　　　. 10<br>　　　　　. 9<br><br>　　　　. 8<br>　　　　. 11<br>Hopeful<br>Care for me<br><br>Dependent on Jesus<br>Some hope<br>Ask Jesus for help | 　. 1　　Bad-tempered<br>No fighting spirit<br>Won't care for others<br>A burden<br><br>Irresponsible　　. 3　. 4<br>Difficult to communicate with |

**Diagram 10-4  Kong's Post-conversion Status**

| | |
|---|---|
| 　　　　　　. 8<br>Mature<br><br>Soft-hearted<br>Care for others　　. 5<br>Satisfied<br>Fraternal<br>Purposeful　　　. 6<br>Responsible | <br><br><br><br><br>Undignified<br>Care about self<br>Pretending　　. 4 |
| Proper<br>Mutual encouragement　.10　. 11/12<br>Dignified<br>　　　　. 9　. 2<br>　　　　　　. 1 | . 3　　　　　Irresponsible<br>　. 7　　　　Phony<br>Poor relationships<br>Selfish<br>Doubtful<br>Tough at heart<br><br>Facing daily drudgeries |

willing to do what the others did, like pray, read the Bible, and worship, etc., he was frank in admitting that so far he had not experienced anything special. While he had witnessed a brother displaying hand tremors, which was considered a sign of being filled with the Holy Spirit, he himself had no such experience. While he remained sceptical of what could be achieved, he was willing to stay and learn more about Jesus' way.

Referring to Kong's pre-conversion profile, again it displays essentially the same basic pattern of having the Actual Self, Social Self and the Drug Self being together, yet the Actual Self is isolated at the same time. Its description is again negative, being seen as bad-tempered, a burden, no fighting spirit and uncaring. On conversion, the Drug Self is abandoned, but still described as undignified, selfish and a pretender, while the Actual Self moves close to the Ideal Self and the Relatives, and is seen as dignified, proper and sharing mutual encouragement with the others. However, Kong sees himself as seen by others not as positively as he sees himself, as his Social Self is rather removed from the Actual Self and is closer to the Brother, and evaluated as much more negative. By his own admission, Kong had not been able to immerse himself totally into the religious scene, despite his willingness to try. Such a psychological barrier could render him to be seen within the Home as still in need of reform, and, it is possible that his perception of his Social Self reflects his feeling of being seen by other people in the Home as non-conforming.

Kong's perception of his family members is generally much more positive than that of King. In contrast to King, the wife is seen in a positive light together with other family members. The wife, in actual fact, has been supportive of his stay in the Home. Jesus and the helper are most positively seen as caring, fraternal, responsible etc.

The above analyses of individual profiles not only substantiate the group data in terms of mapping cognitive changes upon conversion, but also show that the profiles can be seen to have therapeutic value in guiding therapy work (Lau, 1994).

To conclude the analysis, excerpts from all eleven participants in the longitudinal sample are presented below, as they reveal best what they have experienced.

## Individual Narratives of Participants in the Longitudinal Sample

To highlight the changes observed in the participants of the cross-sectional sample, individual narratives with reference to perceived changes after conversion from each of the participants in the longitudinal sample are given below. Of the 11 participants only one fails to notice any significant change in himself as a result of conversion (Kong). Roughly three types of changes have been mentioned:

1. Cognitive change — when the participants were in their drug-dependent state, their thinking was muddled or they thought only of drugs which in turn blocked their ability to really face problems. After conversion, their thinking has become clear, and they can see further ahead. Jesus' words serve to teach them, guide them, and are a source of encouragement.
2. Interpersonal relationships — from a conflict-ridden existence, they now learn to be patient, cooperative, forgiving, accommodating, humble, as well as tolerant of other people.
3. Emotional change — from being angry and discontented, they now have peace and happiness.

The following eleven excerpts illustrate these changes:

1) 感到好平安，煩燥時，諗有其他人幫緊自己，咁就會平安。如果諗住有藥物，就會有依賴……。接受祈禱，能夠係心理上平服一D，隔絕左白粉，所以唔再去諗佢……。我喜歡留係度，至少無出面咁多紛爭，暫時離講，感到平安，好多野學，例如點包容D弟兄，點同人合作，工作而家點樣，學下做野認真，都係以前疏忽左……。太專注白粉，而疏忽左生活中之趣味同生活細節……學倒好多野，建立番自己好有幫助。(B)

Feels very peaceful, when I get grumpy, I think of others helping me, then I feel peaceful. If I keep thinking of drugs, there will be dependence … Accepting prayer can be psychologically soothing, isolated from heroin, so I don't think of it any more … I like to stay here, at least there is less conflict in here, for the time being, I feel peaceful, a lot to learn, for example, how to accommodate other brothers, how to cooperate with others, how to get a job done, learn to do things seriously, all these I have neglected in the past … Too focused on heroin, I neglected the pleasures in life and the small details … Learn a lot, very helpful in rebuilding myself.

2) 食白粉係唔想諗番個D問題，用食白粉蓋過問題，跟耶穌用佢D話語開解自己，睇聖經時可學會克制自己，中和番……。

Taking heroin means not wanting to think about problems, use heroin to cover up problems, following Jesus, using His words to inform, pacify myself, reading the Bible one can learn to control oneself, harmonizing....

你知信耶穌係好，有人認同，食白粉唔好，無人認同。
You know believing in Jesus is good, people accept you, taking heroin is no good, no one accepts you.

唔食白粉會辛苦，唔認同，唔尊重你，信耶穌係佢比力量變番好你，如果心信，行出去作榜樣，會有喜悦及公認你。
Not taking heroin one suffers, no acceptance, no respect, believing in Jesus gives you strength to change into something good, if you believe Him in your heart, walk out and be a model, there will be joy and acceptance.

藉著佢令自己轉變咁大，呢世都會記得，……如果你藉住佢，佢會比話語你，教你點做，諗番個D鼓勵倒自己，警惕倒自己，好有用。
On account of Him I am greatly changed, will remember this all my life ... if you depend on Him, He will give you words, teach you what to do, thinking about this is encouraging for me, can help me to become alert, very useful.

3) 現階段睇唔倒神係我身上工作。
At this stage I don't see God working on me.

4) 要學識應附人際關係。
Need to learn to deal with interpersonal relationships.

接受佢先……寬恕人之態度，以前嬲，打得就打。
Accept Him first ... a forgiving attitude, in the past when I was angry, I would get into a fight if it were possible.

悶時學下點滿足自己，要學寬恕，要學滿足，都要係耶穌身上學番離。白粉係蓋住人D思想，耶穌係清析D，思想比你睇遠D。
When bored learn how to satisfy myself, need to learn to forgive, need to learn to be satisfied, all of these are learned from Jesus. Heroin covers up a person's thinking, Jesus is clear, makes you see further ahead.

5) 諗法已經改晒，以前的嬲怒，以前個的心情，性格有改變……對人對事謙卑D，唔會咁多衝突。
My way of thinking has changed completely, the anger in the past, the kind of feelings in the past, there is change in my personality ...

more humble towards things and people, there will not be so many conflicts.

6) 倚賴白粉，肉體上辛苦典癮，先依賴佢，基督唔同，開心同唔開心都依賴佢，諗住有耶穌基督，唔開心都變返開心，開心令你更加開心，呢種係無條件架。

Dependent on heroin, the body suffers from withdrawal pains, so need to depend on it, Jesus is different, whether happy or sad one depends on Him, thinking there is Jesus, one becomes happy when sad, when happy He makes you even happier, this is unconditional.

7) 個時倚賴白粉，依加倚賴信仰來維持生命，有班弟兄姊妹關心，代替左白粉，耶穌係填補我地心靈，醫治我地。

Dependent on heroin in the past, now depend on faith to maintain life, there is care from the brothers and sisters, substituting heroin, Jesus fills up my heart, healing us.

係監房，XXX (name of an agency for drug rehabilitation) 度戒，但你個思想，心呀無變到，表面上心態康復，但無真正改變，呢度除左身體康復，心態亦能改變，呢D最可以幫倒我地，同埋有一班弟兄維繫住，好緊要。

Quitting drug in prison, in XXX, but your thinking, your heart have not changed, superficially one seems to have been healed, but there is no real change, here, besides the body becoming healed, the mental state is also changed, this is what is most helpful to us, also there is a group of brothers sustaining you, very important.

XXX 度戒無人理你，食煙，講粗口，你戒完白粉就得，因為佢無一種信仰鼓勵同支持你，(信仰) 帶來一種鼓勵同信心，一種平安同喜樂……唔會胡思亂想，諗番舊生命D野。

Quitting drug in XXX no one cares about you, smoking, speaking foul language, as long as you quit heroin, because there is not a form of belief to encourage and support you, (belief) brings encouragement and confidence, a kind of peace and joy … won't think wild, won't think of the past life.

8) 信耶穌好少少，好包容，忍讓人，有愛。

Believing Jesus is a little bit better, accommodating, tolerating others, have love.

9) 學倒忍耐別人，忍讓，個人樂觀左，開朗左，同埋D人溝通多左，D人好，大家開開心心……唔講粗口，對人善良D。

Learn to be patient with others, be tolerant, one gets more optimistic, happier, communicating more with other people, people are nice, everybody happy ... no foul language, kind to others.

10) 靠白粉一塌糊塗，無白粉搵白粉，個人亂晒籠，但靠耶穌清醒一
D。

One gets all mixed up, being dependent on heroin, when there is no heroin, one searches for it, makes the person very confused, but relying on Jesus makes one clear-headed.

11) 係改思想，斬釘截鐵，拔根，改掉壞思想，唔好再接近舊時 D 生
活，D 人。打算行耶穌條路，安樂茶飯，唔好有爭鬥，有野心。

It's changing how one thinks, ultimately, uprooted, get rid of the bad thoughts, not to go back to the old life, the same kind of people any more. Plan to walk Jesus' way, secure life, no more conflicts, no more ambition.

According to the participants, conversion is seen to bring about cognitive, emotional and behavioural changes, turning a confused, unhappy, tempestuous person into one who thinks clearly, is happy, and can relate to other people.

Thus far, the three sets of data used in the study, namely, the mental health measures, the grid data, and the individual narratives reveal, in different ways, the kinds of changes present in the participants as a function of their conversion in the religious drug rehabilitation programme. In what ways has the programme brought about such changes? Is it the nature and the structure of the programme? Is it Jesus who does wonders?

# CHAPTER 11

# Religious Drug Rehabilitation: St. Stephen's Society

To understand the self transformation reported by our participants as they go through religious drug rehabilitation, we first return to "where the client is", that is, their love affair with heroin in order to understand how St. Stephen's Society's drug rehabilitation programme brings about such a transformation.

## Drug Experience

Judging from the participants' narratives on their drug career (Chapter 7), their initial use of heroin was more due to psychosocial reasons such as being with friends who did drugs, and being curious or bored, given that the first dose is inevitably unpleasant physiologically speaking, as it induced nausea and vomiting for practically all of them. But then the chemical properties of the drug soon take their course on subsequent use, producing the typical *High* which maintains its continuous use, as argued by Bozarth (1990). According to him, the acquisition phase of drug addiction may be influenced by factors such as drug exposure and the expectation of pleasure from drugs; the pharmacological actions of the drug, however, will predominate during repeated drug use, and he concluded by regarding a drug's pharmacological effects as being primary in causing addiction. But Peele (1985, 1989, 1991), and others have argued otherwise. They see drug taking as volitional, and how a person interprets the event as far more important for addiction than biological determinism. Present data agree with this position, as argued below.

Examining the participants' narratives on the euphoria derived from heroin, it can be seen that the beliefs about heroin held by the participants when they were still active abusers centred mainly on heroin offering them an easy escape from reality, that it provides an instant form of catharsis, it relieves boredom, improves sexual prowess, and is energy giving and identity enhancing. Heroin reduces tension and leads to a state of superb blissful existence in which the user feels totally care-free and trouble-free. Recalling that the first smoke is inevitably reported as bringing bodily discomfort for all participants, most commonly in the form of vomiting, the subsequent pleasure derived from taking heroin must be seen as learned, hence a function of individual interpretation of events.

As for continuing drug use, the theme of coping with life stress is a major one. In the case of heroin, it has been well documented that its effect on time perception and the insulation of the users from the outside world are two important properties for inducing users further onto the road to "H", as Chein et. al. (1964) dubbed it, H being Heaven, High, and Hell. During the High, users feel they are in a world of their own where they can do as they wish, their harsh environment cannot penetrate them, and as time flies effortlessly, so will their problems.

However, as Chein et. al. (1964) reminded us, not all drug users progress to a state of addiction. At some stage, a few of the participants would not have been seen as heroin abuser when they could keep their heroin habit under control, and had regular employment to maintain it. C19 even managed to remain drug free for eight years before he relapsed. However, when they hit rock bottom and come forward for help, whether voluntarily or due to coercion, the problem for those eager to help is one of being able to offer these people what they need most — to be rid of their drug habit. To do so requires an understanding of what it means to be addicted and re-addicted, so that drug abusers can be helped to behave differently. A further look at the participants' relapse experience informs us of the strong hold heroin has on its users.

## Relapse

There is a popular belief endorsed by many participants that it is easy to kick heroin, but extremely difficult to stay off it after quitting, as almost all of them have done it cold turkey style, either when they were imprisoned, or when they left for Mainland China in times when heroin supply was low in Hong Kong. Hence, the two clichés "白粉棺材" (heroin coffin), "既成道友，一世道友" (once an addict, always an addict) denote their belief in the inevitability of relapse. Indeed, why do they relapse?

If the views on relapse from Shiffman (1989) and Stimson and Oppenheimer (1982) are accepted, that is, seeing a person's decision to continue with drug-taking or to quit it as the eventual outcome of the overall balance between temptation and resistance to temptation, then looking at the participants' reasons for returning to heroin (Table 7-4) should give some ideas about the possible relapse promoting factors. The data indicate that apart from the overwhelming effect of the social pressure exerted by their returning to old acquaintances who are mostly prepared to offer them a fix, which in turn also means the easy availability of heroin, the other reasons are: being bored, having bad moods, being aware of their psychological dependence on heroin, being troubled by problems, and having a low status in society. All of these can be seen as problems in life that the participants believe heroin can help eradicate by sending them into a world of oblivion, an instant relief from life's depressing circumstances. It should also be noted that very few cited the chemical impact of heroin as a reason for relapse, i.e., the fear of withdrawal pain and the High.

Because of forced treatment as a result of imprisonment, some participants remarked that as their body had been cleansed of heroin, they thought they would be better able to re-experience the High. Prior to their release from captivity, they would typically engage in drug talk with each other, discussing how and where they could go for heroin, what the quality of the supply would be like etc. These ideas and actions are important in tipping the balance towards relapse. Bradley (1989) also found what he called cognitive factors, meaning an intention or plan to use drugs again, together with negative states such as loneliness, boredom, tension and anxiety, as important factors leading to renewed opiate use. Brown, Guavey, Meyers and Stark (1971) also found in their study of drug abusers of both sexes and male juvenile drug abusers that "they had given up drugs only physically, and that a psychological need remained" (p. 639). Relief of personal problems, easy availability of heroin and the influence of friends were also cited. Rhoads (1983) and Judson and Goldstein (1983) found that heroin abusers relapsed mainly because of negative emotional states and lack of social support. Similarly Kosten, Rounsville, and Kleber (1986) found that relapsed heroin abusers had more negative life experiences post-treatment and more depression at intake. As is the case for the present study, craving is relatively unimportant in relapse (Bradley, 1989; Heather, Stallard, & Tebutt 1991).

Given the emphasis on personal meaning in interpreting drug taking activities by the participants, it is not surprising that the chemical aspects of heroin is de-emphasized in relapse. The psychological gains obviously outweigh the physiological ones in the participants' experience. Towards the later stages of their drug career, most participants become locked into a maladaptive life style that spells little but repeated failure, given the constructs of a Drug Self for anticipating life events. Recalling that Group A participants see them (Actual Self) as well as regarding others as seeing themselves (Social Self) to be inadequate, immoral, and with little tender feeling, these attributes are further exaggerated in their image of their Drug Self which is described as isolated from other people and from their own ideals (actual self isolation, self alienation, and social alienation). Their low self convergence, that is, seeing themselves as very different from their own ideal, however, as noted earlier, is contrary to overseas observations (Stojnov, 1990). This may signal something positive at the time when the participants come forward for help, since it would be highly unlikely for people who see themselves as having reached their own ideal to desire change.

What does the rehabilitation programme offer to chronic heroin abusers in so far as they stay with the programme?

## The Programme

### Stage One

The first attempt towards conversion occurs at the very first meeting at the Prayer Meeting Stage, where all participants are initiated into receiving Jesus as their saviour. This practice is said to have its biblical root in the Letter of Paul to the Romans 10:9, which reads: "If the confession 'Jesus is Lord' is on your lips, and the faith that God raised him from the dead is in your heart, you will find salvation" (Revised English Bible, 1989, p. 142). Such a verbal declaration of faith is taken by all participants as a formality contingent upon their attending the meetings. None admitted to having been converted at the first meeting. Rather, they accounted for their willingness to make such a declaration as an indication of their motivation to seek change and of their need for help. The raising of hope for the future is also important for those who feel they are at rock bottom. At this stage, confession of sins, drug taking being but one, and catharsis for past miseries, hurt, and pain, are carried out through prayers, which include the use of glossolalia, worship, singing, and Bible lessons, all of which are core activities throughout the entire programme. Such activities are experienced as conducive to positive affect, even when the participants have not been converted, since some Stage One participants also found joy, comfort, peace and relief after prayer or worship. The general effect brought about by these religious activities is seen as soothing to a troubled mind and heart.

## Stage Two

While rituals such as prayer, worship, and Bible reading continued during Stage Two, a unique experience is also brought about during the detoxification period. It is here that the image of Jesus becomes a living experience, whereas prior to this, he is perceived more as a figure in the Bible to be talked about.

Looking at the basis for conversion (Table 8-3), it is Jesus' love as manifested through the helpers and fellow brothers during the first ten days of the participants' experience in the New Boys Home that overwhelmed them, together with events which they interpreted as miracles performed by Jesus; these two occurrences bring many of them to Jesus. The ten days are unique in that none of the participants have ever experienced the kind of continuous care and concern given during that period. Furthermore, it breaks immediately the isolation and alienation felt by the Stage One participants. The lesson learned here seems to be twofold for the participants: (a) that Jesus lives amongst his converts and, (b) the fact that someday the person being served is expected to serve others. The participants' own experience gives them a model for future action, as personal testimony works as another powerful validation experience in the conversion process. While only two out of the entire sample claimed to have been converted consequent upon a single critical event, all others talked of being aware of a gradual change in their belief in Jesus, most of which occurs within the first three months of their stay in the New Boys Home.

While confession and catharsis begin at Stage One, these activities continue in Stage Two. Mutual identification is encouraged between brother and helper through identification with Jesus. Indeed the image of Jesus is held as the ideal. Thrust into a community with fixed beliefs (Antze, 1976), new attitudes and behaviours are induced and maintained by putting the participants into close proximity with others already committed to the Christian faith. The function of a religious community is seen by Berger and Luckmann (1967) in this way:

> To have a conversion experience is nothing much. The real thing is to be able to keep on taking it seriously; to retain a sense of its plausibility. This is where the religious community comes in …

> The partners in significant conversation change. And in conversation with the
> new significant others subjective reality is transformed. It is maintained by
> continuous conversation with them, or with the community they represent.
> (pp. 158–159)

It is also through daily living with other people that participants are
forced to face the kinds of stress that occur in ordinary life, stresses which
in the past they used to block out with heroin. Having been detoxified, and
now living in a drug-free environment, Stage Two participants must learn
to cope without drugs. A lot of learning takes place by using Jesus as a
model. Rather than blocking out all personal and interpersonal conflicts
with the use of the wonder drug called heroin, these are now solved through
feeling, thinking, and talking about them, and then acting on them according
to Jesus' teaching. The learning that begins in the New Boys Home and
continues thereafter is one of opening up alternatives for behaviour based
on the dominant ideology of being a follower of Jesus.

While the character sketch of Jesus is given to them for emulation,
most participants also realize that He is just too perfect. This is noted in the
perfect rating for Jesus on all positive constructs; further, it is only at Stage
Three and Four that the participants see their Actual Self as significantly
much closer to Jesus. However, at Stage Two, the helpers, who are successful
models serve as intermediaries. In fact, a large part of the learning and
identification in the participants can be seen to take place within their
exchanges with the helpers whose role they might one day adopt, should
they choose to remain in the Society to serve Jesus, which is one obvious
option given to them.

While mention has been made of some of the structural elements in the
programme, such as the use of religious rituals like prayer, worship and
Bible reading, and the unique experience of detoxification in the New Boys
Home which are experienced as contributive to the participants' conversion,
ideologically it can also be noted that what conversion is taken to mean is
related to the changes reported by the participants, that is, what beliefs
about the Christian faith have the participants acquired that lead to changes
in them?

Conversion is first and foremost taken to mean *change* (Table 8-4),
which entails hope and a new life. This is consistent with the discussion in
the literature on religious conversion, from Stanley Hall, Starbuck, William
James, through to the more recent writers Moore and Gillespie, whose views
have been summarized in Chapter Four. Conversion is next seen to bring to

the converts emotional security, which includes love, happiness, peace, strength and confidence etc., feelings and personal qualities that are lacking in a chronic drug abuser's life. These highly positive gains are seen to result from the healing brought about by Jesus, the great healer.

The third interpretation of the meaning of conversion may be regarded as more practical, in the sense that Jesus is to be depended upon, and will also provide moral guidance and act as a model for emulation; the latter has been emphasized throughout the entire programme.

Conversion as change, as hope and as the beginning of a new life would be consistent with the changes in the self identity indices and with the grid measures indicating changes in the four self elements; the kind of emotional security recorded is reflected in the three mental health measures, all of which show positive changes, turning the severely depressed and hopeless drug abuser into a person full of hope and vision for the future. The emphasis on morality and positive behaviour as exemplified in Jesus is seen in the changes in the constructs in relation to the self elements.

### Stage Three

Progressing onto Stage Three, there is a significant role reversal for the participants, in that as long as they retained their status as brothers in the New Boys Home, they would continue to be regarded as still needing the service of the helpers. Getting on to the training team of the Help Mobile indicates that one is ready to learn to serve. Further, it also means that the participants will be exposed to the temptation offered by heroin, despite the fact that they will be accompanied by well reformed leaders, because in their outreach duties they will come into contact with active drug users and visit places where heroin is available.

With regard to the attraction of heroin, 48% of the participants (excluding Group A) in Group B and Group C still admitted to being uncertain of whether they could be tempted by heroin (Table 9-5). Group B is in one sense in a better position, because they are restricted to a drug free environment most of the time. The real test comes for Group C, when the participants are led out to serve other people, including drug addicts. They also have more private time, as they can take home leave. Recalling that one of the major reasons for relapse is that of returning to old associates because one is bored or has little to do to pass the time, being left alone could be risky for these people. How are they coping?

After conversion, Jesus is regarded by all participants as what Shiffman

(1989) called a relapse-protective factor in that living according to Jesus' way gives meaning and purpose to life, mainly in the serving of others. In place of idleness and under the protection of the group, Group C participants engage in outreach work helping the needy, or serving the brothers in the New Boys Home when necessary. It has been noted that for them the Ideal Self is seen as closest to Jesus across all groups, perhaps reflecting the intensity with which the message of learning to walk in Jesus' way has been taken by them. However, this emphasis on striving towards perfection with Jesus as the perfect ideal might have brought about some unexpected repercussions, which is discussed later with reference to relapse.

### Stage Four

Group D participants are all involved in leading roles in the daily running of the rehabilitation programme, full time on a voluntary basis. On average, they have served for five and a half years in the Society, indicating the high degree of their commitment to their faith in Jesus and the work of the Society. On all measures they come out as the healthiest in terms of their mental adjustment, even when compared to available local normative data. They see themselves as happy, full of vision and hope for the future. Their rating of self elements, except for the Drug Self, matches closely with that for Jesus (Table 9-3), indicating a strong identification with Jesus. Heroin no longer poses a threat to them. Rather, for some of them at least, Jesus seems to be fulfilling a role that heroin once occupied in their former life as a heroin abuser. As four specific individual participants put it (D1, D2, D4, and D10 in Chapter 9), Jesus gives them the kind of satisfaction that surpasses that once given by heroin.

## A Summary: Religious Conversion and Drug Rehabilitation

A chronic heroin abuser who approaches the Society for help is most likely to be depressed, desperate, isolated, rejected by other people and even rejected by himself. He lives by rules that bring him into conflict with others, which is why many of the participants first contacted the Society. For those who stay long enough, the nature of the rehabilitation programme is such that it responds to their immediate needs for acceptance, self-confidence, self-esteem, companionship, love, hope, direction, proper rules for behaviour etc., all embodied in their conversion. D3 summarized what he sees as the basic ingredients of the programme: (a) Jesus gives people self-confidence;

(b) a group of self sacrificing and dedicated individuals; and (c) a good place to stay. For D7 the most successful ingredient in the programme is love.

In their own words as summarized in Table 9-4, the participants are helped to get rid of their drug habit through Jesus' love and the comradeship within the brotherhood of Christ and, equally importantly, through the emotional security they received from Christian brotherhood. Some also acknowledged changes in their own attitude and outlook on life as resulting from conversion. The moral guidance that flows from Jesus' teaching is also important for some in binding them to a drug-free state. What helps them is hence phrased in entirely psychological terms, and has little to do with the chemistry of the drug, despite the fact that they all framed their need for heroin at the later stage of their drug taking in physiological terms, that of withdrawal pains. This brings the situation back to Peele's (1991) position that addiction is a matter of what the drug taking experience means to a person. As gathered from the present sample of chronic heroin abusers, addiction seems to mean a masking of their dissatisfaction in life and of their need for human contact in the later stages of their drug taking. It may well be that this is a long-term consequence of prolonged drug addiction, in that chronic abusers have short-circuited their place in society by opting out, by escaping into dope, so that they end up isolated and alienated from society. There are drug users who can maintain their habit without ever seeking treatment, such as Hanson, Beschner, Walters, & Bovell's (1985) sample of black male heroin users. However, when they do come in for help, it is important for the service providers to first understand what addiction means to these people at different stages of their drug career, before they can be properly served.

Although for specific relapse episodes, different clients may have different relapse patterns, owing to the imbalance between the temptation of, and resistance to drugs (Shiffman, 1989), Annis (1990) found recognizable profiles of conditions of relapse. Some might relapse after encountering unpleasant emotions and conflict with others, some may respond to pleasant emotions and pressures. Using the lifestyle approach in viewing addiction, as formulated by Walters (1996), one would also suggest greater commonalities amongst chronic drug abusers, who, through prolonged drug use, have probably developed a very similar negative lifestyle which lands them in troubles from which they may desire relief, as is the case for the present sample. St. Stephen's Society's drug rehabilitation programme apparently answers the need of those chronic heroin abusers who come forward for help: their need for love, emotional security, a change for the better, and guidance.

From this insider's perspective of what the rehabilitation programme does for the participants, the following chapter develops an outsider's perspective for an understanding of addiction and rehabilitation. In other words, how can psychology, in the form of Kelly's (1955) Personal Construct Theory, help to make sense of the participants' rehabilitative experience? And yet, the uniqueness of Kelly's theory is that the grid method is able to generate data that remain close to the insider's account. A constructional perspective on addition and rehabilitation so formulated is also able to bridge religion and therapy on the basis of a mutual focus on the importance of belief in affecting human actions.

# CHAPTER 12

# A Personal Construct Theory of Drug Addiction and Drug Rehabilitation

A constructional perspective for understanding drug addiction is first formulated. The religious drug rehabilitation programme at St. Stephen's Society is then conceptualized in Kellyian terms. Implications for drug rehabilitation are drawn for secular settings.

## Personal Construct Theory of Drug Addiction

Kelly's (1955) theory explores the ways in which the beliefs (constructs) held by people can shape their lives. A personal construct view of drug abuse can be derived from an understanding of chronic heroin-addicted persons through their construing. Group A participants see their Actual Self as very much like their Drug Self, and the constructs used are those that speak of low morality, personal inadequacy, isolation and social rejection, an image that they themselves referred to as "dope fiend". Such a perception is presumably derived from a lifestyle of repeated arrests, incarceration, relapse and re-addiction, isolating and locking them up in perpetual misery, as construing the self in these terms is very maladaptive when used in a drug free world. This very negative self-perception can have far reaching consequences.

As argued by Klion (1993) and Klion and Pfenninger (1997), drug addicted persons end up with a role constriction that proves to be maladaptive in normal daily life. How has this come about? This study provides data to explain such a development.

Norris and Makhlouf-Norris (1976) argued that a person construes in order to reduce uncertainty so as to maintain his/her self-identity. To construe the self negatively is then self-validating for active drug addicted individuals such as Group A participants. Yet they appear to be in a double-bind situation in that, in order to prevent invalidation of their very negative construct system, they have to construe themselves in the worst possible ways. Such construing further invalidates them as social actors in the wider context beyond their drug world. In this sense, the chronically drug addicted person is in a state of disorder as defined by Kelly: "From the standpoint of the psychology of personal constructs we may define a disorder as any personal construction which is used repeatedly in spite of consistent invalidation" (1955, p. 831). The following excerpts come from three Group A participants talking about the futility of quitting drugs:

> 戒得掂又咪咁，都係一個人，你個社會地位都係咁，都係廿四小時做野啦，唔會話我"meet"左，當我大爺咁丫嘛。你一樣做翻你，只不過唔需要再接觸個樣野。(A2)
>
> What's the big deal about quitting drugs, it's still me being alone, your status in society is the same, still working for twenty-four hours a day, no one will say since I have quit heroin, I will be treated as a big shot. You are the same you, it's just that there is no need to touch it (meaning heroin).

> 出到離，又無工作做，戒咗都無用，食番機會好大。(A19)
>
> When I was released (from prison), there was still no job. No point in quitting (heroin), the chance of taking it again is very high.

> 做人無乜目標，需要食又係咁，唔食又係咁，完全無目標，食咗白粉同唔食白粉都係咁做人。(A16)
>
> There is little purpose in life, whether I take drugs, or I don't take them, it's the same, absolutely no purpose at all. Taking heroin or not taking heroin, it is still the same me.

The sense of futility or, in construct terms, the invalidation of oneself, is succinctly captured by the popular self-description of "白粉棺材" (heroin coffin) by chronic heroin abusers.

In one sense, the very low cognitive complexity indices for the participants also indicate the disturbed nature of their construing. Apart from having fewer constructs to deal with things, a further problem with a constricted construct system is that the invalidation of virtually any construct would carry implications for the predictiveness of the person's core constructs and is therefore very threatening. The simple construer may then become extremely resistant to modifying his or her construing, even if presented with disconfirming evidence. Any one who has worked with chronically drug-addicted persons can appreciate the difficulties involved in motivating them towards change. This is the negative aspect of constricted construing.

In examining the reasons for drug use, another form of constriction may be seen in the participants while at their active drug taking stage, in that their existence is dictated by the use of heroin in order to escape from reality, and later on in order to avoid withdrawal. Antze's (1976) discussion of the relapse process sheds light on how such a constriction could come about. He argued that the high from heroin, which produces a feeling of insulation or detachment from the environment, becomes associated with the relief of stress, and this strong association tends to shape the drug addicted person's response to all kinds of stresses, so that instead of confronting stress, he shuts it out, or as the majority of participants see it, continuing heroin use provides a route to escape from reality. Further, as life becomes nothing more than daily hassles, the instant and solitary relief that heroin gives becomes a panacea. This constriction crystallizes over the long years of heroin use. As the person gets used to the pleasure and relief obtained from heroin, he gradually extends the use of heroin to cope with all forms of stress, to such an extent that it seems irrelevant to him that different kinds of stress require different ways of handling it. Finally, any emotional tension will trigger the threat of withdrawal pains that can only be alleviated by heroin intake. In other words, the next fix, and then the next, can obliterate all problems in life.

As Karst and Groutt (1977) pointed out, the power of drug experience can serve to validate a particular construct as a channel for perception and behaviour, and make it more difficult for the person to experiment with other constructs and/or develop new ones. It serves to stifle the development of a large repertory of personal constructs useful in coping with a variety of life experiences. Escaping from reality and avoiding withdrawal have come to dominate the participants' functioning in life. As Dawes (1985) suggested, the constriction of the drug-addicted person's construct system can result in the development of a subsystem of constructs that relate to drug taking.

In their drug-taking state, Group A participants see their Actual Self as overlapping with the Drug Self, which is seen in terms of being low in social interaction, morality, self sufficiency, tenderness, and involvement with other people. As the person anticipates events mostly using the Drug Self as a reference, this subsystem of constructs would have little implication for him when he is sober. In other words, he finds life increasingly stressful when not on drugs, since his constructs fail to help him cope when he is not stoned. This results in a further constriction of his world to that of drug taking, giving him little chance to develop the alternative constructions of a drug-free life. Such constriction in construing is indicated by the very low cognitive complexity found in Group A participants.

To recapitulate, there are two problems involved in helping chronically addicted persons out of their sufferings: their tendency to reduce all forms of stress to withdrawal pains, and their learnt habit to opt out rather than to cope with stress, or to cope by getting drugged. Seen from the personal construct view which emphasizes a person's anticipation of environmental events, heroin has come to mean two things for the user: it embodies all of life's stresses, and at the same time, it provides a way of coping with life stresses, hence the extreme constriction of all that is in life to a heroin fix. In Kellyian terms, the chronically addicted person's whole being is psychologically channelized by his anticipation that heroin will bring him instant relief from all of life's problems, because heroin is life, and life is heroin. Therefore, in personal construct terms, a re-construction of life is necessary. In religious terms, conversion brings about a re-orientation to life (Gillespie, 1991).

## A Constructional Interpretation of St. Stephen's Society's Drug Rehabilitation Programme

To bring about a Christian identity is the goal of conversion. This process may be understood using Kelly's philosophy of Constructive Alternativism, in that therapy is a reconstruction of a person's beliefs, or ways of anticipating events. It is "an experimental process in which constructions are devised or delineated and then tested out" (Kelly, 1969b, p. 220).

Seen from a therapeutic angle, St. Stephen's Society's programme resembles a form of peer psychotherapy within a therapeutic community, as it is largely administered by former heroin abusers who are now helpers in a residential setting. Antze (1976), apart from highlighting the importance of ideologies in shaping behaviour in these contexts, has also identified a cluster of social-psychological processes used. These are also found in the Society's programme, namely confession, catharsis, mutual identification and the removal of stigmatization. This approach has been summarized by Clinard (1963):

> In each case the group helps to integrate the individual, to change his conception
> of himself, to make him feel again the solidarity of the group behind the

individual, and to combat social stigma. These group processes, it is felt, replace "I" feelings with "we" feelings, give the individual the feeling of being in a group, and redefine certain norms of behaviour. (p. 647)

In essence, this approach has the same aim as Kelly's reconstruction of the self in psychotherapy. In their study of shared and personal constructs generated in a religious commune, Karst and Groutt (1977) referred to the commune as offering a type of fixed-role therapy to their participants, in that new patterns of behaviour are introduced and a new role relationship with other people is aimed at. These changes, furthermore, are also expected after a conversion experience, given that conversion is seen to bring about changes in self-identity through identification with Jesus Christ and the sharing of Christian solidarity (Kurewa, 1980). Therapy and conversion, then, meet in the potential transformation of their clients or believers. The post-conversion changes in the participants clearly indicate a gradual movement towards identification with Jesus. The conversion process is now discussed in terms of Kelly's fixed-role therapy.

## *Fixed-role Therapy and Religious Drug Rehabilitation*

Fixed-role therapy aims at a reconstruction of self by asking the client to play a role that is different from the self-characterization of the client. He/she is to experiment with different role behaviours that are unlikely to be elicited by the usual "self". Through playing out this fixed role, the person will be forced into a detailed psychological examination of this imaginary person and thereby becoming less self-centred. The emphasis is on personal exploration and experimentation by the client, so that he/she may realize that being stuck in one's old ways is not inevitable. Alternatives are thus opened up for the person within this role experimentation.

Kelly first devised fixed-role therapy as a set of techniques within individual therapy, but later extended it to group therapy, since group situations are particularly facilitative of experimentation, as they provide more opportunities for social experiments and validational evidence for the individual, than is possible if only the therapist and the client were involved.

As details of the technique of fixed-role therapy are available in Kelly (1955) and others' work (Karst and Trexler, 1970; Viney, 1981), the present discussion will only highlight those features which have parallels within the rehabilitation programme, in order to draw practical implications regarding social work intervention in the addiction field and in clinical practice.

### Writing the Fixed-role Sketch

As originally conceived, a fixed-role sketch for a client is written by the therapist from material gathered from the client's self-characterization. The role should not deviate drastically from what the client is like, so that therapeutic goals can be achieved with as little disturbance to the client as possible. As Kelly himself later discovered, his clients would rather play the opposite of who they were than move little by little, and they tended to think in terms of either black or white. Therefore, he later deliberately advanced sharply contrasting behaviour for a client to explore.

In the programme, the promulgation of the image of Jesus can be seen as a given fixed-role which all programme participants are to emulate. This is done right from Stage One through Bible reading, personal testimonies and worship activities, during which the character and deeds of Jesus are narrated. As shown in the grid data (Table 9-3), the image of Jesus is seen as perfect by all participants. To reach such a state of near perfection is possible only at Stage Four, when the leaders of the programme rate themselves as almost as perfect as Jesus. Ideologically speaking, then, Jesus serves as the model, but in the actual role learning, the helpers/leaders themselves act as intermediaries for the new boys at Stage Two.

### Role Enactment

Opportunities for role learning by the participants are inherent in everyday routines whether in the New Boys Home or in the Help Mobile team, but more intensely so in the Home. Here, Kelly's two corollaries, that of Commonality and Sociality, are seen to be at work.

Individuals may differ from each other and see a particular event differently, but they can also be similar to each other when they have a construct system similar to that of others (commonality corollary). This seems to be borne out by the consistently very low cognitive complexity indices found throughout the four stages, suggesting that the structural aspects of the cognitive system as a whole remains unchanged for the participants, despite a change from negative to positive affectivity in content. This means the participants use much the same sorts of constructs to describe their world, and in this sense they are very similar to each other. Such high uniformity in worldview of course facilitates mutual identification.

Kelly's Sociality corollary is also exemplified in the conversion process. For him, to be in a role relationship with another, is for a person to act according to his/her understanding of the other person, and also for the person to construe others' construction of him or her, that is, to anticipate other people's views in order to adjust to changing demands. Role playing for Kelly is thus social, because it requires the testing of personal constructs against the consequences of others' reactions to the construer.

In the constant exchanges between brothers and helpers, the helpers, who are predominantly recovered individuals, are expected to use their past experiences to help anticipate the needs of the brothers whom they serve, as they are considered to have the best understanding of what the brothers have gone through or will go through. One frequent problem encountered in the New Boys Home is the tendency for the new brothers to leave after detoxification. A lot of persuasion is evident from the helpers, and also from other brothers who have stayed longer, when they are alerted to a new brother's intention to leave. The need to construe a new brother's motives and actions is necessary for successful persuasion to occur. In turn, the new brothers have to learn to deal with personal and interpersonal conflicts without the benefit of heroin. Jesus' teaching is upheld; in particular, love, compassion, humility, and tolerance are emphasized in everyone's dealings with people and events.

In the conversion process, the participants' identification with Jesus is mediated through learning to play the role of helpers. Helpers are expected to live out a Christian image in serving the brothers. The participants, having been served, are in turn expected to serve yet other new brothers. Conversion in this sense echoes James' (1958) notion of conversion as a lived experience. To be converted is "to experience religion, to gain assurance ... and consciously right, superior, and happy ..." (p. 157). It has been found that individual conversions take place predominantly within the first three months of stay in the New Boys Home, the occasion usually being marked by baptism. The consequences of conversion are in line with James' description. The converts now see themselves as significantly happier and morally righteous, gaining in self-esteem and starting to relate to other people. The significant uplifting of depression, the increase in hope and purpose in life are noted in the changes in the three mental health measures from Group A to Group B status, while identification with Jesus and the shedding of the Drug Self image are evident in the grid measures. Changes in self descriptions from very negative terms to positive ones can be seen in the changing use of the constructs with reference to the self elements. The above findings corroborate overseas data on personal changes in people as a result of their religious encounters, for example, in the studies done by

Paloutizian (1981), Ridway (1972), and Bennett and Rigby (1991), which have already been mentioned.

In acting out the new role, Kelly also appealed to the "make-believe" quality of dramatics and regarded it as most important to fixed-role therapy, in that it serves as a protective mask for the actor so that he/she is free to explore the world without irrevocable commitment to the role given. The enactment is also for a pre-fixed period of time (two weeks is recommended by Kelly, to begin with).

In the programme, participants are in a protective environment. Most of them did in fact acknowledge that they were sealed off from temptation, as long as they stayed in the New Boys Home. Their non-committal attitude as to whether they could resist temptation from heroin, or from the colourful lifestyle they once had, is indicative of such awareness. The real test comes to many when they either leave the programme prematurely, or when they move on to Stage Three when they will be led back into their familiar world of the dope fiend as part of their outreach work, though with the support of the helpers. Based on the participants' accounts of their experiences, within the therapeutic community of the New Boys Home, they may be regarded as learning to experiment with themselves under the protective mask of make-believe, as when they model worship, and other forms of behaviour, *prior* to their conversion. This preparedness to experiment with themselves is expressed when all are ready to say "yes" to the questions asked in the very first meeting at Stage One, about whether they believe in Jesus.

### Changing Constructs

The grid data have demonstrated clearly that participants change their perception of themselves in relation to other people as they progress through the programme. The essence of change, in narrative form, can be seen in the excerpts from the longitudinal sample (Chapter 10). The post-conversion changes are that their thinking has become clearer and future-oriented, having Jesus as a guide. Their relationships with other people are less conflict-ridden and friendlier; emotionally they feel peaceful and happy.

In helping to revise the client's constructs, Kelly (1955) gave several pointers, some of which can be seen in the operation of the programme.

1. To generate new constructs, novel experience is needed. Kelly advised that this must be done selectively so as not to overwhelm the client. The clearest example of a completely new experience is definitely the ten-day detoxification period during which

unconditional regard and continuous care are given to the participants. Fifty percent of participants (excluding Group A) take that experience as an evidential force for conversion (Table 8-3). Together with the subsequent care and concern that the participants continued to receive during their stay in the New Boys Home, these experiences contribute to the development of new constructs. Kelly's concern about the client mishandling new experiences is apparently safeguarded by the fact that immediate feedback is available, as the participants and helpers live with each other in a closely knitted community. In their daily exchanges, both helper and client are able to adjust to each other's anticipations of events much more easily than when individual therapy is conducted in the clinician's office, the venue in which fixed-role therapy was first practiced.

2. Though Kelly (1955) emphasized that his approach stresses the present, he acknowledged that the past also needs to be worked on, because "it is the stuff which the client's construct system must have been designed to make sense out of ..." (p. 592). He asked, therefore, that therapists help clients to reconstrue certain events and figures in their past and apply adult thinking to these, rather than reacting in an infantile manner. In the conversion process, a person's past is absolved through confession and repentance; then he is reborn through the grace of God, with Jesus as his saviour. In essence, dealing with the past means looking at certain events in the past, examining the mistakes, and then reconstruing the situation in order that the possibilities of repeating past mistakes are minimized in the future. Throughout the programme, the participants are helped to shed their past selves, to adopt a Christian identity, and to maintain it. This is evident in the changes in their perception of their four self elements — as the Drug Self is dropped and the Actual Self and Social Self move towards Jesus, the Ideal Self and others. This is especially apparent on reaching Stage Two, where conversion most frequently occurs within two months of residence in the New Boys Home. For a self-transformation to take place within such a short span of time would be unheard of in any form of therapy. The programme's religious context with its appeal to supernatural powers is obviously more powerful than anything a mortal therapist can do.

3. Kelly required the therapist to design and implement experiments for the client; for example, asking the client to try out a fixed-role sketch with his boss or girl friend, and then bringing back the

experience for discussion in the therapy room. In the programme, Stage Three can be considered as an important experiment for the testing out of the drug-free state. There, participants again face temptation from heroin, either by returning to heroin-infested areas in their outreach work, or when they are on home leave without supervision. Those who can withstand the test gain further experiential evidence and validation of their identity as a Christian. In a sense, this is a form of in vivo behavioural rehearsal, desensitizing the participants to the attraction of heroin.

4. As the client tries out new constructs leading to new behaviours, the therapist, representing a sample of the client's social world, is expected by Kelly to validate those behaviours. For the programme participants, the whole of the community of believers validates their new behaviours constantly and continuously throughout their stay in the programme, and, in this way, the whole community is more powerful than a single therapist in the therapy room. However, the possibility of potential conflicts may also be high in view of the sheer number of people involved in the validation process. Conflicts amongst brothers and between brothers and helpers occur, particularly when the brothers are at different stages in their conversion process. Hence the attrition rate tends to be highest at Stage Two.

The above analysis of the conversion process in terms of Fixed-Role Therapy in a group context affirms the thesis that religion and therapy are compatible, in that both offer a cure of souls, and both target changes in individual lives. This is possible in view of the powerful role played by a person's beliefs on his/her actions. To highlight the interconnectedness between religion and psychotherapy, the discussions so far on the findings, the religious programme, and the constructional approach to addiction and drug rehabilitation are integrated and summarized in the following two tables, Tables 12-1 and 12-2, showing parallel relationships between the psychological status of the participants, features in the religious programme and the corresponding constructional (PCT) interpretation, first with reference to the pre-conversion status, and then to the post-conversion status, of the participants.

In summary, the comparative view given in Tables 12-1 and 12-2 of the participants' psychological status, the religious programme, and a PCT interpretation of the participants' experience of the programme suggests

**Table 12-1  Pre-conversion Status, Religious Programme, and PCT**

| Pre-conversion Status | Features in the Religious Programme | PCT Interpretation |
|---|---|---|
| **Context**<br>Crime-related<br>Other drug abusers | Community of believers | Constructs' range of convenience applicable only to a drug abuser's life |
| **Individual**<br>Isolated, alienated<br>Low self-esteem<br>Immoral, inadequate<br>Severely depressed<br>Hopeless, purposeless | Sinner | Negative self construal<br>Self invalidation<br>Low cognitive complexity (tight construer) |
| **Experience**<br>Escape from reality<br>Withdrawal distress<br>Heroin as coping | Offers hope<br>Confession<br>Repentance<br>Redemption<br>Religious activities (prayer, Worship etc.) bring relief | Constriction in construal leads to all life stresses experienced as withdrawal<br>Drug Self subsystem fails to anticipate events<br>Believe heroin brings relief |

several features in the two approaches that may be conducive to therapeutic change in the participants. Some of these may be common to both a religious programme and the secular approach (PCT); some may be unique to a religious programme that may serve as a challenge to secular workers in the addiction field:

1. A change in social context is brought about when a client enters a supportive religious community/therapeutic group. Hope is raised in the chronic drug abusers when they first join the prayer meetings. Their verbal declaration of being converted serves to indicate their desire for change, raising their hope that help is available. This brings the issue of how to maintain a person's commitment to long term treatment into focus, as the drop-out rate in clients attending a residential therapeutic community is high (Bale et al., 1980). In the religious programme, the fact that the participants are exposed en mass to successful models giving personal testimonies of their experiences, helps to sustain their desire to pursue change, recalling that personal testimony has been cited as the third most frequent reason as a basis for conversion. What is the parallel in a secular approach?

**Table 12-2  Post-conversion Status, Religious Programme, and PCT**

| Pre-conversion Status | Features in the Religious Programme | PCT Interpretation |
|---|---|---|
| **Context** | | |
| Therapeutic community | Community of believers<br>Unconditional care<br>Structured Environment | Therapeutic group<br>Acceptance, concern<br>Structured Environment |
| **Individual**<br>Drug self disowned<br>Isolation & alienation decrease<br>Self-esteem increases<br>Moral, self sufficient<br>Hopeful, purposeful | Reborn as Christians | Therapeutic group members |
| **Experience**<br>Disown Drug Self<br>Identify with Jesus (Christian identity)<br>Involved with others<br>Learning to care and help<br>Emotional security (love, strength, joy etc.) | **Religious Conversion**<br>Jesus & helpers as models<br><br>Continuous care (first ten days in particular)<br><br>Confession<br>Repentance<br>Catharsis<br>Removal of stigma<br>Conversion upon Jesus' love & community solidarity<br><br><br>Learning to cope<br><br><br>Religious activities<br><br>Religious community validates Christian identity | **Fixed Role Therapy**<br>Fixed role sketches<br><br><br>Therapist and group attention<br><br>Observing incidents<br>Formulation of constructions<br><br>Removal of stigma<br>Role enactment in protective environment<br><br>Sociality<br>Commonality<br>Changing constructs through novel experience, reconstrue the past<br>Therapist implements experiments for client<br>Therapist & therapeutic group validate new identity |

2. The care and concern received by the participants contributes to breaking the sense of isolation and alienation felt. The use of religious rituals, which many participants find soothing and cathartic, is unique to the religious approach. Further, the total care (particularly in the

detoxification period) practiced in the programme also poses a challenge to secular practice.

3. Conversion, or in PCT terms, a reconstruction of self, brings about a change in identity, disengaging the participants from their negative Drug Self stereotype. The use of Jesus as an identity model for emulation is a clear message given on first contact with the programme. What is the fixed role sketch that could serve as an alternative in secular practice?

4. The reconstruction of self is brought about by changing the participants' beliefs about themselves; this is done through intensive conversations (Bible lessons, sharing personal testimonies and prayers) and practicing new behaviours such as helping other new brothers. Also from believing that heroin is the cure all for life's problems, the participants come to believe in Jesus as a cure all. What beliefs in the secular context would best serve the participants in their continual struggle in life?

5. The narrowing of focus onto drug-related activities is replaced and expanded by being religiously involved or engaging in novel activities all of which relate the person to other people. What social experiments in particular would be therapeutic for drug abusing clients in the secular setting?

6. The changed self requires validation by other people, whether in the person of a therapist, therapeutic group, or a religious community. Is there a need to expand the validating context to a wider frame, given that re-integration into society is a stated goal in rehabilitation?

The practice implications that follow from these observations are discussed in Chapter Fourteen, the final chapter. As relapse is possible in spite of conversion, and as human frailty is a condition of life, there is a need to understand those who fail to acquire or maintain change in spite of help, be it human or spiritual in nature. The question of relapse and conversion is examined in the following chapter.

# CHAPTER 13

# Relapse

While some participants find fulfilment in Jesus in lieu of heroin, others return to drugs even after conversion, given that 35% of the participants are repeaters of the programme. Examining the role of religious experience in individual lives may offer some insight in understanding such differences in the conversion experience. Womack's (1981) study raises some interesting hypotheses that are relevant to the present discussion.

## Physiological Pre-disposition

Womack (1981) did an anthropological study on a classical Pentecostal church in the United States. In particular, she interviewed a group of converts who had been alcohol and drug abusers before their conversion. Taking the experience of *having the Holy Ghost* as a manifestation of an ecstatic/trance experience, or an equivalent of an altered state of consciousness (ASC), she maintained that drug abuse and the trance experience of being visited by the Holy Ghost were generically related, because they were both ASC as manifested in similar psycho-physiological states of excitement, euphoria, and sometimes analgesia. She thus hypothesized that ecstatic religion satisfies a triad of social, psychological, and psycho-physiological needs similar to those which drive people to drug abuse, and that there is an easy transition from drugs to church for some people, since the same needs are now being fulfilled by the church. One hypothesis is that religious trance continues to satisfy certain psycho-physiological needs that have been present in drug abuse. Hence, ecstatic religion can be as addictive as drugs and alcohol use. She concluded that: "There must be a connector between drugs and religion in order to explain why trance can substitute for drugs as well as one drug can substitute for another" (p. 29).

In the present sample, a variety of religious experiences have been reported which resemble the ecstatic states described by Womack. These experiences have been regarded by some participants as their being touched by the Holy Spirit. Physically, these may involve the body shivering, shaking, or a feeling of dizziness; psychologically, the reported emotions are feelings of joy or relief. Both D1 and D10, who found Jesus completely satisfying, reported such experiences. That drug experiences and religions have a substantial affinity, particularly in the East, is evident from the use of drugs such as hashish by Eastern spiritual masters. Allegro (1971) even argued that the origin of the Judeo-Christian tradition may have been heavily influenced by altered states facilitated by the use of naturally occurring psychedelic substances, such as the mushroom Amanita muscaria or fly agaric. Kramrisch, Otto, Ruck, and Wasson (1986) held a similar view and argued further that all religions originated from the use of psychedelic mushrooms. Timothy Leary (1968) had earlier also concluded from his experimentation with LSD, that in the psychedelic era religion without drugs would be as pointless and unnatural as astronomy without telescopes. Drug-induced religious experience is therefore not unknown. More recent attempts have also been made to uncover a neurophysiologic basis of religious experience. For example, Fenwick (1996) hypothesized that religious experience may be a mainly right hemisphere experience, given that the right side of the brain is dominant for emotion.

Returning to Womack's thesis (1981), it could be that for certain individuals like D1 and D10, their susceptibility to mystical experiences facilitates their religious conversion, and subsequently binds them to their religious commitment. A low level of religious commitment, on the other hand, is experienced as related to relapse.

## Religious Commitment

According to the 26 repeaters in the programme, they relapsed when they were pulled away from walking Jesus' way, because of their inability to abandon their worldly desires for women, wine and song, or as they put it, walking according to their own selfish ways inevitably led them to relapse, since the secular and highly materialistic lifestyle hardly left them room for devotional activities such as prayer, Bible reading and worship within the community of believers. In other words, lacking religious commitment is seen to lead to relapse.

A lack of religious commitment means of course that the person will lose the religious community that protects him from drug exposure, given that the return to old associates has been taken as a major reason for relapse. There are many addiction workers who believe that their clients cannot solve their problems without a change in their environment to promote a drug-free lifestyle. Maddux and Desmond (1980) and Schasre (1966) reported that drug abusers who did well after treatment cited relocation from their usual drug sources and decreased drug supplies as the major factor in recovery. Waldorf (1983) also found that once a person decided to quit, he/she had to give up old friends, avoid drug using situations, and develop leisure or recreational interests in order to be successful. These observations point to the importance of having a validating context for maintaining a person's newly acquired beliefs through conversion. The nature of conversion itself, however, may affect subsequent behaviour in the convert as well.

## The Nature of Conversion

Returning to the twenty-six repeaters, eleven were converted in their subsequent admissions to the programme. One might conveniently argue that their relapse was a function of their not having been converted. However, Hefner (1993), after making a comparative analysis of several authors' accounts of various conversion experiences in different cultural contexts, offered the following insight, which is worth considering. According to him:

> The most necessary feature of religious conversion, it turns out, is not a deeply systematic reorganization of personal meanings but an adjustment in self-identification through the at least nominal acceptance of religious actions or beliefs deemed more fitting, useful, or true ... conversion implies the acceptance of a new locus of self-definition, a new, though not necessarily exclusive, reference point for one's identity. (p. 17)

This view, that conversion does not necessarily lead to a complete reformulation of oneself is also shared by Merrill (1993) and Keyes (1993). Having studied Christian conversion in New Mexico and Thailand respectively, they concluded that conversion does not necessarily entail a reformulation of one's understanding of the ultimate conditions of existence, but it does involve commitment to a new moral authority and a new or re-conceptualized social identity.

Leaving aside the repeaters who had not been converted prior to their relapse, reversion to old ways of thinking and behaving does occur in converts. Although there is clear evidence of an identity transformation, as indicated by the grid measures after the participants have been converted, if Hefner's (1993) observation is tenable that, despite conversion to Christianity, it is possible for a convert to endorse an inclusive view about himself, then the balance between temptation from, and resistance to drugs remains unstable for some individuals. Given the appropriate environmental or socio-psychological factors, the balance could be tipped. Jordon's (1993) study of Chinese conversion offers further insight into understanding the phenomenon of conversion in Chinese communities.

Jordan (1993) sees conversion as "being a self-conscious change in more or less enduring religious belief and affiliation from one religious system to another. 'Religious system' includes both a system of belief and a social structure of believers" (p. 285). This brings the problem of creating and sustaining religious beliefs and membership in a community of believers. Beginning with the background of a traditional China where religious sectarianism flourished, and with adherents of different cults competing with each other in claims of efficacy (Topley, 1967), Jordan argues that conversion in traditional China has been a matter of moving from one deity to another, such as from a village god like the Earth god to Kwan Yin, the Buddhist saviour of souls, depending on how a person experienced a cure from the pantheon of gods available, whether for arthritis, infertility, or bad fortune. The characteristics of Chinese conversion arising from such a background, then, are that of conditionality, additivity, and pantheon interchangeability. Conditionality refers to the evaluation of a new religious belief against a belief that one already holds, and if incompatibility exists between the two, then the new belief would be discarded. Additivity is the addition of beliefs and practices onto the original ones, not as their replacement. Pantheon interchangeablility is the substitution of one deity for another. Hence, conversion across competing alternatives has always been an option in Chinese history. Depending on personal experience, conversion can be facilitated by the subordination of old beliefs to new ones, all of which need not be ultimately true, and some of which can be interchangeable with one another, with little change in cosmology or values for the individual.

As the majority of participants have been involved in triad activities, this has necessarily entailed their worship of Chinese popular deities like Kwan Kung, Wong Tai Sin, and other traditions practiced within triad organizations. Family practices of ancestor worship or worship of Kwan

Yin or other deities are also found. Although six participants claimed they were baptized as Christians when they were very young and a minority had attended Christian schools, they all claimed these experiences meant very little to them. Exposure to Chinese popular religions for the participants is thus high. While it is mandatory that the participants sever their ties with non-Christian beliefs and practices, given Jordan's observations, the possibility of an uneasy balance between the deities could well remain with some of the participants. Additivity and conditionality have been observed in many participants who remarked that all religions are compatible since they lead people to goodness (導人向善), suggesting that the need for a total abandonment of old beliefs may not be necessary. A25 is an example.

In the second interview for A25, held eight weeks after he entered the New Boys Home, he was talking about his conversion experience. Since he had been a devotee of shamanic practices (神打), he was asked if he still retained faith in other deities upon his conversion to the Christian faith , to which he said yes. He elaborated that he believed Jesus could help him, but he would not say other people's gods were false or no good ("我信耶穌幫倒我，但我無話人地 D 神係假或唔好，我唔會咁講。") Because in his past experience he found the practice of inviting Chinese deities (請神) and writing paper talisman (寫符) were effective for things like stopping bleeding after a gang fight, he would still use such methods in future if he were involved in similar situations. However, since he found that Jesus had responded to his plea regarding his kicking heroin, he would rely on Jesus in this particular matter. Additivity seems to apply for him. It should be noted that it took only three days in the New Boys Home for his conversion to take place, an unusually brief period when compared to the norm of around one to two months for most participants. Such little resistance to a new faith might imply additivity is at work.

The question of under what conditions a person would resolve his divided loyalty to Chinese deities upon conversion to Christianity is an interesting one. A future study of those who relapse after conversion would also be informative for their rehabilitation. Obviously there are participants who are able to remain drug free after one admission to the programme. For example, only five in Group D required multiple admissions and all remained drug free at least beyond two years, and some for well over a decade. It may be asked what factors relate to successful transfer of learning acquired through conversion? What leads to some being able to remain committed to their faith while others cannot?

## Successful Rehabilitation

Apart from the conversion experience, there may be psychosocial factors that relate to the maintenance of a person's religious commitment. Research on relapse and relapse prevention have produced a variety of matrices of risk factors (Platt, 1995), depending on whether emphasis is put on background factors, pre- or post-treatment variables, or the approach used in conceptualizing relapse. Joe, Chastain, Marsh, and Simpson (1990) have offered the tentative hypothesis that an underlying concept reflecting the degree of socialization into a supportive network and to a conventional lifestyle is significant in predicting later recidivism to opiate addiction. But then factors relating to the degree of socialization could be numerous, for example, age, educational attainment, degree of criminality prior to, or during drug taking, or the length of drug career. Emerging from conversations with the participants are some suggestions for why relapse occurs after conversion such as the age of the person and the social support available. The younger the person is, the more alternatives he will consider himself to have in terms of making a comeback to a previous life style of fame and glory in the secular world; this is presumably related to the stage of drug career he is at, in that again, the younger he is, the less likely it is that he will see himself as having hit bottom. Then pressure from the environment, such as the family putting pressure on the person for not contributing to their livelihood, could push him towards a quick return to the hustle and bustle of secular life, in the same way that he was driven towards heroin use in the first place. The Society's open invitation to the participants to join its work as full-time volunteer helpers after rehabilitation is of course serving a relapse protective function, as large scale studies elsewhere also found that the strongest predictor of successful drug treatment outcome is in fact time in treatment (DeLeon and Jainchill, 1982; DeLeon, 1986; Hubbard et al., 1989).

Group D participants form a unique group in that they have chosen to stay with the Society. Taking conversion as entailing a re-socialization into a Christian lifestyle, according to Joe et al.'s (1990) thesis, they would be regarded as highly socialized. They apparently enjoy optimum mental health according to the indices employed in the study. They rate themselves highly and identify closely with Jesus. Furthermore, they live according to Jesus' way. They see themselves as happy, hopeful, and fulfilled, despite cognitive simplicity in their construct system, a condition seen as related to maladjustment. There is some research evidence to suggest that cognitive structure changes are found after therapy, although the results are inconclusive. For example, Raz-Duvshani (1986) argued that as a restructuring of the construct system towards greater complexity results from therapy, the more freedom a person will have in anticipating events, hence the greater the possibility of choice of alternative forms of behaviour for him/her. Yet for Group D participants (the same argument applies to Groups B and C) who are obviously not maladjusted individuals, their simple construct system and good adjustment may reflect Kelly's (1955) positive view of constriction in construing. He said, "If one wishes to view constriction positively, he can see it as a way of making one's world manageable by shrinking it to a size he can hold in his own two hands" (p. 901). Jesus is the answer to life's problems for his followers. For Group D participants, their sustained religious commitment centres on their single-minded devotion to Jesus.

That sustained religious commitment is correlated with effective rehabilitation is found by Peters (1980) in her follow-up study of graduates from the Teen Challenge programme in New York, a drug rehabilitation programme initiated by Wilkerson (1963) using baptism by the Holy Spirit to help teenagers in the New York slums to combat their drug habit, a programme not unlike the one run by St. Stephen's Society. Peters (1980) located twelve subjects who had left the programme for five years and stayed drug-free, and compared them to ten who relapsed. She concluded that all twelve positive cases expressed a verbal commitment to Christian beliefs as taught in their programme, with nine of them maintaining regular practices of prayer and Bible study, either on an individual or a group basis, while the other three did so irregularly. Eight of the twelve were employed by a religious organization. She, however, questioned whether this employment reflected a deep religious commitment, or an inability to cope in a more threatening environment. The ten who relapsed reverted to drugs when they discontinued their religious practices, though when they re-entered a therapeutic community of a similar nature, or the same programme, they managed to remain drug-free again, except for one who smoked marijuana despite his religious commitment.

To summarize, the possibility that physiological predispositions may render certain individuals more susceptible to religious experiences is worth exploring. On the other hand, particular to Chinese conversional experience, the ability to maintain an inclusive self-identity, which encompasses both old and new beliefs, may render a person susceptible to old temptations, despite religious conversion having taken place. In any case, successful rehabilitation would imply the need for a continuous validation of beliefs within a supportive context, demonstrating again the impact of beliefs on behaviour. This brings the discussion back to the role of religion in healing, our final chapter.

# CHAPTER 14

# Religion and Healing

What practice implications can be drawn from our examination of the religious dimensions in St. Stephen's Society's drug rehabilitation programme for addiction work, as seen within the context of the role of belief in therapeutic change?

As Eliade (1963) reminded us, "obviously there are no *purely* religious phenomena … because religion is human it must for that very reason be something social, something linguistic, something economic — you cannot think of man apart from language and society" (p. xiii). While this study takes a psychological perspective in understanding the believers' religious experience, the data obtained is the expression of a relationship the believer has to the Transcendent. Questions regarding the nature of the Transcendent remain outside the scope of the study.

## Religious Beliefs as Cognitive Mediators

In discussing relapse prevention with drug abusers, amongst other things, Daley (1987) urged that clinicians should be willing to evaluate the clients' personal beliefs and assumptions about relapse in order to improve their service to their clients. Religion is about beliefs, ethical codes, and practices (Spencer, 1956, Lewis, 1984; Joseph, 1988). After conversion, the participants believe that they have been healed and given a new life (symbolically marked by baptism). Jesus is with them and gives them moral guidance, and their behaviour changes for the better. In other words, they have acquired a new set of beliefs about themselves that entail a very different worldview from that of old, which is the dope fiend's world. Researchers are still debating which specific, identifiable aspects within a person's religious experience, contribute to life satisfaction (Ellison, 1991), that religious beliefs contribute to positive mental health is now well recognized, though one must not lose sight of the fact that religion can also have negative impacts on people. Schumaker (1992) lists some of these as generating high levels of guilt, creating anxiety and fear by way of belief in hell or a punishing god, or encouraging dependency and conformity. However, for chronic drug abusers who have been locked in misery, even risking such effects may not be a total violation of mental soundness, as Taggart (1994) remarked: "A religion that would seem harsh and punitive to someone with a flexible superego and a reliable emotional support system may offer welcome strength, companionship, and structure to an impulse-ridden individual living in a chaotic environment ... there are many recipes for wholeness". (p. 116)

Taggart (1994) captures perhaps unknowingly Kelly's whole approach to understanding life, that there are always alternative constructions one can have for any experience. This is the impact of what religious belief, or for that matter, secular, or any other form of belief, can have on people's behaviour. In other words, beliefs offer a worldview, an interpretation of how events should be seen and of what actions to take. They serve as cognitive mediators (Dull and Skokan, 1995), or in Kellyian terms, they provide particular constructs for shaping experience, an ideology, in short, for guiding behaviour. Waldorf (1973) considered that an ideology:

> ... gives the ex-addict a framework within which to understand and interpret his past behaviour — he was a sinner, childish, a victim of his environment; it helps temper whatever guilt or remorse he may feel for undoubtedly many antisocial acts; and it provides him with rough guidelines for how to live in the future. It becomes a philosophy of life. (p. 154)

A positive religious framework can induce feelings of control, self-enhancement, optimism or other forms of life satisfaction through giving meaning to events. For example, prayer can induce feelings of control for a person by changing his/her perception of events (McIntosh and Spilka, 1990). D11 was converted on the basis of a single event involving praying for his son's recovery from an illness, a situation within which he felt he was unable to help. The praying gave him the conviction that Jesus would intervene, thereby making the incident manageable for him. The continuous increase in self-esteem (indicated by high self convergence) is clearly seen in the participants after conversion. Being a child of God means one is lovable and valued, as so amply demonstrated by the unconditional care and concern given to the new boys during detoxification. A concomitant view towards a positive future is indicated by results from the C-HOPE and the C-PIL. The message in Luke, Chapter Eleven, verses nine to ten, is of course hope inducing: "So I say to you, ask, and you will receive; seek, and you will find; knock, and the door will be opened to you. For everyone who asks receives, those who seek find, and to those who knock, and the door will be opened to them". The belief that one is within God's plan, and that Jesus helps during times of trouble is equally consoling. Emotional security based on love, strength, confidence, peace, etc. acquired after conversion also contributes to a sense of well-being.

Just as addiction provides a way of life for some people (Gorsuch and Butler, 1976) such as the participants whose need for heroin got them out of bed and onto the streets, religion may offer them another approach to a total life commitment. Such religious commitment could be seen to meet a similar need for a focus and purpose in life that some may find in the lifestyle of a dope fiend, or as Womack (1981) sees it, religion satisfies certain psychophysiological needs that may be present in drug use. There are those who have even approached addiction as essentially spiritual crises (Grof, 1993; May, 1988, Van Kaam, 1966). Carl Jung was quoted to say this of one of his clients, "his craving for alcohol was the equivalent, on a low level, of the spiritual thirst of our being for wholeness, expressed in medieval language: the union with God" (cited in Sikorsky, 1990, p. 14). May (1988), having worked with drug abusers for years, came to see addiction of all kinds as a deep-seated form of idolatry that draws people away from God's love, because the objects of our addictions become our false gods. Our true desire, however, is God's love, and it is grace that heals, grace being the outpouring of God's "healing, love, illumination, and reconciliation" (p. 17). Jesus' love forms the basis for conversion for half of our participants.

How are the participants socialized into a Christian way of thinking and living that may have parallels within therapeutic work?

## Religious Healing and Therapy

In discussing the role of ministers as healers, Robinson (1986) sees all forms of healing to have the following features:

1. The healer is seen to have the power and authority to heal;
2. Previous healing or other divine events endorses such healing power;

3. Healing is performed in response to a request from the sick person, or friends, or relatives. Hence, expectant trust (Frank, 1974) is already present;
4. A supportive context exists within which healing takes place;
5. Suggestions and authoritative conversations are part of the healing method; and,
6. Physical means are used to deliver the healing action.

Others have uncovered even more specific parallels between the therapeutic process and religious healing (Csordas, 1990; Jacobs, 1992; Kilbourne & Richardson, 1988). Maton and Wells (1995, p. 183) summarized these as follows:

1. Changing deeply held, maladaptive cognition;
2. The sharing of pain, reduction of anxiety, and emotional release within a context of trusting relationships; and,
3. Behavioural change follows from altered cognition and emotions.

The therapeutic community model used in St. Stephen's Society's programme may be seen to encompass a number of practice measures in achieving the above three therapeutic goals which may inform social work practice.

### *Acceptance*

The trio of attributes of *understanding*, *acceptance*, and *sincerity* (Traux & Carkhuff, 1967; Carkhuff & Bereson, 1967) as fundamental counsellor dimensions need no debate in their being adopted by therapists of any orientation, the operationalization of each on the part of the therapist, however, can be controversial. Counsellor training manuals abound as to how best these may be delivered. The training of social workers through skill laboratories or field placement is taken as essential, particularly in casework service where the worker-client encounter is most intense. The continuous care model practiced in the Society's programme, during the detoxification period, exemplifies a unique form of promise to its participants of the care and attention they will receive. Such an experience has indeed brought many of them to Christ and a new life. This ideology of care should challenge the more traditional form of care delivery via the office set-up. The possibility of its being practiced in a non-religious residential treatment setting should be explored.

## The Use of Rituals

Prayer is a central activity in the programme. Apart from it being central in worship services, participants are encouraged to pray as often as the need arises. It can be an individual and/or a group activity. Apart from thanks-giving, the worship sessions allow for confession and catharsis to take place. Participants are free to talk about their problems and fears, healing is then done through prayer. Individuals who practice praying, chanting, or meditating have reported that these strategies help to clear their mind and even reduce physical discomfort (Ramaswami & Sheikh, 1989). Similar effects have also been reported by our participants, particularly during the detoxification period. The therapeutic value of Christian ritual has been highlighted by Griffith and Young (1988), for example, in helping people through mourning.

The therapeutic value of using ritual in therapy work has been recognized in recent years. Imber-Black and Roberts (1992) see rituals as symbolic rites that help people do the work of relating, healing, believing, and celebrating. They can be impregnated with symbolic meaning that can serve to liberate or condemn. Parker and Horton (1996) suggest that clients can be helped to develop personal rituals using words, names, and the sense of touch. It should be noted that rituals need not be of a religious kind. Personal rituals can be found in everyday customary actions such as in taking a meal, or in drinking, singing, dancing, game playing, or bed time routines.

## Talking Cure

In the professional field constructivism as a paradigm is heatedly discussed and debated. For example, an entire volume of the *Journal of Teaching in Social Work*, (volume 8, Numbers 1/2 in 1993) has been devoted to revising social work education from a social constructivist approach. The emphasis on cognition is paramount, and is vital for the understanding, and therefore treatment, of all forms of problems, physical or otherwise. Although the use of the talking cure is not new, and has its root in the Biblical tradition, as Proverbs Chapter 15 verse 4 states: "A soothing word is a tree of life …", how it works is still being studied. Bankart (1997) has given a very competent treatise on the history of the talking cure in both western and eastern traditions. It is through conversations that reality is transformed for the participants, whether in the form of confession, the giving of testimonies, praying, singing, reading the Bible, or receiving messages from the Holy

Spirit through images and pictures. Research on cognitive control seems to suggest that controlling beliefs can affect physical experiences. Cognitive strategies for reducing pain have long been found effective in the form of using imagery, distraction, or self-talk (Spanos, Horton, & Chaves, 1975; Kanfer & Goldfoot, 1966; Kanfer & Seider, 1973; Langer, Janis, & Wolfer, 1975). The use of prayer for detoxification in reducing withdrawal pains for the participants further confirms the efficacy of cognitive controls. Changing wholly and entirely a person's belief system, of course, represents the cognitive approach on a grand scale. The whole ideology of the programme thus poses searching questions about value perspectives in therapy, for example, the issue of client self-determination, and the logical positivistic view of a value-free world. Fisher (1991) has discussed eloquently the problems involved in the pursuit of the ideal of self-determination in social work practice, and ends with a constructive perspective to resolve the issue. Apart from re-sensitizing practitioners to the issue of values, the power of the word as used within a total healing community presents yet another challenge to social work practice.

### Ideology

The use of the therapeutic community in drug treatment has been favourably reviewed (DeLeon, 1984, 1986, 1990–91). While the aims and the structural aspects in this form of treatment are familiar to many, for example, the emphasis on personal growth, the use of a highly structured environment, and the use of peer therapists, the role of ideology as an important dimension is rarely mentioned. Antze (1976) attributed this neglect on the part of social scientists to the fact that ideologies often appeared shallow, incoherent and thus of little importance. He subsequently argued for the essential importance of the role of ideologies in peer psychotherapy in a community setting, in that ideologies serve as a cognitive antidote to combat the particular conditions shared by the residents, in the case of addiction, it would be the relapse process.

In St. Stephen's Society's programme, that Jesus can be seen as serving as a cognitive antidote to relapse is a clear message given to the participants during the very first meeting. A clear message is conducive to the persuasive process (conversations) in that "clear conceptual organizers" and "frameworks for how to change" have been found to relate to therapeutic benefits (Lieberman, 1973, pp. 238 & 442). Given that a person's constructs, or beliefs, are important in guiding behaviour, making these explicit not only help in their transmission, presumably they also facilitate consensual validation of the beliefs by the group, which in turn serves to reinforce the clarity of group beliefs.

To recapitulate, the characteristics of the religious approach found in St. Stephen's Society's programme are as follows:

1. It conveys a sense of total care to the individual, from the unconditional continuous care given, particularly prominent in the detoxification period, to the promise of salvation. Practically speaking, the Society offers shelter to a person as long as he/she remains in the Society and serves Jesus.
2. The use of rituals for healing, the immediate experience being the sense of relief these rituals bring to the individual. More importantly though, through the processes involved in confession, prayer, Bible reading, worship, and ultimately baptism, beliefs about oneself are changed, from that of a sinner, to that of a new-born Christian.
3. The religious community, in which intensive encounters between helpers and clients occur, also serves the function of what Berger and Luckman (1967) see as transforming the subjective reality of the help-seekers, through their continuous conversations with new significant others who are their brothers and sisters in Christ.
4. The presence of a clear ideology, phrased as Jesus' way, serves as a cognitive antidote to human suffering.

How may social workers incorporate the religious/spiritual dimension into their practice?

## Religion and Social Work Practice

As a person's belief system represents his/her view of reality, it is important for the therapist to attempt to learn and understand the client's religious beliefs and how they may contribute to, or maintain the problem he/she presents. Religious beliefs may also act as a resource for solutions. For example, for Christians, the image of a sinner may contribute to a strong sense of guilt in a client, but at the same time, the concept of salvation may be most therapeutic. Prest and Keller (1993) have advocated the use of spiritual beliefs, myths, and metaphors for working with clients. They have identified several strategies such as eliciting fundamental beliefs that are contributing to the presenting problem, identifying discrepancies between beliefs and behaviour, or the use of quotations from religious texts giving directions for change.

As a religion necessarily entails a value perspective for its believers, which in turn mediates their actions, value clarification can be an important therapeutic goal. Data, in terms of construct use by the participants in the present study, clearly indicate their moral concerns which, upon conversion, change from the endorsement of negative values to positive ones. Studies have been made of the values held by alcoholics and drug abusers, with some writers postulating a relationship between values and addiction (Freed, 1968; Jacobson, Ritter, & Mueller, 1977; Martini & Brook, 1978; Toler, 1975). While Maslow (1964) regarded alcoholism and addiction to be examples of valueless-ness or value pathology, Eckhardt (1976) observed a change in recovering AA members from egocentric values to ethical values, and Maxwell (1984) noted that recovery in AA involved basic changes in "ideas, attitudes, and values" (p. 70). The existence of a probable relationship between value and addiction prompted Rokeach (1981) to propose the use of self-confrontational value therapy in drug abuse treatment. Brown and Peterson (1990) have also developed specific procedures for value therapy. Briefly, the first step involves identifying and clarifying held values; the second step is that of self-evaluation or behavioural monitoring; the third step is to arouse self-dissatisfaction by producing contradictions between a person's values and related behaviours through confrontational feed-back. Such cognitive-behavioural interventions need not be confined to the treatment of addiction, as studies by Rokeach (1971) and Rokeach and Cochrane (1972) have shown that when self-confrontational pro-cedures bring about cognitive dissonance between existing held values or value/behaviour conflicts, this may result in long-term value and behaviour change. Thus, helping a client clarify his/her religious values can be therapeutic.

A religious/spiritual perspective also provides techniques that can be used therapeutically. That prayers bring about positive, cathartic effects has been acknowledged by the participants of this study. Taggart (1994) advocated the use of journaling, meditation, and dialogues.

As a religion may exercise powerful controls over a person's behaviour (Taggart, 1994), participation in religious groups can have a significant psychosocial impact on people. Lewandowski and Canda (1995) have developed a typological model for the assessment of religious groups for use in social work practice, utilizing leadership style and recruiting methods as indicators of social control. This serves to inform practitioners of the possible impacts on clients participating in different religious groups.

In social work practice, the impact of religion on a person may be understood by examining those beliefs the client holds that are derived from a religious framework, and how these may relate to his/her problem. For example, how may the image of the sinner in Christian terms contribute to negative behaviours, such as stealing and lying, manifested by an adolescent? Applying the grid method to elicit constructs from the client regarding roles and situations related to his/her misbehaviour is one way of investigating the issue from an insider's perspective. Thus, understanding religion as providing cognitive mediators, and from the "active viewpoint of believers" (Paden, 1992) opens up a potential area in therapeutic work hitherto very much neglected in social work practice (Loewenberg, 1988; Marty, 1980).

Returning to addiction work, for some participants, religious conversion does not necessarily entail a cure. As reminded by Muffler et al. (1992), religion is not a panacea or a perfect solution, but the present study of a religious approach to drug rehabilitation raises a series of questions for drug counsellors.

## Drug Counselling

When addiction is seen as a question of maladjustment to life circumstances, the cure must go beyond detoxification and towards helping the person to deal with life. Waldorf's (1983) study of heroin addicts who achieved remission on their own, and of those who succeeded via treatment, found that the factors identified with cure represent the basic building blocks in human functioning, such as improvement in intimate relationships (like marriage), changes in social networks, increased work opportunities, health concerns, and more global factors such as maturation and a sense of who the abuser is or wishes to be. If these factors are seen to provide the aims and purposes of drug treatment and rehabilitation, then it rightfully belongs to the realm of social work in that it aims at restoring people's capacity for social functioning (Zastrow, 1999).

Barber (1995a), following the emerging trends in drug abuse treatment in adopting a Trans-theoretical Model of Change, has integrated a social work perspective into such a model, drawing particularly on the potential of social work's *person-in-environment* tradition to guide intervention through the various stages in the addiction cycle, extending intervention beyond the individual drug abuser. Barber (1995b) also rightly argued for moving resistant drug abusers into treatment. Several issues are raised from the constructional interpretation of St. Stephen's Society's programme:

    I.   Question of motivation and commitment to treatment and rehabilitation.

    II.   Question of a care delivery model.

    III.   Question of a fixed-role sketch.

    IV.   Question of what beliefs to inculcate in clients.

    V.   Question of what social experiments to implement.

    VI.   Question of a validating context.

The aim of this discussion is to draw implications for practice from lessons learned from the participants' rehabilitative experience in the religious programme, in order to inform practices in non-religious drug rehabilitation, viewed from a personal construct perspective.

For Stage One participants, joining the programme and verbally admitting to being converted signifies to them a hope for change, this raises the issue of sustaining motivation for change in people in drug rehabilitation. The probability of a caring community being able to sustain motivation more effectively than a lone drug counsellor is reflected in the fact that nearly half of the participants came to the programme involuntarily on account of their involvement with the court, but then stayed on. The abundance of live models of success, presented by recovered persons now serving as helpers in the programme, serves very much as an anchorage for many. The question of motivating people to receive, and then stay in drug treatment, is a major concern, Miller's whole concept of motivational interviewing being one example (Miller, 1983; Miller & Rollnick, 1991). Kelly's (1955) answer to the question of motivation is that "the organism is delivered fresh into the psychological world alive and struggling" (p. 37). The question is, to what direction will it turn? In terms of those drug abusing individuals who go in and out of treatment agencies, instead of looking at the problem as a matter of their lacking motivation for change, and seeing it as Miller and Rollnick (1991) do in their formulation of motivational interviewing as: "... a particular way to help people recognize and do something about their present or potential problems ..." (p. 52), the question for service providers becomes one of thinking of ways to keep them in treatment, and of pointing them in a direction that society would like them to move towards. This has much to do with the nature of the interface between the individual and his/her environment.

The importance of the social context for sustaining the direction of movement of the individual has been demonstrated by the initiation of and the quitting of drug taking activities, in that the first contact with drugs predominantly takes place through experimenting within the context of peer or sub-cultural groupings, and that the social context is often made use of in drug rehabilitation, such as therapeutic communities or self-help groups (Wells, 1990). While the "power of the group" is vital in terms of the persuasive force it generates on the individual, the participants' experience of the religious programme has demonstrated that that force need not be didactic. They were moved instead by *love*, Jesus' love as expressed initially through the continuous care they received in the detoxification period, and subsequently, the total care offered by the Society, if they decide to remain in it. This raises two issues.

First, the care and concern (Jesus' love, comradeship) received by the participants helps break their sense of isolation and alienation, and contributes to their sense of emotional security (love, security, strength, confidence, joy). This is seen to relate directly to their rehabilitation. The continuous care model practiced in the religious programme particularly challenges secular approaches in addiction work, in the sense that the need for dedicated professionals in this field is clearly indicated. More specifically, such a practice of continuous care in the initial stage of drug rehabilitation is worth exploration by workers in a non-religious context.

The second issue is that the concept of total care challenges the idea of rehabilitation as a "time-limited process". In any case, that the attraction of heroin to its users ceases completely only for Stage Four participants (at least three years after detoxification) also indicates the need for long-term treatment. Concomitantly, the need for a change in the social context within relapse prevention is indicated when a return to old associates is cited as the major reason for relapse. This again affirms that individual therapy is unlikely to succeed in treating chronic addiction, an observation already made by addiction workers (Ch'ien, 1994; Washton, 1995). Further, as relapse is an inherent feature in addiction, a "revolving door" policy in treatment must be allowed to cater for people to return to treatment.

In successful cases, the dramatic disowning of the Drug Self after conversion (at Stage Two), which continues throughout the rehabilitative process, indicates the need for an identity change to combat chronic addiction. The significant change in mental status beginning at Stage Two (lifting of depression, increase in hope and purpose in life) also suggests that treatment criteria must go beyond the sole emphasis on abstinence. Other indices for change should be considered as treatment goals. The three areas of change reported by the longitudinal sample may provide a guide for consideration: clear thinking, pro-social behaviour, and positive emotions.

A change of self identity entails global lifestyle changes. In Kellyian terms, self transformation involves a change in beliefs about oneself, as so clearly indicated in the participants' change in self descriptions: from being immoral to highly moral, being of low self sufficiency to being highly self-sufficient. Identity change is in turn related to increase in self esteem and pro-social behaviours, bringing the person closer to other people. Hence, to transform the lone drug abuser, the importance of a positive social environment within which the person can experiment with new roles is indicated.

The presence of an identity model for emulation and a clear ideology that provides a direction for change are important to changing beliefs about oneself. This is reflected in the convergence of the Actual Self, Ideal Self, and Jesus, and the increasing trend in Purpose-in-Life scores, which begin at Stage Two and continue through Stage Three and Four. In the religious programme, an ideal and a purpose in life are given in the image of Jesus, supported by personal testimonies from those who have been successfully reformed. This implies that non-directive therapy emphasizing catharsis and maximizing self-determination in clients is inappropriate in treating chronic addiction. The need for moral guidance is indicated.

The low cognitive complexity found for all participants irrespective of stage of rehabilitation, suggests that simple rules for action may be a better guide for chronic drug abusers under treatment, recalling that the major reason for their continual drug use was that of escape from reality, meaning that heroin solved all problems for them, requiring little thinking on their part in dealing with life problems. Learning to think in a complex manner may prove difficult for them. The importance of an ideology as a cognitive antidote (Antze, 1976) is demonstrated in the emulation of the Christian way in the religious programme. An alternative would need to be found by exploring cultural values appropriate to the type of clients a secular programme serves. This relates to the choice of role models.

In order to facilitate self transformation, against the model of Jesus being the ideal, what fixed role sketch, what beliefs may prove effective for emulation in drug treatment in secular contexts? This brings attention back to the basic thesis of the present study, that of the role of belief in therapeutic change, and the value basis for people's actions. The grid method would be a way to research this area in order to derive an alternative role model and sets of beliefs in the process of self transformation. The relevance of value clarification in prevention work (De Haes, 1987) may also be put into practice using the grid.

Upon the adoption of a new identity, the need for continual validation of the transformed self is important, since the present study indicated that positive changes are still found beyond the immediate stage of conversion (Stage Two), in particular, greater improvement in mental status (being depression free, hopeful and purposeful) is found the longer the participants stay in the programme (Stage Four participants). Apart from implying again the need for long-term treatment in chronic addiction, the kinds of social experiments needed for validating experiences in the converts, either through religious conversion, or through therapy, would be related to the acquisition of new values in them. In the religious programme, serving other people as part of a Christian way of life, brings the participants back into society at large, through their outreach work with the destitute, including active drug abusers. Apart from it being a testing ground to gauge their resistance to heroin, such experiences would also be self validating. In secular treatment, the possibility of involving clients in self-help groups or community service would be alternatives worth exploring. However, the question of the stigmatization of drug abusers as mentally ill people will have to be combated. In St. Stephen's Society's model of care, the extensive use of volunteers as helpers in all stages of the rehabilitative process serves to counteract stigmatization. A greater use of volunteers in secular addiction work may serve to enlarge the validating context for clients in recovery, and in this way, lowering the impact of stigmatization.

Given the potential therapeutic values of religious healing then, how would a social scientist resolve the tension between religion and science, social science included?

## Belief and Therapeutic Change

Warren (1993) sees the tension created in the personal construct approach to understanding religion to lie in Kelly's formulation of people as *inquiring* scientists, versus the *absolutist* position inherent in adopting a religious faith. A personal construct analysis of religion attempts to understand how individual believers construe religion to be, and what implications it will have for them. For example, Kelly (1969a) himself has offered an analysis of the story of Eden in his discussion of sin and psychotherapy. Todd (1987) used the grid to ask people what they believe and to help them to reflect on their beliefs. He advocated the use of the grid for analysing growth in belief.

Seen from this angle, the present study can be regarded as another such attempt, as the participants' experience of self and others, including their image of Jesus, unfolds across the different rehabilitative stages. However, Warren (1993) raises the thorny issue that such an approach verges on equating religion with relativism, which is incompatible with the absolutist claims of most religions. He appeals to Hegel's work for a solution, in that instead of pointing out the futility of trying to answer questions about the truth value of religious statements, as no agreement can be reached about them, Hegel (1798–99/1961) suggested that instead the consequences of acquiring religious beliefs should be considered.

Judging from the present data, believing in Jesus means change for the participants, a new life as a Christian. Yet there is also a tendency for some participants to see religion as a matter of obeying commands (the notion of Jesus as a moral guide). This perhaps, may lead to an understanding of relapse when it occurs after conversion, in that the repeaters in the programme return to drugs when they obey their inner desires for their old life rather than Jesus' command not to take drugs. Hegel argued that this view of basing morality on commands is mistaken. Rather, he proposed the idea of love as an emotion that leads to natural goodness as if a command had been necessary. With reference to the Sermon on the Mount which traditionally has been taken to symbolize taking Jesus' teaching as reverence for the law, Hegel argued:

> The Sermon does not teach reverence for the laws; on the contrary, it exhibits that which fulfills the law but annuls it as law and so is something higher than obedience to law and makes law superfluous. (1798–99/1961, p. 212)

Hegel made a distinction between the ethical life as contrasted with morality, a contrast between a free (autonomous) and an unfree (enslaved) state of mind. Warren (1993) takes Hegel's point to mean "we must look to the 'good' as a quality of mind initially expressed in the concept of love and developing (as he saw the wider ramifications) into the notion of the ethical life (Sittlichkeit)" (p. 486).

If the essence of religion is rediscovered as the "progressive unfolding of love or as a more general principle of uncoerced, free, spontaneous social life" (Warren, 1993, p. 487), Warren then argues, this is a "natural sociality" (p. 486) which leads to a harmonious social life. Here, Kelly's (1955) Commonality and Sociality corollaries point to the complex inter- actions between person and environment in the individual's constructions of the world. Personal Construct Theory and religion would have met in the living out of an ethical life. Indeed, the idea of love has been taken by the participants in this study as leading them to Jesus and away from drugs.

In reviewing outcome research on the effectiveness of psychotherapy, Lambert and Bergin (1994) concluded that while there is no strong evidence that any one system of psychotherapy is consistently superior to all others, they found "Interpersonal, social, and affective factors common across therapies still loom large as stimulators of patient improvement" (p. 181), and that improvement in clients can be greatly facilitated by "a therapeutic relationship that is characterized by trust, warmth, acceptance, and human wisdom" (p. 181), an observation pointing to attributes not unlike the basic core counsellor dimensions promulgated by humanistic therapists decades ago (Carkhuff & Bereson, 1967; Traux & Carkhuff, 1967), attributes which are conducive to Warren's (1993) notion of the unfolding of love and a free and spontaneous social life.

If the ethical life is basic to human living, then the business of psychotherapy is to assist clients in achieving it. Values, which are inherent within a person's beliefs, or constructs in Kellyian terms, must be involved in the reconstruction of tragic lives. Value neutrality would then be an untenable position. Long ago Maslow (1969) warned that "the classical philosophy of science as morally neutral, value free, value neutral is not only wrong, but is extremely dangerous" (p. 724). In the social work field, Pilseker (1978) wrote: "social workers cannot be nonjudgmental and they should not attempt to be so. They are merchants of morality and should acknowledge this fact openly instead of talking as if they believed that 'anything goes'" (p. 55). Glasser (1984) also considered that the non-judgmental approach might lead "to a practice that at best is not helpful to our clients and at worst can be quite harmful to them...the worker has both the right and the obligation to place the client's decision-making process in a moral context" (p. 8).

To clarify one's values is to understand what one believes in. In this study, chronic heroin abusers are seen to have developed beliefs that heroin is able to help them cope with life in the course of their drug taking, a belief structure which ultimately caused them misery. Believing in Jesus has led some of them away from drugs. Kelly's (1955) Personal Construct Theory has been demonstrated to provide a viable framework for understanding people's beliefs. The constructional approach is able to exemplify psychotherapy as a scientific and moral enterprise (London, 1964), in its ability to unravel beliefs, and to provide a methodology for doing so. The cognitive perspective on addiction taken in the study is also compatible with such an approach, as it seeks to understand drug taking behaviour in terms of what such an activity means to the drug user, and what beliefs the person holds regarding drugs and drug use. Peele (1988, 1990) has also advocated a values approach to addiction. He criticized the war on drugs approach as ineffective because it ignores personal values and assumes addiction to be a medical problem which can be remedied by reducing drug supply and providing medical treatment to those in need. Instead, he argued that people must be taught constructive values such as work, responsibility, achievement, and a sense of community involvement. When positive alternatives are opened to them, their priority in life should switch from drugs to other more pro-social concerns, as is seen happening to the participants of this study.

Admittedly, there can be more than one way to bring about change, as Kelly (1969b) says: "There is no particular kind of psychotherapeutic relationship — no particular kind of feelings — no particular kind of interaction that is itself a psychotherapeutic panacea ..." (p. 223), so there is no one form of treatment for all forms of addictive behaviour. However, in discussing the source of change in psychotherapy, and arguing from a constructivist position, while accepting that psychotherapeutic techniques and methods may be classified as affective, cognitive, or behavioural operationally speaking, Rosen (1991) asserts that:

> ... what accounts theoretically for substantial and durable therapeutic change is cognitive modification and reorganization. It is the revision and reintegration of knowledge structures that produces significant long-range gain. No matter how cathartic an affective technique proves to be or rewarding a behavioural strategy, unless the patient's knowledge structures are modified, I would not expect enduring improvement. (p. 167)

A meaningful framework for social work research and practice requires that it encompasses contemporary scientific thought and is consistent with the values of the profession (Witkin & Gottschalk, 1988). Kelly's postpositivist personal construct approach is seen to provide such on both epistemological and methodological grounds. Given the onslaught against the positivist paradigm in social work research (Heineman, 1981), Personal Construct Theory provides a viable alternative, in that seen from the point of view of the critical realist, maintaining that reality exists would safeguard against epistemological anarchy, given that relativism is seen to be entailed by the other end of the paradigm choice, the constructivistic position (Fisher, 1991; Nigel & O'Byrne, 2000). While the epistemological dilemma regarding how truth claims can ever be made is still unresolved, and some suggest that there is merit in its being unresolved, since premature closure of the issue would prevent progress in the discussions (Thomas & Roghaar, 1990), the case of religion would require the search for universals which the postpositivist stance can well accommodate. Methodologically, Kelly (1955) has provided the grid method, which has inherent flexibility in its usage, whether as a quantitative or a qualitative technique. This falls in line with the current thinking on combined methodology (Brannen, 1992; Tashakkovi & Teddlie, 1998). Furthermore, Kelly's (1955) approach gives prominence to respect for the uniqueness and dignity of the individual in attempting to achieve understanding from the insider's perspective. While his therapy is growth-oriented, it also requires that both therapist and client be jointly held responsible for actions negotiated. Such an approach is consistent with the values of the social work profession.

This study has demonstrated that the impact of religion can be considerable on individuals. It is all the more important when social work, or any profession aiming at effecting change in people's lives, is seen as a moral undertaking. Religion is about values, or as Warren (1993) puts it, the ethical life. Taking the religious dimension seriously in our work with clients would be mandatory. Christian conversion brings a particular set of values to the converts. It would be very relevant to discover the kinds of values that sustain individuals who have made successful recovery in secular forms of treatment, bearing in mind again Kelly's (1969b) wisdom that there cannot be but one psychotherapeutic panacea for all problems. The search for the most effective forms of treatment for particular types of clients is still an urgent task in addiction work for all concerned. Our story of ascension from Coffin to Heaven remains one such search for answers to life's misery.

# Grid Measurements

## The Measurement of Self-Identity

Norris and Makhlouf-Norris (1976) have devised a Self-Identity System to indicate how a person sees himself/herself. They see self-conception to have at least three important components: the *Actual Self*, which is the representation of the person now; the *Social Self*, which is the representation of how other people see the person; and the *Ideal self*, being the representation of a person's desired aim. From there, a self-identity plot can be constructed as follows:

1. Constructs are elicited by using the method of self-identification (Kelly, 1955, p. 219), which is the basic triadic procedure but using the *Actual Self* as one of the three elements in every presentation of elements.
2. The elements are then rated using the standard procedure.
3. The resulting grid (constructs x element ratings) is then subjected to the INGRID programme (Slater, 1972) which performs principal components analysis on the ratings of the elements by constructs, generating, amongst other indices, values for the distances between any pair of elements as a ratio of the expected distance between all pairs of elements in the grid. These measures of *distances between elements* can be used to examine how people identify themselves as being similar or dissimilar to certain people, given that the element list consists of people. Conventionally, these element ratios have a minimum of 0, a mean of 1, and rarely exceed 2. A pair of elements with a distance close to 0 is construed as virtually identical, a distance close to 2 will be seen as being dissimilar, and a distance close to 1

is construed as being neither similar nor dissimilar but indifferent to each other. Element distances, between 0.8 to 1.2, have been taken as an area of indifference. Several indices are derived to indicate how a person sees himself/herself:

a. *Self convergence* means great similarity between the Actual Self and the Ideal Self. In terms of element distance, the Actual Self is separated from the Ideal Self by a distance of less than 0.8.

b. *Actual Self isolation* means the Actual Self is not similar to any non-self elements. A person in such a state suffers uncertainty as to what kind of person he/she is, is alone and has little basis for social interaction. There are no non-self elements within a distance of 0.8 from the Actual Self.

c. *Self alienation* occurs when the Actual Self and the Ideal Self are completely dissimilar, that is, defined in opposition to each other. The Actual Self is separated from the Ideal Self by a distance greater than 1.2, and no more than two non-self elements are further away from the Ideal Self.

d. *Social alienation* is when neither Actual Self nor the Ideal Self is defined in terms of its similarity to non-self elements. The person is representing himself/herself as unlike all other people. There are not more than two non-self elements within a distance of 0.8 from either the Actual Self or the Ideal Self.

## Analysis of Constructs

### Cognitive complexity

Some people see things and relate to others in a very simple way, other people may look at things in very complex ways. The index of *cognitive complexity* refers to how complicated a person's construct system is. It is "... the capacity to construe social behaviour in a multidimensional way. A more cognitively complex person has available a more differentiated system of dimensions for perceiving others' behaviour than does a less cognitively complex individual" (Bieri et al., 1966, p. 185). One measure, amongst others, for measuring cognitive complexity is to use the principal components generated from the INGRID programme as an indicator in terms of percentage of variance, in that the higher the percentage of variance that is accounted for by the first component, or the first two components, the lower the complexity of the cognitive system. Alternatively, a lesser degree of variance is taken to indicate greater complexity (Chetwynd, 1977). This means that a person with low cognitive complexity will have fewer constructs to describe more things.

## *Categorization of constructs*

Elicited constructs from individuals can be categorized for comparison purposes. Landfield's (1971) scheme for the classification of constructs is the most commonly used for construct categorization, according to Winter (1992), as it gives in details guidelines for the categorization, and a scoring manual for practice. His categories also cover a wide range of descriptions of behaviour. The method has been employed to investigate constructs used by clinical groups, such as the suicidal, or sexual abusers (Horley, 1988; Landfield, 1976), and in investigating constructs that are found to be predictive of psychotherapy (Caine, Wijesinghe, & Winter, 1981; Landfield, 1971). His scheme of twenty categories with their sub-categories is listed below. Detailed descriptions are available in his manual (1971, pp. 165–175):

Social interaction (active vs inactive)
Forcefulness (high vs low)
Organization (high vs low)
Self sufficiency (high vs low)
Status (high vs low)
Factual description
Intellective (high vs low)
Self reference
Imagination (Low)
Alternatives
Sexual
Morality (high vs low)
External appearance
Emotional arousal
Egoism (high)
Tenderness (high vs low)
Time orientation (past, and future)
Involvement (high vs low)
Extreme qualifiers
Humour (high vs low)

Only constructs with a loading of .32 or larger are considered as meaningful and used for classification (Tabachnick and Fidell, 2001). In the study, the categorization was done by two judges after training in using Landfield's system. Inter-judge agreement reached 94% on all cases. The ratings of the elements with reference to the constructs in these categories have been re-coded and standardized along a six-point scale, with one denoting the negatively evaluated end of a category, e.g., low morality, and six as the positively evaluated end of the category, e.g., high morality. The relationship between elements and constructs could then be reflected in the ratings along a scale of one to six. Further, in group comparisons, only categories with at least 30 cases have been used for statistical analysis.

## Analysis of Elements

Using Norris and Makhlouf-Norris' (1976) convention of using distance between elements as an indicator, changes in perception of self and others can be mapped across the different rehabilitative stages of the participants by examining how they position the various elements in relation to each other. The analysis of elements can also be performed in relation to the constructs, giving a description of the different worldviews of the participants by searching for group patterns in the use of constructs with reference to the elements, for example, how is the Drug Self (one of the elements used in the study) described as against that for the Actual Self.

A graphic way of expressing the relationship between elements and elements, and then elements and constructs is also possible as the INGRID programme provides data for constructing a plot of elements in construct space, as explained below.

### *Plot of Element in Construct Space*

The INGRID programme, which performs a principal component analysis of the ratings of an individual grid, gives, amongst other forms of data, a table of loadings of each element and construct on each component. By plotting the loadings on the first two components, a two-dimensional visual representation of a participant's construct system can be obtained (Slater, 1977, Winter, 1992). Table I-1 gives the element and construct loadings of one participant (A2):

Based on the loadings given above, the participant's construct system is drawn by locating the positions of the elements and constructs. This is

**Table I-1  Loadings of Elements and Constructs**

| Element | Component 1 Loadings | Component 2 Loadings | Construct | Component 1 Loadings | Component 2 Loadings |
|---|---|---|---|---|---|
| 1 | −5.23 | 1.82 | 1 | −5.18 | −2.14 |
| 2 | 3.49 | 1.44 | 2 | −5.97 | −2.43 |
| 3 | −8.51 | 0.54 | 3 | −6.94 | −0.97 |
| 4 | −10.05 | −0.15 | 4 | 7.40 | −1.62 |
| 5 | 6.64 | −0.38 | 5 | 6.91 | −1.12 |
| 6 | 5.22 | −0.27 | 6 | −6.41 | −0.19 |
| 7 | −8.72 | −0.19 | 7 | −6.00 | 0.12 |
| 8 | 5.88 | −0.27 | 8 | −6.33 | 1.13 |
| 9 | 4.90 | 0.46 | 9 | −6.80 | −1.21 |
| 10 | 3.12 | −0.36 | 10 | −3.48 | 1.32 |
| 11 | −1.42 | −3.73 | 11 | 6.10 | −0.56 |
| 12 | 4.67 | 1.07 | 12 | −5.59 | 1.13 |

done by plotting the sets of element and construct loadings against Components One and Two as coordinates. An example is given for the plotting of Element One in Diagram I-1 that is self-explanatory, and for Construct One in Diagram I-2.

**Diagram I-1    Location of Element One**

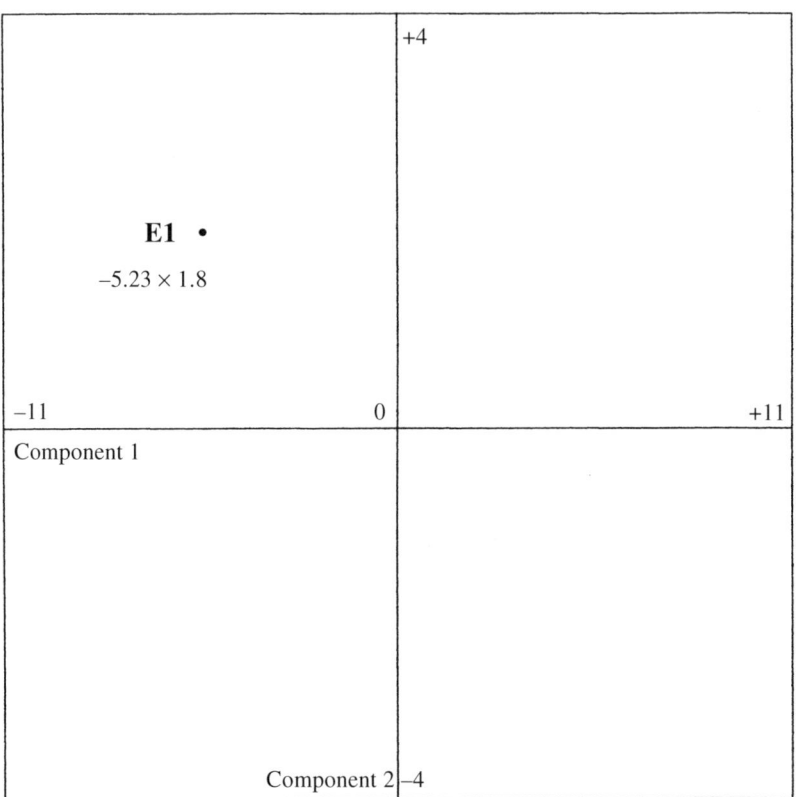

As constructs are dimensions rather than points like the elements, each construct is located by drawing a straight line through the centre of the diagram to the point corresponding to the construct's loadings on the two components. In diagram I-2, "•" represents the point of the loadings for Construct Three (–6.94 for Component One, and –0.97 for Component Two). This point locates the high end of the rating scale, i.e., the emergent pole (defined by ratings of 6 on a six-point scale), the position of which is obtained by further extending the line joined from 0 to "•", shown in the diagram, to the edge of the diagram. This gives the location of Construct Three (muddled) for Participant A2. The location of the contrast pole (hard working) for Construct Three is found by having the line thus drawn to be further extrapolated to the edge of the opposite quadrant of the diagram.

## Diagram I-2  Location of Construct Three

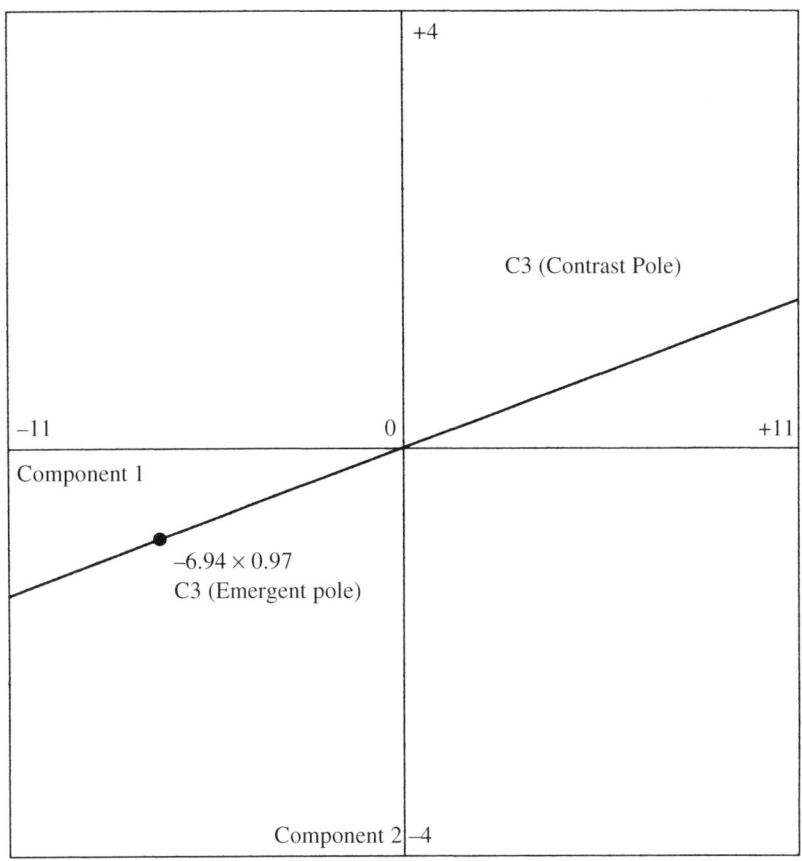

+4

C3 (Contrast Pole)

−11

0

+11

Component 1

−6.94 × 0.97
C3 (Emergent pole)

Component 2 −4

# Bibliography

AA World Services, Inc. (1952). Twelve steps and twelve traditions. New York: Author.

Abramowitz, L. (1993). Prayer as therapy among the frail Jewish elderly. *Journal of Gerontological Social Work, 19*(3/4), 69–75.

Action Committee Against Narcotics (1998). *Eleventh quarterly progress report (covering the period 1 December 1997 to 28 February 1998.* Hong Kong: Government Secretariat.

Adams-Webber, J.R. (1989). Some reflections on the "meaning" of repertory grid responses. *International Journal of Personal Construct Psychology, 2,* 77–92.

Alaszewski, A., & Harrison, L. (1992). Alcohol and social work: A literature review. *British Journal of Social Work, 22,* 331–343.

Allegro, J. M. (1971). *The sacred mushroom and the cross.* New York: Bantam.

Allison, M., Hubbard, R., & Rachal, J. V. (1985). *Treatment process in methadone, residential and out-patient drug free programmes.* Rockville, MD: National Institute on Drug Abuse.

Allport, G.W. & Ross, J.M. (1967). Personal religious orientation and prejudice. *Journal of Personality and Social Psychology, 5*(4), 432–443.

Anastas, J. W. (1999). *Research design for social work and the human services,* 2$^{nd}$ Ed. New York: Columbia University Press.

Annis, H. M. (1986). A relapse prevention model for treatment of alcoholics. In W. E. Miller & N. Heather (Eds.). *Treating addictive behaviours: Processes of change* (pp. 407–434). New York: Plenum Press.

Annis, J. M. (1990). Relapse to substance abuse: empirical findings within a cognitive-social learning approach. *Journal of Psychoactive Drugs, 22,* 117–124.

Antze, P. (1976). The role of ideologies in peer psychotherapy organizations: Some theoretical considerations and three case studies. *The Journal of Applied Behavioural Science, 12,* 323–346.

Argyle, M., & Beit-Hallahmi, B. (1975). *The social psychology of religion*. London: Routledge & Kegan Paul. (Original work published 1958.)

Arnkoff, D. B., & Glass, C. R. (1993). Cognitive therapy and psychotherapy integration. In D. K. Freedheim, *History of psychotherapy: A century of change* (pp. 657–693). Washington, DC: American Psychological Association.

Ashworth, C. M., Blackburn, I.M. & McPherson, F.M. (1982). The performance of depressed and manic patients on some repertory grid measures: A cross-sectional study. *British Journal of Medical Psychology*, *55*, 247–255.

Bahr, S. J., & Hawks, R. D. (1995). Religious organizations. In Coombs, R H., & Ziedonis, D. M. (Eds.), *Handbook on drug abuse prevention — a comprehensive strategy to prevent the abuse of alcohol and other drugs* (pp. 159–179). Boston: Allyn & Bacon.

Bakan, D. (1968). *On method — Toward a reconstruction of psychological investigation*. San Fransciso: Jossey-Bass.

Bale, R. N., Van Stone, W. W., Kuldau, J. M., Engelsing, T. M., Slashoff, R .M., & Zarcone, V. P., Jr., (1980). Therapeutic communities vs. methadone maintenance. *Archive of General Psychiatry*, *37*(2), 179–193.

Bankart, C. P. (1997). *Talking cures — A history of western and eastern psychotherapies*. Pacific Grove, CA: Brooks/Cole Publishing Company.

Barber, J. G. (1994). Alcohol addiction: Private trouble or social issue? *Social Service Review*, *68*(4), 521–35.

Barber, J. G. (1995a). *Social work with addictions*. London: Macmillan.

Barber, J. G. (1995b). Working with resistant drug abusers. *Social Work*, *40*(1), 17–23.

Bateson, G. (1972). *Steps to an Ecology of Mind*. New York: Ballantine Books.

Batson, C. D., & Ventis, W. L. (1982). *The religious experience: A social-psychological perspective*. New York: Oxford University Press.

Beail, N.(1985). *Repertory grid technique and personal constructs — Applications in clinical and educational settings*. London: Croom Helm.

Beck, A. T., Ward, C.H., Mendelson, M., Mock, J., & Erbaugh, (1961). An inventory for measuring depression. *Archives of General Psychiatry*, *12*, 57–62.

Beck, A. T., Wright, F. D., Newman, C. F., & Liese, B. S. (1993). *Cognitive therapy of substance abuse*. New York: The Guilford Press.

Beck, A.T., Weissman, A., Lester, D.,& Trexler, L. (1974). The measurement of pessimism: The Hopelessness Scale. *Journal of Consulting and Clinical Psychology*, *42*(6), 861–865.

Beck, R. N., (1965). Hall' s genetic psychology and religious conversion. *Pastoral Psychology*, *16*, 47.

Becker, H. S. (1953). Becoming a marijuana user. *American Journal of Sociology*, *59*, 235–42.

Bednarz, D. (1985). Quantity and quality in evaluation research. *Evaluation and Program Planning*, *8*, 289–306.

Beecher, H.K. (1959). *Measurement of subjective responses: Quantitative effects of drugs*. NY: Oxford University Press.

Bennett, G., & Rigby, K. (1991). Psychological change during residence in a rehabilitation centre for female drug misusers. Part I. Drug misusers. *Drug and Alcohol Dependence*, *27*, 149–157.

Bennett, G., Rigby, K., & Owers, D. (1990). Assessment of psychological change within a residential rehabilitation centre for drug users. In P. Maitland (Ed.), *Personal construct theory deviancy and social work*. London: Inner London Probation Service Centre for Personal Construct Psychology.

Benson, H., & Stark, M. (1996). *Timeless healing: The power and biology of belief*. New York: Scribner.

Benson, P. L. (1990). *The troubled journey: A portrait of 6th-12th grade youth*. Minneapolis: Lutheran Brotherhood.

Benson, P. L. (1992). Religion and substance use. In J. F. Schumaker (eds.) *Religion and Mental Health* (pp. 211–220). New York: Oxford University Press.

Benson, P. L., Wood, P. K., Johnson, A. L., Eklin, C. H., & Mills, J. E.(1983). *Report on 1983 Minnesota survey of drug use and drug-related attitudes*. Minneapolis: Search Institute.

Benson, P. L., Yeager, R. J., Wood, P. K., Guerra, M. J., & Manno, B. V.(1986). *Catholic high schools: Their impact on low-income students*. Washington, DC: National Catholic Educational Association.

Berger, P, & Luckman, T. (1967). *The social construction of reality*. London: Penguin Press.

Bergin, A. E. (1980). Psychotherapy and religious values. *Journal of Consulting and Clinical Psychology*, *48*, 95–105.

Bergin, A. E. (1985). Values and psychotherapy. In D.G. Benner (Ed.), *Baker encyclopedia of psychology* (pp. 1191–1194). Grand Rapids, MI: Baker Book House.

Bergin, A. E. (1991). Values and religious issues in psychotherapy and mental health. *American Psychologist*, *46*, 4, 394-403.

Bergin, A. E. & Garfield, S. L. (Eds.). (2002). *Handbook of Psychotherapy and Behaviour Change*, 5th Ed. New York: Wiley.

Berthold, S. M. (1989). Spiritism as a form of psychotherapy: implications for social work practice. *Social Casework: The Journal of Contemporary Social Work*, *70*(8), 502–09.

Berzins, J. I., Ross, W. F., English, G., E., & Haley, J. V. (1974). Subgroups among opiate addicts: A typological investigation. *Journal of Abnormal Psychology*, *83*(1), 65–73.

Bianchi, E. C. (1989). Psychotherapy as religion: Pros and cons. *Pastoral Psychology*, *38*(2), 67–81.

Bieri, J., Atkins, A. L., Briar, S., Leaman, R. L., Miller, H., & Tripodi, T. (1966). *Clinical and social judgement*. New York: Wiley.

Blowers, G. H. (1991). Some Hong Kong Chinese perceptions of pornography: A repertory grid study. *Bulletin of the Hong Kong Psychological Society, 26/27*, 47–58.

Blowers, G. H., & Bacon-Shone, J. (1994). On detecting the differences in jazz: A reassessment of comparative methods of measuring perceptual veridicality. *Empirical Studies of the Arts, 12*(1), 41–58.

Blowers, G. H., & McCoy, M. M. (1986). Perceiving cinematic episodes: A cross-cultural repertory grid study of a narrative film segment. *International Journal of Psychology, 21*, 317–332.

Blum, K. (1991). *Alcohol and the addictive brain: New hope for alcoholics from biogenic research.* New York: Free Press.

Boehm, W. (1958). The nature of social work. *Social Work, 3*, 10–19.

Boisen, A. T. (1936). *The exploration of the inner world.* New York: Harper & Row.

Bozarth, M. A. (1990). Drug addiction as a psychobiological process. In D.M. Warburton (Ed.), *Addiction controversies* (pp. 112–134). Chur, Switzerland: Harwood Academic Publishers.

Bradley, B.P. (1989). Heroin and the opiates. In M. Gossop (Ed.), *Relapse and addictive behaviour* (pp. 73–85). London: Tavistock.

Brannen, J. (1992). Combining qualitative and quantitative approaches: an overview. In Brannen, J. (Ed.). *Mixing Methods: qualitative and quantitative research* (pp. 3–37). Aldershot, England: Avebury.

Brennan, J. F. (1982). *History and systems of psychology.* Englewood Cliffs, NJ: Prentice-Hall.

Breton, M. (1989). Liberation theology, group work, and the right of the poor and oppressed to participate in the life of the community. *Social Work With Groups, 12*(3), 5–18.

Brewer, D. D., Catalano, R. F., Haggerty, K., Gainey, R. R., & Fleming, C. B. (1998). A meta-analysis of predictors of continued drug use during and after treatment for opiate addiction. *Addiction, 93*, 73–92.

Brickman, B. (1988). Psychoanalysis and substance abuse: Toward a more effective approach. *Journal of the American Academy of Psychoanalysis, 16*(3), 359–379.

Bridgman, P. W. (1927). *The logic of modern physics.* New York: Macmillan.

Brook, J. S., Whiteman, M., Gordon, A. S., & Brook, D. W. (1984). Paternal determinants of female adolescents' marijuana use. *Developmental Psychology, 20*, 1032–1043.

Brooner, R. K., King, V. L., Kidorf, M., Schmidt, C. W., & Bigelow, G. E. (1997). Psychiatric and substance use comorbidity among treatment-seeking opioid abusers. *Archive of General Psychiatry, 54*, 71–80.

Brown, B. S., Guavey, S. K., Meyers, M. B., & Stark, S. D. (1971). In their own words, addicts' reasons for initiating and withdrawing from heroin. *International Journal of the Addictions, 6*, 635–645.

Brown, H. P., & Peterson, J. H. (1990). Rationale and procedural suggestions for defining and actualizing spiritual values in the treatment of dependency. *Alcoholism Treatment Quarterly, 7*(3), 17–47.

Brown, L. B. (Ed.). (1994). *Religion, rersonality, and mental health.* New York: Springer.

Brown, S. A. (1985). Expectancies versus background in the prediction of college drinking patterns. *Journal of Consulting and Clinical Psychology, 53*(1), 123–30.

Bryman, A. (1992). Quantitative and qualitative research: further reflections on their integration. In J. Brannen (Ed.). *Mixing Methods: qualitative and quantitative research.* (pp. 57–78). Aldershot, England: Avebury.

Buchanan, D. R. (1992). An Uneasy Alliance: Combining qualitative and quantitative research methods. *Health Education Quarterly, 19*(1), 117–135.

Bullis, R K. & Harrigan, M. P. (1992). Religious denominational policies on sexuality. *Families in Society: The Journal of Contemporary Human Services, 73*(5), 305–12.

Bullis, R. K. (1996). *Spirituality in social work practice.* Washington, DC: Taylor & Francis.

Bumberry, W., Oliver, J. M., & McClure, J. N. (1978). Validation of the Beck Depression Inventory in a university population using psychiatric estimate as the criterion. *Journal of Consulting and Clinical Psychology, 46,* 150–155.

Burke, A. C., & Clapp, J. D. (1997). Ideology and social work practice in substance abuse settings. *Social Work, 42*(6), 552–562.

Burkett, S. R. & White, M. (1974). Hellfire and delinquency: Another look. *Journal for the Scientific Study of Religion, 13,* 255–462.

Button, E. (1985). *Personal construct theory and mental health: theory, research and practice.* London: Croom Helm.

Cahalan, D. (1970). *Problem drinkers: a national survey.* San Francisco: Jossey-Bass.

Caine, T. M., Wijesinghe, O. B. A., & Winter, D. A. (1981). *Personal styles in neurosis: Implications for small group psychotherapy and behaviour therapy.* London: Routledge & Kegan Paul.

Canda, E.R. (1988). Spirituality, religious diversity, and social work practice. *Social Casework, 69*(4), 238–47.

Canda, E.R. (1989). Religious content in social work education: a comparative approach. *Journal of Social Work Education, 25*(1), 36–45.

Canda, E. R. & Furman, L. D. (1999). *Spiritual diversity in social work practice: the heart of helping.* New York: Free Press.

Canda, E. R., & Smith, E. D. (Eds.). (2001). *Transpersonal perspectives on spirituality in social work.* New York: Haworth Press.

Caplis, R. (1983). Catholic social service and transcendental values. *Social Thought, 9*(1), 3–16.

Carkhuff, R. R., & Berenson, B. G. (1967). *Beyond counselling and therapy*. New York: Holt, Rinehart & Winston.

Chamberlain, K. & Zika, S. (1992). Religiosity, meaning in life and psychological well-being. In J. F. Schumaker (Ed.), *Religion and mental health*. (pp 138–148). New York: Oxford University Press.

Chan, C. M., & Tsoi, M. M. (1984). The BDI and stimulus determinants of cognitive-related depression among Chinese college students. *Cognitive Therapy and Research, 8*, 501–508.

Chappel, J. N. (1990). Spirituality is not necessarily religion: A commentary on "Divine intervention and the treatment of chemical dependency." *Journal of Substance Abuse, 2*, 481–483.

Chein, I., Gerard, D.L., Lee, R.S., and Rosenfeld, E. (1964). *The road to H: Narcotics, delinquency, and social policy*. New York: Basic Books.

Chetwynd, J. (1977). The psychological meaning of structural measures derived from grids. In P. Slater (Ed.). *The measurement of interpersonal space by grid technique*, vol. 2. *Dimensions of interpersonal space* (pp. 175–194). Chichester: Wiley.

Cheung, R. (1994). A non-residential treatment model in rehabilitating psychotropic substance abusers. In The Hong Kong Council of Social Service, *Proceedings of the 15th IFNGO conference for the prevention of drug and substance abuse* (p. 172). Hong Kong: The Hong Kong Council of Social Services.

Ch'ien, J. M. N. (1994). Community based self-help networking in reducing the private demand and risks of drug abuse. *Conference proceedings — the 15th IFNGO conference for the prevention of drug and substance abuse (December 5–9, 1994, Hong Kong)* (pp. 62–76). Hong Kong: The Hong Kong Council of Social Service.

Christensen, C. W. (1963). Religious Conversion. *Archives of General Psychiatry, 9*, 207–216.

Citron, P (1978). Group work with alcoholic, polydrug-involved adolescents with deviant behaviour syndrome. *Social Work with Groups, 1*(1), 39–52.

Clark, E. T., (1929). *The psychology of religious awakening*. NY: Macmillan.

Clarke, P. B. & Byrne, P. (1993). *Religion defined and explained*. New York: St. Martin's Press.

Clayton R. .R., (1992). Transitions in drug use: Risk and protective factors. In M. Glantz, & R Pickens, (Eds.). *Vulnerability to drug use* (pp. 15–51). Washington D.C.: American Psychological Association.

Clement, P. W., & Warren, N. C. (1973). Can religion and psychotherapy be happily married? An experiment in education. In R. H. Cox (Ed.), *Religious systems and psychotherapy* (p. 417–426). Springfield, IL.: Thomas.

Clinard, M. (1963). *Sociology of deviant behaviour*. New York: Holt, Rinehart & Winston.

Cook, T. (1985). Postpositivist critical multiplism. In R. Shotland & M. Mark

(Eds.). *Social science and social policy* (pp. 21–62). Beverly Hills: CA: Sage.

Corrigan, E. M. (1979). Alcohol knowledge and practice issues. *Health and Social Work, 4*(4), 9–40.

Cox, D. R. (1983). Religion and the welfare of immigrants. *Australian Social Work, 36*(1), 3–10.

Cox, R. H. (1973). *Religious Systems and Psychotherapy*. Springfield, IL.: Thomas.

Cronbach, L.J. (1975). Beyond the two discicplines of scientific psychology. *American Psychologist, 30,*(1), 116–127.

Croughan, J. L., Miller, J. P., Wagelin, D., Whitman, B. Y. (1982). Psychiatric illness in male and female narcotic addicts. *Journal of Clinical Psychiatry, 43,* 225–228.

Crumbaugh, J. C. (1968). Cross-validation of purpose in life test based on Frankl's concepts. *Journal of Individual Psychology, 24,* 74–81.

Csordas, T. J. (1990). The psychotherapy analogy and charismatic healing. *Psychotherapy, 27,* 79–90.

Cummings, C., Gordon, J., & Marlatt, G. A. (1980). Relapse: strategies of prevention and prediction. In W. R. Miller (Ed.), *The addictive behaviours: Treatment of alcoholism, drug abuse, smoking, and obesity* (pp. 291–321). Oxford: Pergamon Press.

Cushman, P. (1993). Psychotherapy to 1992:A historically situated interpretation. In D. K. Freedheim (Ed.). *History of psychotherapy: A century of change.* (pp. 21–64). Washington, D.C.: American Psychological Association.

Dackis, A., & Gold, M. S. (1983). Opiate addiction and depression — cause or effect? *Drug Alcohol Dependence, 11,* 105–109.

Daley, D. C. (1987). Relapse prevention with substance abusers: clinical issues and myths. *Social Work, 32*(2), 138–142.

Datta, L. (1994). Paradigms wars: A basis for peaceful coexistence and beyond. In C. S. Reichardt & S. F. Rallis (Eds.), *The qualitative‑quantitative debate: New perspectives* (pp. 53–70). San Francisco: Jossey-Bass.

Dawes, A. (1985). Construing drug dependence. In E. Button (Ed.). *Personal construct theory and mental health* (pp. 182–194). London: Croom Helm.

De Haes, W. F. (1987). Looking for effective drug education programmes: Fifteen years exploration of the effects of different drug education programmes. *Health Education Research, 2,* 433–438.

DeLeon, G., (1974). Phoenix house: Psychopathological signs among male and female drug-free residents. *Addictive Diseases, 1*(2), 135–151.

DeLeon, G. (1984). The therapeutic community: Study of effectiveness. *National Institute on Drug Abuse Treatment Research Monograph Series*, DHHS Publ. (ADM), 85–1286. Rockville, MD: NIDA, 95pp.

DeLeon, G. (1986). The therapeutic community for substance abuse: Perspective and approach. In G. De Leon & J. Ziegenfuss (Eds.), *Therapeutic communities*

*for addictions: Readings in theory, research and practice* (pp. 5–18).
Springfield, IL: Charles C. Thomas.

DeLeon, G. (1990–91). The therapeutic community and behavioural science. *The International Journal of the Addictions, 25*(12A), 1537–1557.

DeLeon, G., & Jainchill, N. (1982). Male and female drug abusers: social and psychological status 2 years after treatment in a therapeutic community. *American Journal of Drug Alcohol Abuse, 8*, 465–497.

DeLeon G., Skodol, A., & Rosenthal, M. S. (1973). Phoenix house: Changes in psychopathological signs of resident drug addicts. *Archives of General Psychiatry*, 28(1), 131–135.

Denzin, N. K. (1970). *The research act: A theoretical introduction to sociological methods*. London: Butterworth.

Dittes, J.E. (1969). The psychology of religion. In G. Lindzey & E. Aronson (Eds.), *The handbook of social psychology* (vol. 5) (pp. 602–659). Reading, MA: Addison-Wesley.

Dole, V. P. & Nyswander, M. E. (1965). A medical tratment for diacetylmorphine (heroin) addiction. *Journal of the American Medical Association, 193*, 646–650.

Donahue, M. J. (1987). *Religion and drug use: 1976–1985*. Paper presented at the annual meeting of the Society for the Scientific Study of Religion, Louisville, Kentucky.

Dorus, W., & Senay, E. C. (1977). *Severity and course of depression in opiate-dependent patients*. Paper presented at the Fourth National Drug Abuse Conference, San Francisco, CA.

Dudley, R. L., Mutch, P. B., & Cruise, R. J. (1987). Religious factors and drug usage among Seventh-day Adventist youth in North America. *Journal for the Scientific Study of Religion, 26*(2), 218–223.

Dull, V. T.,& Skokan, L. A. (1995). A cognitive model of religion's influence on health. *Journal of Social Issues, 51*(2), 49–64.

Easthope, G. (1993). Perceptions of the causes of drug use in a series of articles in The International Journal of the Addictions. *The International Journal of the Addictions, 28*(6), 559–569.

Eckhardt, W. (1976). Alcoholic values and Alcoholics Anonymous. *Quarterly Journal of Studies on Alcohol, 28*, 277–288.

Edgington, E.S. (1966). Statistical inference and nonrandom samples. *Psychological Bulletin, 66*, 485–487.

Eliade, M. (1963). Patterns in comparative religion. R. Sheed (Trans.). Cleveland: World Publishing Co.

Ellis, A. (1966). The case against religion: A psychotherapist's view. In B. Ard (Ed.). *Counseling and therapy: Classics on theories and issues* (pp. 271–282). Palo Alto, CA: Science & Behavior Books.

Ellis, A. (1980). Psychotherapy and atheistic values: A response to A. E. Bergin's

"Psychotherapy and religious issues." *Journal of Consulting and Clinical Psychology, 48*, 635–639.

Ellison , C. G. (1991). Religious involvement and subjective well-being. *Journal of Health and Social Behaviour, 32*, 80–99.

Erikson, E. H. (1950). *Childhood and Society*. NY: Norton

Erikson, E. H. (1968). *Identity: Youth and crises*. NY: Norton

Falk, J. L. (1983). Drug dependence: Myth or motive? *Pharmacology Biochemistry and Behaviour, 19*, 385–391.

Faver, C.A. (1986). Religion, research, and social work. *Social Thought, 12*(3), 20–29.

Fenwick, P. (1996). The neurophysiology of religious experience. In D. Bhugra (Ed.), *Psychiatry and religion: Context, consensus and controversies* (pp. 166–177). London: Routledge.

Fischer, J. (1993). Empirically-based practice: The end of ideology? *Journal of Social Service Research, 18*(1/2), 19–64.

Fisher, D. D. V. (1991). *An introduction to constructivism for social workers*. New York: Praeger.

Flournoy, T. (1903). Les principes de la psychologie religieuse. *Archives de Psychologie, 2*, 33–57.

Fowler, F. W. (1981). *Stages of faith*. San Francisco: Harper & Row.

Frank, J. (1961). *Persuasion and healing: A comparative study of psychotherapy*. New York: Schodren Books.

Frank, J. (1974). *Persuasion and healing*. New York: Schocken Books.

Frank, J. D. (1978). Psychotherapy and the healing arts. In J. L. Fosshage, & P. Olsen (Eds.), *Healing implications for psychotherapy* (pp. 31–47). New York: Human Sciences Press.

Fransella, F. & Bannister, D. (1977). *A manual For repertory grid technique*. London: Academic Press.

Fransella, F. & Thomas, L. (1988). *Experimenting with personal construct psychology*. London: Routledge

Fraser, C. & Gaskell, G. (Eds.) 1990. *The social psychological study of widespread of beliefs*. Clarendon Press, Oxford.

Fraser, M., Taylor, M. J., Jackson, R., & O'Jack, J. (1991). Social work and science: Many ways of knowing? *Social Work Research and Abstracts, 27*, 5–15.

Freed, E. X. (1968). Interpersonal values of hospitalized alcoholic psychiatric patients. *Psychological Reports, 22*, 403–406.

Freud, S. (1959). A religious experience. In *Sigmund Freud: Collected Papers*, Vol. 5 (pp. 243–246). (J. Strachey, Trans.). New York: Basic Books. (Original work published 1928).

Freud, S. (1964/1927). *The future of an illusion*. New York: Anchor Books. (Original work published 1927.)

Fromm, E. (1950). *Psychoanalysis and religion*. New Haven: Yale University Press.

Fuller, R. (1982). *Mesmerism and the American cure of souls*. Philadelphia: University of Pennsylvania Press.

Gartner, J., Larson, D., & Allen, G. (1991). Religious commitment and mental health: a review of the empirical literature. *Journal of Psychology and Theology*, *19*, 6–25.

Geerlings, P. J. ,van Limbeck, J. Wouters, M., de Leeuw, M., van Iperen, H. J., Bouman, H. K., Stichting, F. A., d'Hont, F. A., Edelbroek, W., van Rooyen, T., & Goris, A. (1990). Psychopathology and drug abuse. In J. J. Plattt, C. D. Kaplan & P. J. Mekin (Eds.), *The Effectiveness of Drug Abuse Treatment. Dutch and American Perspectives* (pp. 147–159). Florida: Robert E. Krieger Publishing Co.

George, L. K., Larsons, D. B., Koenig, H. G., & MuCullough, M. E. (2000). Spirituality and health. *Journal of Social and Clinical Psychology*, *19*(1), 102–116.

Gerald, M. (1992). Working with alcoholics and drug abusers in private practice: A psychoanalytic-chemical dependencey model. *Psychology of Addictive Behaviour*, *6*(1), 5–13.

Gergen, M. M. (1988). Toward a feminist metatheory and methodology in the social sciences. In M. Gergen (Ed.), *Feminist thought and the structure of knowledge*, (pp. 97–104). New York: New York University.

Gilbert, J. G., & Lombardi, D. N. (1967). Personality characteristics of young male narcotic addicts. *Journal of Consulting Psychology, 31*(5), 536–538.

Gillespie, V. B. (1991). The dynamics of religious conversion, identity and transformation. Birmingham, Alabama: Religious Education Press.

Glantz, M., & Pickens, R. (Eds.). (1992). *Vulnerability to drug abuse*. Washington, D.C: American Psychological Association.

Glasser, P. H. (1984). Being honest with ourselves: What happens when our values conflict with our clients? *Practice Digest*, *6*(4), 6–10.

Goggins, S. (1988). *An examination of the construing of drug dependence and abstinence by heroin addicts going through detoxification and ex-heroin addicts going through rehabilitation using an implication grid technique*. Unpublished BSc dissertation, University of Surrey.

Googins, B. (1984). Avoidance of the alcoholic client. *Social Work*, *29*(1), 161–166.

Gordis, E. (2000). Alcohol, the brain, and behavior: Mechanisms of addiction. *Alcohol Research & Health*, *24*(1), 12–15.

Gorski, T. T. (1986). Relapse prevention planning: A new recovery tool. *Alcohol Health and Research World*, *63*, 6–11.

Gorsuch, R. L. (1995). Religious aspects of substance abuse and recovery. *Journal of Social Issues*, *51*(2), 65–83.

Gorsuch, R.L., & Bulter, M. (1976). Initial drug abue: A review of predisposing social psychological factors. *Psychological Bulletin*, *81*, 120–37.

Gossop, M., Green, L., Phillips, G., & Bradley, B. P. (1987). What happens to opiate addicts immediately after treatment: a prospective follow-up study. *British Medical Journal, 294,* 1377–80.

Grensted, L. W. (1930). *Psychology and God: A study of the implications of recent psychology for religious belief and practice.* London: Longmans, Green.

Griffith, E. E, & Young, J. L. (1988). A cross-cultural introduction to the therapeutic aspects of Christian religious ritual. In L. Comas-Diaz, & E. E. Griffith (Eds.), *Clinical guidelines in cross-cultural mental health* (pp. 69–89). New York: Wiley & Sons.

Griffin, R. E. (1991). Assessing the drug-involved client. Families in Society: *The Journal of Contemporary Human Services, 72*(2), 87–94.

Grof, C. (1993). *The thirst for wholeness: Addiction, attachment and the spiritual path.* New York: HarperCollins Publishers.

Grof, S. (1985). *Beyond the brain: Birth, death and transcendence in psychotherapy.* Albany, NY: SUNY Press.

Guba, E.G. (1990). *The paradigm dialog.* Newbury Park: Sage.

Hadaway, C. K., Elifson, K. W., & Petersen, D. M., (1984). Religious involvement and drug use among urban adolescents. *Journal for the Scientific Study of Religion, 23*(2), 109–128.

Haertzen, C. A., & Hooks, N. T. (1969). Changes in personality and subjective experience associated with the chronic administration and withdrawal of opiates. *Journal of Nervous and Mental Disease, 148*(6) 606–614.

Hammersley, M. (1992). Deconstructing the qualitative-quantitative divide. In J. Brannen,. (Ed.). *Mixing methods: Qualitative and quantitative research* (pp. 39–55) Aldershot, England: Avebury.

Hanson B., Beschner, G., Walters, J.M., and Bovell, E. (1985). *Life with heroin - Voices from the inner city.* Massachusetts: Lexington Books.

Harpur, T. (1994). *The uncommon touch.* Toronto: McClelland & Stewart.

Harré, R. & Secord, P. F. (1972). *The explanation of social behaviour.* Oxford: Basil Blackwell.

Hawkins, J.D., Catalano, R. F., & Miller, J. Y. (1992). Risk and protective factors for alcohol and other drug problems in adolescence and early adulthood: Implications for substance abuse drug prevention. *Psychological Bulletin, 112,* 64–105.

Heather, N., Stallard, A., & Tebutt, J. (1991). Importance of substance abuse cues in relapse among heroin users: comparison of two methods of investigation. *Addictive Behaviours, 16,* 41–49.

Hefner, R. W. (1993).World building and the rationality of conversion. In Robert W. Hefner (Ed.), *Conversion to Christianity* (pp. 3–46) Berkely: University of California Press.

Hegel, G. W. F. (1961). *On Christianity: Early theological writings.* (T. M. Knox, trans.) New York: Harper Torchbooks. (Original essays published 1798–1799).

Heineman, M.B. (1981). The obsolete scientific imperative in social work research. *Social Service Review*, September: 371–97.

Hoffmann, N. G., Harrison, P. A., & Belille, C. A. (1983). Alcoholics Anonymous after treatment: Attendance and abstinence. *International Journal of the Addictions, 18*, 311–318.

Holmes, A. (1999). *The mental effects of heroin*. Philadelphia: Chelsea House Publishers.

Hong Kong Government. (1996). *By-census summary report*. Hong Kong: Author.

Horley, J. (1988). Cognitions of child sexual abusers. *Journal of Sex Research, 25*, 542–545.

Horsburgh, M. (1988). Words and deeds: Christianity and social welfare, *Australian Social Work, 41*(2), 17–23.

Houston, J., & Adshead, G. (1993). The use of repertory grids to assess change: Application to a sex offenders group. *Issues in Criminological and Legal Psychology, 19*, 43–51.

Hoy, R. M. (1973). The meaning of alcoholism for alcoholics: A repertory grid study. *British Journal of Social and Clinical Psychology, 12*, 98–9.

Hoy, R. M. (1977). Some findings concerning beliefs about alcoholism. *British Journal of Medical Psychology, 50*, 227–35.

Hubbard, R. L., Marsden, M. E., Rachal, J. V., Harwood, H. J., Cavanaugh, E. R., & Ginzburg, H. M. (1989). *Drug abuse treatment: A national study of effectiveness*. Chapel Hill, N. C.: The University of North Carolina Press.

Hundleby, J. D., (1987). Adolescent drug use in a behavioral matrix: A confirmation and comparison of the sexes. *Addictive Behaviors, 12,* 103–112.

Hunt, W. A., Barnett, L. W., & Branch, L. G. (1971). Relapse rates in addiction programmes. *Journal of Clinical Psychology, 27*, 455–456.

Imber-Black, E., & Roberts, J. (1992). *Rituals for our times*. New York: HarperCollins.

Imre, R. W (1982). *Knowing and caring: Philosophical issues in social work*. Lanham, MD: University Press of America.

Imre, R. W. (1984). The nature of knowledge in social work. *Social Work, 29*(1), 41–45.

Jacobs, J. L. (1992). Religious ritual and mental health. In J. F. Schumaker (Ed.), *Religion and mental health* (pp. 291–299). New York: Oxford University Press.

Jacobson, G. R., Ritter, D. P, & Mueller, L. (1977). Purpose in life and personal values among adult alcoholics. *Journal of Clinical Psychology, 33*(1), 314–316.

James, W. (1902). *Varieties of religious experience*. New York: Longmans, Green.

James, W. (1958). *The varieties of religious experience*. New York: Mentor Books, New American Library of World Literature. First Published in the United States of America by Longmans, Green, & Co., 1902.

James, W. (1961). *The varieties of religious experience*. New York: Collier. First Published in the United States of America by Longmans, Green, & Co., 1902.

Jessor, R., & Jessor, S. L. (1977). *Problem behaviour and psychosocial development: A longitudinal study of youth.* New York: Academic.

Jilek, W. G. (1994). Traditional healing in the prevention and treatment of alcohol and drug abuse. *Transcultural Psychiatric Research Review, 31,* 219–258.

Joe, G. W., Chastain, R.L., Marsh, K. L., & Simpson, D. D. (1990). Relapse. In D. D. Simpson & S. B. Sells (Eds.). *Opioid addiction and treatment: A 12-year follow-up* (pp. 121–136). Malabar, FL: Krieger.

Jones, S. L. (1988). A religious critique of behavior therapy. In W. R. Miller & J. E. Martin (Eds.). *Behaviour therapy and religion-integrating spiritual and behavioral approaches to change* (pp.139–170) Newbury Park: Sage Publications.

Jordan, D. K. (1993). The glyphomancy factor: Observations on Chinese conversion. In Robert W. Hefner (Ed.). *Conversion to Christianity* (p. 285–304). Berkeley: University of California Press.

Joseph, M. (1998). The effect of strong religious beliefs on coping with stress. *Stress Medicine, 14,* 219–224.

Joseph, M. V. (1987). The religious and spiritual aspects of clinical practice: A neglected dimension of social work. *Social Thought, 13*(1), 12–23.

Joseph, M. V. (1988). Religion and social work practice. *Social Casework, 69*(7), 443–52.

Judson, B. A., & Goldstein, A. (1983). Episodes of heroin use during maintenance treatment with a stable dosage of acetyle-methadol. *Drug and Alcohol Dependence, 11,* 271–278.

Jung, C. (1972). *Psychological types.* Princeton, NJ: Princeton University Press.

Kanfer, F., & Seider, M. L. (1973). Self-control: Factors enhancing tolerance of noxious stimulation. *Journal of Personality and Social Psychology, 25,* 381.

Kanfer, J. H., & Goldfoot, D. A. (1966). Self-control and the tolerance of noxious stimulation. *Psychological Reports,* 18, 79–85.

Karp, D. (1996). *Speaking of sadness: Depression, disconnection, and the meanings of illness.* New York: Oxford University Press.

Karst, T. O. & Groutt, J. W. (1977). *Inside mystical heads: Shared and personal constructs in a commune with some implications for a personal construct theory of social psychology,* In D. Bannister: New perspectives in personal construct theory (pp. 67–92). London: Academic Press.

Karst, T. O. & Trexler, L. D. (1970). Initial study using fixed-role and rational-emotive therapy in treating public-speaking anxiety. *Journal of Consulting and Clinical Psychology, 34,* 360–366.

Kelly, G. (1955). *The psychology of personal constructs.* New York: Norton.

Kelly, G. A. (1969a). Sin and psychotherapy. In B. Maher (Ed.), *Clinical psychology and personality* (pp. 165–188). New York : Wiley.

Kelly, G. A. (1969b). The psychotherapeutic relationship. In B. Maher (Ed.).

*Clinical psychology and personality: The selected papers of George Kelly* (pp. 216–223). New York: Wiley.

Keyes, C. F. (1993) Why the Thai are not Christians: Buddhist and Christian conversion in Thailand. In Robert W. Hefner (Ed.), *Conversion to Chrisitanity* (pp 259–284) Berkeley: University of California Press.

Khantzian, E. J., Halliday, K. S., & McAuliffe, W. E. (1990). *Addiction and the vulnerable self: Modified dynamic group therapy for substance abusers.* New York: Guilford Press.

Kilbourne, B. K., & Richardson, J. T. (1988). A social psychological analysis of healing. *Journal of Integrative and Eclectic Psychotherapy, 7,* 20–34.

King, G., & Lorenson, J. (1989). Alcoholism training for social workers. *Social Casework: The Journal of Contemporary Social Work, 70,* 375–382.

Klass, D. (1992). Religious aspects in the resolution of parental grief: solace and social support. In K .I. Pargament, K.I. Maton, & R. E. Hess (Eds.), *Religion and prevention in mental health: research, vision, and action.* (pp. 156–178). New York: The Haworth Press.

Klion, R. E. (1993). Chemical dependency: A personal construct theory approach. In L. Leitner & G. Dunnett (Eds.), *Critical issues in personal construct psychotherapy* (pp. 279–302). Malabar, FL: Krieger.

Klion, R. E., & Pfenninger, D. T. (1997). Personal construct psychotherapy of addictions. *Journal of Substance Abuse Treatment, 14*(1), 37–43.

Koenig, H. G. (Ed.) (1998). *Handbook of religion and mental health.* San Diego, Calif.: Academic Press.

Koenig, H. G., Ford, S., George, L. K., Balzer, D. G., & Meador, K. G.. (1993). Religion and anxiety disorder: An examination and comparison of association in young, middle-aged, and elderly adults. *Journal of Anxiety Disorders, 7,* 321–342.

Koenig, H. G., George, L. K., & Siegler, I. C. (1988). The use of religion and other emotion-regulating coping strategies among older adults. *The Gerontologist. 28*(3), 303–310.

Koenig, H. G.., Hays, J. C., George, L. K., & Blazer, D. G.. (1997). Modeling the cross-sectional relationships between religion, physical health, social support and depressive symptoms. *American Journal of Geriatric Psychiatry, 5,* 131–143.

Koenig, H. G.., McCullough, M. E., & Larson, D. B. (2001). *Handbook of religion and health.* New York: Oxford University Press.

Kosten, T. R., Rounsville, B. J., & Kleber, H. D. (1986). A 2.5 year follow up of depression, life crises and treatment effects on abstinence among opiate addicts. *Archives of General Psychiatry, 43,* 733–738.

Kramrisch, S., Otto, J., Ruck, C., & Wasson, R. (1986). *Persephone's quest: Etheogens and the origin of religion.* New Haven, CT: Yale University Press.

Kreek, M. J. (1991). Using methadone effectively: Achieving goals by application of laboratory, clinical, and evaluation research. In R. Pickens, C. Leukefeld, &

C. Schuster (Eds.), *Improving drug abuse treatment* (pp 245–266). Rockville, MD: National Institute on Drug Abuse.

Kuhn, T. (1970). *The structure of scientific revolutions.* Chicago: University of Chicago Press.

Kurewa, J. N. Z. (1980). Conversion in the African context. *The International Review of Missions, 68,* 164.

Kvan, E. (1989). The Cantonese perception of food. *Bulletin of the Hong Kong Psychological Society, 22/23,* 78–90.

Lai, B. (1997). *A retrospective study and a prospective study of psychoactive substance abusers of PS33.* Hong Kong: Department of Psychiatry, CUHK.

Lambert, M. J., & Bergin, A. E. (1994). The effectiveness of psychotherapy. In Bergin, A. E., & Garfield, S. L. (Eds.), *Handbook of psychotherapy and behaviour change* (4ᵗʰ ed.) (pp. 143–189). New York: Wiley.

Landfield, A. W. (1971). *Personal construct system in psychotherapy.* Chicago: Rand McNally & Company.

Landfield, A. W. (1976). A personal construct approach to suicidal behaviour. In P. Slater (Ed.), *The measurement of intrapersonal space by grid technique* Vol. I. *Explorations of intrapersonal space* (pp 193–107). London: Wiley.

Langer, E. J., Janis, E. L., & Wolfer, J. A. (1975). Reduction of psychological stress in surgical patients. *Journal of Experimental Social Psychology, 11,* 155–165.

Larson, D. B., Sherrill, K. A., & Lyons, J. S. (1992). Associations between dimensions of religious commitment and mental health reported in American Journal of Psychiatry and Archives of General Psychiatry. *American Journal of Psychiatry, 149,* 557.

Lau, N.H.Y. (1994). Exploring family belief systems: A constructional approach to therapy and change. *The Hong Kong Journal of Social Work, 28*(1), 13–21.

Lea, G. (1982). Religion, mental health, and clinical issues. *Journal of Religion and Health. 21,* 336–351.

Leary, T. (1968). *The politics of ecstasy.* New York: Putnam.

Lee, Y. P., & Ng, L. G. (1989). Student and staff perception of language needs. *Bulletin of the Hong Kong Psychological Society, 22/23,* 46–56.

Leiby, J. (1977). Social welfare: History of basic ideas. In J. B. Turner et al. (Ed.), *The Encyclopedia of Social Work* (17ᵗʰ ed., pp. 1513–18). Washington, D.C.: National Association of Social Workers.

Lewandowski, C. A., & Canda, E. R. (1995). A typological model for the assessment of religious groups. *Social Thought, 18*(1), 17–38.

Lewis, G. R. (1984). The attributes of God. In W. Elwell (ED.). *Evangelical dictionary of theology* (196–200). Grand Rapids: Baker.

Lewis, K. N., & Lewis, D. A. (1985). Impact of religious affiliation of therapists' judgements of patients. *Journal of Consulting and Clinical Psychology, 53,* 926–32.

Lieberman, M. A. (1973). *Encounter groups: First facts.* New York: Basic Books.

Lincoln, Y. S. & Guba, E. G. (1985). *Naturalistic inquiry.* Newbury Park, CA: Sage.

Lincoln, Y.S. & Guba, E. G. (2000). Paradigmatic controversies, contradictions and emerging confluences. In N. K. Denzin, & Y. S. Lincoln (Eds.), Handbook of qualitative research (2nd ed., pp. 163–188). Thousand Oaks: Calif.: Sage.

Lindesmith, A. R. (1968). *Addiction and opiates.* Chicago: Aldine.

Litman, G. K., Eiser, J. R., & Taylor, C. (1979). Dependence, relapse and extinction: A theoretical critique and a behavioural explanation. *Journal of Clinical Psychology, 35,* 192–199.

Loewenberg, F. M. (1988). *Religion and social work practice in contemporary American society.* NY: Columbia University Press.

Lombardi, D. N., O'Brien, B. J., & Isele, F. W. (1968). *Journal of Projective Techniques, 32*(5), 479–482.

London, P. (1964). *The modes and morals of psychotherapy.* New York: Holt, Rinehart & Winston.

London, P. (1986). *The modes and morals of therapy* (2nd. Ed.). New York: Norton.

Lovinger, R. J. (1984). *Working with religious issues in therapy.* New York: Jason Aronson.

Maddux, J. F., & Desmond, D. P. (1980). New light on the maturing out hypothesis in opioid dependence. *Bulletin on Narcotics, 32,* 15–25.

Maddux, J. F., & Desmond, D. P. (1981). *Careers of opioid users.* New York: Praeger.

Magura, S. (1994). Social workers should be more involved in substance abuse treatment. *Health and Social Work, 19*(1), 3–5.

Mair, J. M. M. (1977). The community of self. In D. Bannister (Ed.), *New Perspectives in Personal Construct Theory* (pp. 125–149). London: Academic Press.

Mair, J. M. M. & Crisp, A. H. (1968). Estimating psychological organization, meaning, and change in relation to clinical practice. *British Journal of Medical Psychology, 41,* 15–29.

Maltz, M. D. (1994). Deviating from the mean: The declining significance of significance. *Journal of Research in Crime and Delinquency, 31*(4), 434–463.

Manoleas, P. (1992). Should social workers accept a disease model of substance abuse? In E. Gambrill & R. Pruger (Eds.), *Controversial issues in social work* (pp. 124–131). Boston: Allyn & Bacon.

Marlatt, G. A. (1985). Relapse prevention: theoretical rationale and overview of the model. In G.. A. Marlatt & J. R. Gordon (Eds.), *Relapse prevention: Maintenance strategies in the treatment of addictive behaviours* (pp. 3–70). New York: The Guildford Press.

Marlatt, G. A., Demming, B., & Reid, J. B. (1973). Loss of control drinking in alcoholics: An experimental analogue. *Journal of Abnormal Psychology, 81,* 233–241.

Marlatt, G. A., & Gordon, J. R. (Eds.) (1985). *Relapse prevention: Maintenance strategies in the treatment of addictive behaviours.* New York: The Guilford Press.

Martini, J. L., & Brook, R. C. (1978). Value comparisons between alcoholics, non-alcoholics, and therapists. *International Journal of Addictions, 13*(7), 1169–1176.

Marty, M. E. (1980). Social service: godly and godless. *Social Service Review, 54* (4), 462–81.

Maslow, A. H. (1964). *Religions, values, and peak experiences.* New York: The Viking Press.

Maslow, A.H. (1969). Toward a humanistic biology. *American Psychologist, 24.* 724–35.

Maton, K. I., & Wells E. A. (1995). Religion as a community resource for well-being: prevention, healing and empowerment pathways. *Journal of Social Issues, 51,* 177–193

Matson, F. W. (1971). Humanistic theory: The third revolution in psychology. *The Humanist, 31*(2), 7–11.

Maturana, H., & Varela, F. J. (1980). *Autopoeisis and cognition: The realization of living.* Boston: Reidal Publishing Co.

Maxwell, M. A. (1984). *The AA experience.* New York: McGraw-Hill.

May, G. G. (1988). *Addiction and grace.* New York: HarperSanFrancisco.

McAuliffe, W., Feldman, B., Friedman, R., Launder, E., Magnuson, E., Mahoney, C., Santangelo, S., Ward, W., & Weiss, R. (1986). Explaining relapse to opiate addiction following successful completion of treatment. *National Institute on Drug Abuse Monograph Series, 72,* 136–56. Rockville, Maryland: Department of Health and Human Services.

McCartney, J. & O'Donnell, J. P. (1981). The perception of drinking roles by recovered problem drinkers. *Psychological Medicine, 11,* 747–54.

McCoy, M., & Kvan, E. (1979). *Attitudes towards punishment — A repertory grid study of young offenders in Hong Kong.* Hong Kong: Centre of Asian Studies, University of Hong Kong.

McIntosh, D., & Spilka, B. (1990). Religion and physical health: The role of personal faith and control beliefs. In M. L. Lynn & D. O. Moberg (Eds.), *Research on the social scientific study of religion Vol. 2* (pp. 167–194). Greenwich, CT: JAI Press.

McLatchie, B. H., & Lomp, K. G. E. (1988). Alcoholics Anonymous affiliation and treatment outcome among a clinical sample of problem drinkers. *American Journal of Drug and Alcohol Abuse, 14,* 309–324.

McLellan, A., Luborsky, L., Woody, G., O'Brien, C., & Druley, K. (1983). Increased effectiveness of substance abuse treatment: A prospective study of patient-treatment "matching." *Journal of Nervous and Mental Disease, 171,* 597–605.

McLellan, T. (1986). Patient characteristics associated with outcome. In J. Cooper, F. Altman, B. Brown, and D. Czechowicz (Eds.), *Research on the treatment of narcotic addiction: State of the art* (pp. 500–523). Rockwille, MD: National Institute on Drug Abuse.

McNeill, J. T. (1965). *A history of the cure of souls.* New York: Harper & Row.

McShane, C. (1993). Santanic sexual abuse: A paradigm. *AFFILIA — Journal of Women and Social Work, 8*(2), 200–12.

Meadow, M. J. (1986). Current and emerging themes in the psychology of religion. *Journal of Psychology and Christianity, 5,* 56–60.

Mejta, C. L., Naylor, C. L., & Maslar, E. M. (1994). Drug abuse treatment: Approaches and effectiveness. In J. A. Lewis (Ed.), *Addictions: Concepts and strategies for treatment* (pp. 59–81). Gaithersburg, Maryland: Aspen Publishers, Inc.

Merrill, W. L. (1993). Conversion and colonialism in Northern Mexico: The Tarahumary response to the Jesuit mission programme, 1601–1767. In Robert W. Hefner (Ed.), *Conversion to Christianity* (pp 129–164.) Berkeley: University of California Press.

Meystedt, D. M. (1984). Religion and the rural population: implications for social work. *Social Casework, 65*(4), 219–26.

Miller, G. A. (1992). Integrating religion and psychology in therapy: Issues and recommendations. *Counseling and Values, 36,* 112–122.

Miller, N. S. (1995). *Treatment of the addictions: Applications of outcome research for clinical management.* New York: The Haworth Press.

Miller, W. E. (1983). Motivational interviewing with problem drinkers. *Behavioural Psychotherapy, 11,* 147–172.

Miller, W. R. (1990). Spirituality: The silent dimension in addiction research. *Drug and Alcohol Review, 9,* 259–66.

Miller, W. R., & Martin, J. E. (1988). Spirituality and behavioural psychology — Toward integration. In W. R. Miller & J. E. Martin (Eds.), *Behavioural therapy and religion-integrating spiritual and behavioural approaches to change* (pp. 13–23). Newbury Park: Sage.

Miller, W. R., & Rollnick, S. (Eds.). (1991). *Motivational interviewing: Preparing people to change addictive behaviours.* New York: Guilford.

Mol, Hans, (1976). *Identity and the sacred.* NY: Free Press.

Moore, A. J. (1989). *Religious Education as social transformation.* Birmingham, Alabama: Religious Education Press.

Mowrer, O. H. (1961). *The crisis in psychiatry and religion.* New York: Van Nostrand.

Muffler, J., Langrod, J. G., & Larson, D. (1992). There is a balm in Gilead: Religion and substance abuse treatment. In J. H. Lowinson, P., Ruiz, R. B., Millman, & J. G. Langrod (Eds.), *Substance abuse: A comprehensive textbook* (pp. 584–595). Baltimore, MD: Williams & Wilkins.

Nakhaima, J. M. (1994). Family counselling: the overlooked resource. *Arete, 19* (1), 46–56.

Narcotics Division. (1992). *Hong Kong narcotics report — 1992*. Hong Kong: Government Secretariat.

Narcotics Division. (1994). *Report on survey of young drug abusers*. Hong Kong: Government Secretariat.

Narcotics Division. (1995). *Hong Kong Narcotics Report 1995*. Hong Kong: Government Secretariat.

Narcotics Division. (1997a). *1996 survey on drug use among students of secondary school and technical institutes*. Hong Kong: Survey Research Hongkong.

Narcotics Division. (1997b). *Central Registry of Drug Abuse — 40th Report (Jan 1988–Jun 1997)*. Hong Kong Special Administrative Region: Government Secretariat.

Narcotics Division. (1997c). *Hong Kong Narcotics Report 1997*. Hong Kong Special Administrative Region: Government Secretariat.

Narcotics Division. (1997d). *Three-year plan on drug treatment and rehabilitation services in Hong Kong (1997–1999)*. Hong Kong Special Administrative Region: Government Secretariat.

Narcotics Division. (2002a). *Hong Kong Narcotics Report 2002*. Hong Kong Special Administrative Region: Government Secretariat.

Narcotics Division. (2002b). *Central Registry of Drug Abuse 50th Report (Jan 1993–Jun 2002)*. Hong Kong Special Administrative Region: Government Secretariat.

Narcotics Division. (2002c). *The 2000 survey of drug use among students*. Hong Kong Special Administrative Region: Government Secretariat.

Narcotics Division. (2002d). *Report of the task force on psychotropic substance abuse*. Hong Kong Special Administrative Region: Government Secretariat.

Neimeyer, G. J. & Neimeyer, R. A. (1990). *Advances in personal construct psychology: A research manual* Vol. 1. London: JAI Press Inc.

Neimeyer, R. A., Baker, K. D., & Neimeyer, G. J. (1990). The current status of personal construct theory: some scientometric data. In G. J. Neimeyer, & R. A. Neimeyer (Eds.), *Advances in personal construct psychology* (Vol. 1, pp. 3–22). London: JAI Press Inc.

Neimeyer, R. A., & Neimeyer, G. J. (Eds.). (2002). *Advances in personal construct psychology : new directions and perspectives*. Wesport, Conn.: Praeger.

Nelsen, H. M., & Rooney, J. J. (1982). Fire and brimstone, lager and pot: Religious involvement and substance use, *Sociological Analysis, 43*(3), 247–256.

Netting, F.E., Thibault, J.M., & Ellor, J.W. (1990). Integrating content on organized religion into macropractice. *Journal of Social Work Education, 26*(1), 15–24.

Newlin, D. B. (1989). The skin-flashing response: Autonomic, self-report, and conditioned responses to repeated administrations of alcohol in Asian men. *Journal of Abnormal Psychology, 98*, 421–425.

Ng, H. Y., & Kvan, E. (1998). Expanding horizons: Religion in social work education. *Journal of Teaching in Social Work*, 17(1/2), 31–47.

Nigel, P., & O'Byrne, P. (2000). *Constructive social work: towards a new practice.* London : Macmillan Press.

Norris, H., & Makhlouf-Norris, F. (1976). The measurement of self-identity. In P. Slater (Ed.). *Explorations of Intrapersonal Space.* (Vol. 1, pp 79–82). Chichester: Wiley.

Oden, T. (1966). *Kerygma and counseling.* Philadelphia Westminster Press.

Oman, J. (1925). *Grace and Personality.* Cambridge: Cambridge University Press..

Orne, M. (1969). Demand characteristics and the concept of quasi-controls. In R. Rosenthal & R. Rosnow (Eds.), *Artifact in behavioural research* (pp. 143–79). New York: Academic Press.

Paden, W. E. (1992). Interpreting the sacred: Ways of viewing religion. Boston: Beacon Press.

Paloutzian, R. F. (1981). Purpose in life and value changes following conversion, *Journal of Personality and Social Psychology, 41*, 1153–1160

Parker, R. J., & Horton, H. S. (1996). A typology of ritual: Paradigms for healing and empowerment. *Counseling and Values*, January, *40*(2), 82–98.

Pattison, E.M. (1969). Religion in psychotherapy. In E. M. Pattison (Ed.), *Clinical psychiatry and religion* (p. 77–92). Boston: Little, Brown & Co.

Patton, M. Q. (1988). Paradigms and pragmatis. In D. M. Fetterman *Qualitative approaches to evaluation in education: The silent scientific revolution* (pp. 116–137). New York: Praeger.

Payne, I. R., Bergin, A. E., Bielema, K. A., & Jenkins, P.H. (1992). Review of religion and mental health: prevention and the enhancement of psychosocial functioning. In K. I. Pargament, K. I. Maton, & R.E. Hess (Eds.), *Religion and prevention in mental health* (pp. 57–82). New York: The Haworth Press.

Peele, S. (1985). *The meaning of addiction — Compulsive experience and its interpretation.* Massachusetts: Lexington Books.

Peele, S. (1988). A moral vision of addiction: How people's values determine whether they become and remain addicts. In S. Peele (Ed.), *Visions of addiction: Major contemporary perspectives on addiction and alcoholism* (pp. 201–233). Lexington, MA: Lexington Books.

Peele, S. (1989). *Diseasing of America — Addiction treatment out of control.* Massachusetts: Lexington.

Peele, S. (1990). A values approach to addiction: Drug policy that is moral rather than moralistic. *Journal of Drug Issues, 20*, 639–646.

Peele, S. (1991). *The truth about addiction and recovery.* New York: Simon & Schuster.

Peele, S., & Brodsky, A. (1991). *The truth about addiction and recovery: The life process program for outgrowing destruction habits.* New York: Simon & Schuster.

Peltzer, K. (1987). *Some contributions of traditional healing practices towards psychosocial health care in Malawi.* Frankfurt/M.: Fachbuchhandlung für Psychologie Verlag.

Penrod, J. H., Epting, R.F., & Wadden, T. A. (1981). Interpersonal cognitive differentiation and drug of choice. *Psychological Reports, 49*, 752–6.

Perkins, H. W. (1985). Religious traditions, parents, and peers as determinants of alcohol and drug use among college students. *Review of Religious Research, 27*, 15–31.

Peters, T. K. (1980). An investigation into the role of religious experience and commitment as a therapeutic factor in the treatment and rehabilitation of selected drug addicts from Teen Challenge: A follow-up study (Doctoral dissertation, New York University). *Dissertation Abstracts International, 41*, 704A (University Microfilms No. 8017521)

Pieper, M. H. (1985). The future of social work research. *Social Work Research and Abstracts, 21*(4), 3–11.

Pilseker, C. (1978). Values: A problem for everyone. *Social Work, 23*, 54–57.

Platt, J. J. (1995). Heroin addiction — Theory, research, and treatment. (Vol. 2). *The addict, the treatment process, and social control.* Malabar, FL.: Krieger.

Platt, J. J., Widman, M., Lidz, V., & Marlowe, D. (1998). Methadone maintenance treatment: Its development and effectiveness after 30 years. In J. A. Inciardi, & L. D. Harrison (Eds.), *Heroin in the age of crack-cocaine* (pp. 160–187). Thousand Oaks, CA: Sage.

Pope John Paul II. (1989). Science and faith. Address at the University of Pisa, September 24. Reprinted in *Origins, Catholic News Service Documentary Service 19*, October 26.

Prest, L. A., & Keller, J. F. (1993). Spirituality and family therapy: spiritual beliefs, myths, and metaphors. *Journal of Marital and Family Therapy, 19*(2), 137–148.

Price, R. H., Burke, A. C., D'Aunno, T. A., Klingel, D. M., McCaughain, W. C., Rafferty, J. A., & Vaughn, T. E. (1991). Outpatient drug abuse treatment services: Results of a national survey. In R. Pickens, C. G. Leukefkeld, & C. Schuster (Eds.), *Improving drug abuse treatment* (pp. 63-91). Rockville, MD: National Institute on Drug Abuse.

Prochaska, J. O., & DiClemente, C. C. (1983). Stages and processes of self-change of smoking: Toward an integrative model of change. *Journal of Consulting and Clinical Psychology, 51*, 390–395.

Prochaska, J. O., & DiClemente, C. C. (1992). Criticisms and concerns of the transtheoretical model in light of recent research. *British Journal of Addiction, 87*, 825–835.

Propst, T. (1980). The comparative efficacy of religious and nonreligious imagery for the treatment of mild depression in religious individuals. *Cognitive Therapy and Research, 4*, 167–78.

Prugh, T. (1986). Recovery without treatment. *Alcohol Health and Research World*, 24–25.

Pullinger, J. (1980). *Chasing the Dragon.* London: Hodder and Stoughton.

Pullinger, J. (1989). *Crack in the wall: Life and death in Kowloon walled city.* London: Hodder & Stoughton.

Ramaswami, S. R., & Sheikh, A. A. (1989). Meditation east and west. In A. A. Sheikh, & K. S. Sheikh (Eds.), *Eastern and western approaches to healing: Ancient wisdom and modern knowledge* (pp. 427–469). New York: Wiley and Sons.

Rawson, R. A. (1995). Is psychotherapy effective for substance abusers? In A. M. Washton (Ed.), *Psychotherapy and substance abuse — A practitioners' handbook* (pp. 55–75). New York: The Guilford Press.

Raz-Duvshani, A. (1986). Cognitive structure changes with psychotherapy in neurosis. *British Journal of Medical Psychology, 59*, 341–350.

Reamer, F. G. (1993). *The philosophical foundations of social work.* New York: Columbia University Press.

Regier, D. A., Farmer, M. E., Rae, D. S., Locke, B. Z., Keith, S. J., Judd, L. L., & Goodwin, F. K. (1990). Comorbidity of mental disorders with alcohol and other drug abuse. *Journal of the American Medical Association, 264*, 2511–2518.

Reker, G. T. & Guppy, B. (1988). *Sources of personal meaning among young, middle-aged, and older adults.* Paper presented at the annual meeting of the Canadian Association on Gerontology.

*Revised English bible with the apocrypha.* (1989). London: Oxford University Press & Cambridge University Press.

Rhoads, D. (1983). A longitudinal study of life stress and social support among drug abusers. *International Journal of Addictions, 18*, 195–222.

Rhodes, R. (1987). Women, motherhood, and infertility: The social and historical context. *Journal of Social Work and Human Sexuality, 6*(1), 5–20.

Rhodes, R., & Johnson, A. D. (1996). Social work and substance-abuse treatment: A challenge for the profession. *Families in Society: The Journal of Contemporary Human Services, 77*(3), 182–185.

Richards, P. S. (1989). The effects of theistic and atheistic counselor value on client trust: A multidimensional scaling analysis. *Counseling and Values, 33*, 109–120.

Ridgway, J. M. B. (1972). Some attitudinal and motivational changes among heroin addicts involved in a religiously oriented program of rehabilitation (Doctoral dissertation, Drew University). *Dissertation Abstracts International, 33*, 2330B. (University Microfilms No. 72–29, 417).

Robins, L. N.; Helzer, J. E.; & Davis, D. H. (1975). Narcotic use in Southeast Asia and afterwards. *Archives of General Psychiatry, 32*:955–961.

Robins, P. R. (1974). Depression and drug addiction. *Psychiatric Quarterly , 48* (3), 374–386.

Robinson, L. (Ed.). (1986). Minister and healer: Each as the other. In *Psychiatry and religion: Overlapping concerns* (pp. 53–72). Washington, DC: American Psychiatric Association.

Roffman, R. A. (1992). Should social workers accept a disease model of substance abuse? In E. Gambrill & R. Pruger (Eds.), *Controversial issues in social work* (pp. 131–138). Boston: Allyn & Bacon.

Rogers, C. (1951). *Client centered therapy*. Boston: Houghton-Mifflin.

Rokeach, M. (1971). Long-range experimental modifications of values, attitudes, and behaviour. *American Psychologist, 26,* 453–459.

Rokeach, M. (1981). A value approach to the prevention and reduction of drug abuse. In T. J. Glunn, C. G. Leukefeld, & J. P. Ludford (Eds.), *Preventing adolescent drug abuse* (NIDA Research Monograph No. 47, pp. 172–194). Rockville, MD: National Institute on Drug Abuse.

Rokeach, M., & Cochrane, R. (1972). Self-confrontation and confrontation with another as determinants of long-term value change. *Journal of Applied Social Psychology, 2*(4), 283–292.

Roman, S. W. (1992). The treatment of drug addiction: An overview. In T. Mieczkowske (Ed.), *Drugs, crime and social policy* (pp. 222–249). Boston: Allyn & Bacon.

Rosen, H. (1991). Constructivism: Personality, psychopathology, and psycho-therapy. In D. P. Keating, & H. Rosen (Eds.), *Constructivist perspectives on developmental psychopathology and atypical development* (pp. 149–171). New Jersey: Lawrence Erlbaum Asso. Publishers.

Rosenthal, R., & Rosnow, R. (Eds.). (1969). *Artifact in behaviourial research*. New York: Academic Press.

Rotgers, F. (1996). Behavioural theory of substance abuse treatment: Bringing science to bear on practice. In Rotgers, F., Keller, D. S., & Morgenstern, J. (Eds.), *Treating substance abuse — Theory and technique* (174–201). New York: The Guilford Press.

Rounsaville, B. J., Weissman, M. M., Kleber, H., & Wilber, C. (1982). Heterogeneity of psychiatric diagnosis in treated opiate addicts. *Archives of General Psychiatry, 39,* 161–166.

Ruckdeschel, R., & Balassone, M. L. (1994). Does emphasizing accountability and evidence dilute service delivery and the helping role? In W. W. Hudson, & P. S. Nurius (Eds.), *Controversial issues in social work research* (pp 9–21). Boston: Allyn and Bacon.

Salili, F. (1994). Age, sex, and cultural differences in the meaning and dimensions of achievement. *Personality and Social Psychology Bulletin, 6,* 635–648.

Salmon, W. (1971). *Statistical explanation and statistical relevance*. Pittsburgh: University of Pittsburgh Press.

Salzman, L. (1954). The Psychology of regressive religious conversion. *Journal of Pastoral Care, 8*(2), 10.

Sanua, V. D. (1969). Religion, mental health, and personality: A review of empirical studies. *American Journal of Psychiatry, 125,* 1203–1213.

SARDA. Society for the Aid and Rehabilitation of Drug Abusers (1998). *Annual report.* Hong Kong: Author.

Sargent, W. (1957). *Battle for the mind.* New York: Harper & Row.

Scharlack, A. E. & Fuller, T. E. (1994). Coping strategies following the death of an elderly parent. *Journal of Gerontological Social Work, 21*(3/4), pp. 85–100.

Schasre, R. (1966). Cessation patterns among neophyte heroin users. *International Journal of addictions, 1,* 23–32.

Schumaker, J. F. (Ed.). (1992). *Religion and mental health.* Oxford: Oxford University Press.

Scroggs, J. R., & Douglas, W. G. T. (1977). Quoted in V. B. Gillespie, (1991). *The dynamics of religious conversion, identity and transformation* (p. 48). Birmingham, Alabama: Religious Education Press.

Seivewright, N. (2000). *Community treatment of drug misuse: more than methadone.* Cambridge: Cambridge University Press.

Shek, D. T. L. (1986). The Purpose in life questionnaire in a Chinese context: Some psychometric and normative data. *Chinese Journal of Psychology, 28* (1), 51–60.

Shek, D. T. L. (1988). Reliability and factorial structure of the Chinese version of the Purpose in Life Questionnaire. *Journal of Clinical Psychology, 44*(3), 384–392.

Shek, D. T. L. (1990). Reliability and factorial structure of the Chinese version of the Beck Depression Inventory. *Journal of Clinical Psychology, 46*(1), 35–43.

Shek, D. T. L. (1991). Depressive symptoms in a sample of Chinese adolescents: An empirical study using the Chinese version of the Beck Depression Inventory. *International Journal of Adolescent Medicine and Health, 5*(1), 1–16.

Shek, D. T. L. (1993). Measurement of pessimism in Chinese adolescents: The Chinese Hopelessness Scale . *Social Behaviour and Personality, 21*(2), 107–120.

Sheppard, C., Fracchia, J., Ricca, E., & Merlis, S. (1972). Indications of psychopathology in male narcotic abusers, their effects and relation to treatment effectiveness. *Journal of Psychology, 81*(2), 351–360.

Sheppard, C., Ricca, E., Fracchia, J., & Merlis, S. (1973). Indications of psychopathology in applicants to a county methadone maintenance programme. *Psychological Reports, 33,* 535–540.

Sher, K. J., Walitzer, K. S., Wood, P. A., & Brent, E. E. (1991). Characteristics of children of alcoholics: Putative risk factors, substance use and abuse, and psychopathology. *Journal of Abnormal Psychology, 100,* 427–448.

Shereen, M. (1988). The relationship between relapse and involvement in Alcoholics Anonymous. *Journal of Studies on Alcohol, 49,* 104–106.

Sheridan, M. J., Bullis, R. K., Adcock, C. R., Berlin, S. D., & Miller, P. C. (1992).

Practitioners' personal and professional attitudes and behaviours toward religion and spirituality: issues for education and practice. *Journal of Social Work Education*, 28(2), 190–203.

Sheridan, M. J., Wilmer, C. M., & Atcheson, L. (1994). Inclusion of content on religion and spirituality in the social work curriculum: A study of faculty views. *Journal of Social Work Education*, 30(3), 363–76.

Shiffman, S. (1989). Conceptual issues in the study of relapse. In M. Gossop (Ed.), *Relapse and addictive behaviour*, (pp. 149–179). London: Tavistock/Routledge.

Siegler, P. S., & Osmond, H. (1968). Models of alcoholism. *Quarterly Journal of Studies on Alcohol*, 29, 571–591.

Sikorsky, I. I., Jr. (1990). *AA's godparents: Three early influences on Alcoholics Anonymous and its foundation, Carl Jung, Emmett Fox, Jack Alexander*. Minneapolis, MN: CompCare.

Siporin, M. (1986). Contribution of religious values to social work and the law. *Social Thought*, 12(4), 35–50.

Skinner, B. F. (1953). *Science and human behavior*. New York: Free Press.

Skog, O. J. (1992). Correlation and causality: notes on epistemological problems in substance abuse research. In M. Lader, G. Edwards, & D. C. Drummond (Eds.), *The nature of alcohol and drug related problems* (pp. 37–59). Oxford: Oxford Medical Publications.

Slater, P. (1972). The measurement of consistency in repertory grids. *British Journal of Psychiatry*, 121, 45–51.

Slater, P. (1976). Monitoring change in the mental state of a patient undergoing psychiatric treatment. In P. Slater (Ed.), The measurement of intrapersonal space by grid technique, Vol.1. *Explorations of intrapersonal space* (pp. 109–122). London: Wiley.

Slater, P. (Ed.). (1977). The measurement of intrapersonal space by grid technique, Vol.2. *Dimensions of intrapersonal space*. London: Wiley.

Smith, A. & Evans, D. R. (1980). Construct structure associated with alcohol-dependent behaviour in males. *Psychological Reports*, 47, 87–99.

Smith, G. M., & Beecher, H. K. (1962). Subjective effects of heroin and morphine in normal subjects. *Journal of Pharmacology and Experimental Therapeutics*, 136, 47–52

Smith, J. A. (1995). Repertory grids: Interactive, case-study perspective. In J. A. Smith, R. Harre, & L. Van Langenhove (Eds.), *Rethinking methods in psychology* (pp. 162–207). London: Sage.

Spanos, N. P., Horton, C., & Chaves, J. F. (1975). The effects of two cognitive strategies on pain threshold. *Journal of Abnormal Psychology*, 84, 677–681.

Spencer, S. (1956). Religious and spiritual values in social casework practice. *Social Cassework*, 57, 519–526.

Sperry, R. W. (1988). Psychology's mentalist paradigm and the religion/science tension. *American Psychologist*, 43, 607–613.

Spilka, B., Hood, R., & Gorsuch, R. L. (1985). *The psychology of religion: An empirical approach*. Englewood Cliffs, NJ: Prentice Hall.

Spilka, B., & Werme, P. H. (1971). Religion and mental disorder: A research perspective. In M. Strommen (Ed.), *Research on religious development: A comprehensive handbook*, (pp. 161–181). New York: Hawthorn.

Stanley, B. (1985). Alienation in young offenders. In N. Beail (Ed.), *Repertory grid technique and personal constructs: Applications in clinical and educational settings*. (pp. 47–60). ondon: Croom Helm.

Starbuck, E., (1915). *The psychology of religion*. NY: Scribner and Sons.

Stark, R. (1971). Psychopathology and religious commitment. *Review of Religious Research, 12*, 165–176.

Steckler, A., Mcleroy, K. R., Goodman, R. M., Bird, S. T., & McCormick, L. (1992). Toward integrating qualitative and quantitative methods: An introduction. *Health Education Quarterly, 19*(1): 1–8.

Steer, R. A., Emery, & Beck, A. T. (1980). Correlates of self-reported and clinically assessed depression in male heroin addicts. *Journal of Clinical Psychology, 36,* 798–800.

Stewart, T. (1987). *The heroin users*. London: Pandora Press.

Stimson, C, & Oppenheimer, E. (1982). *Heroin addiction: Treatment and Control in Britain*. London: Tavistock.

Stockwell, T. (1985). Stress and alcohol. *Stress Medicine, 1.* 209–215.

Stojnov, D. (1990). Construing HIV positivity amongst heroin addict. In P. Maitland (Ed.)., *Personal construct theory deviancy and social work*. London: Inner London Probation Service/Centre for Personal Construct Psychology.

Strauss, A. L. (1959). *Mirrors and masks: The search for identity*. Glencoe: Free Press.

Straussner, S. L. A., & Spiegel, B. R. (1996). An analysis of 12-step programs for substance abusers from a developmental perspective. *Clinical Social Work Journal, 24*(3), 299–309.

Strunk, O. (1962). *Religion: A psychological interpretation*. New York: Abingdon.

Sutker, P. B. (1971). Personality differences and sociopathy in heroin addicts and nonaddicts prisoners. *Journal of Abnormal Psychology. 78*(3), 247–251

Sutker, P. B., Allain, A.N., & Cohen, G. H. (1974). MMPI indices of personality change following short-term and long-term hospitalization of heroin addicts. *Psychological Reports, 34,* 494–500.

Swan, G. E., Carnelli, D., & Cardon, L. R. (1996). The consumption of tobacco, alcohol, and coffee in Caucasian male twins: A multivariate genetic analysis. *Journal of Substance Abuse, 8,* 19–31.

Sweezy, M. (1991). Why heroin should be legalized? *Smith College Studies in Social Work, 61*(2), 167–178.

Szasz, T. (1978). *The myth of psychotherapy*. New York: Doubleday.

Tabachnick, B. G., & Fidell, L. S. (2001). *Using multivariate statistics*, 4<sup>th</sup>. Ed. Boston: Allyn & Bacon.

Taggart, S. R. (1994). *Living as if*. San Francisco: Jossey-Bass.

Tashakkori, A, & Teddlie, C. (1998). *Mixed methodology: combining qualitative and quantitative approaches*. Thousand Oaks, Calif.: Sage.

Tashakkori, A., & Teddlie, C. (Eds.). (2003). *Handbook of mixed methods in social & behavioral research*. Thousand Oaks, CA: SAGE Publications.

Tebes, J. K., & Kraemer, D. T. (1991). Quantitative and qualitative knowing in mutual support research: Some lessons from the recent history of scientific psychology. *American Journal of Community Psychology*, *19*, 5, 739–756.

Terwee, S. J. S.. (1990). *Hermeneutics in psychology and psychoanalysis*. New York: SpringerVerlag.

Thomas, D. L., & Roghaar, H. (1990). Postpositivist theorizing: The case of religion and the family. In Sprey, J. (Ed.). *Fashioning family therapy: New Approaches* (pp 136–169). New York: Sage.

Thomason, H .H., & Dilts, S. L. (1991). Opioids. In R. J. Frances, & S. I. Miller (Eds.), *Clinical textbooks of addictive disorders* (pp. 103–120). New York: The Guilford Press.

Thompson, A. (1990). *Guide to ethical practice in psychotherapy*. New York: Wiley.

Thouless, R. (1971). *Introduction to the psychology of religion*. Cambridge: Cambridge University Press.

Tillich, P. H. (1963). *Morality and beyond*. New York: Harper & Row.

Tims, F. M., Fletcher, B. W., & Hubbard, R. L. (1991). Treatment outcomes for drug abuse clients. In R. Pickens, C. Leukefeld, & C. Schuster (Eds.). *Improving drug abuse treatment* (pp. 93–113). Rockville, MD: National Institute on Drug Abuse.

Todd, N. (1987). Religious belief and PCT. In F. Fransella & L. Thomas (Eds.), *Experimenting with personal construct psychology* (pp. 483–492). London: Routledge & Kegan Paul.

Toler, C. (1975). The personal values of alcoholics and addicts. *Journal of Clinical Psychology*, *31*, 554–557.

Topley, M. (1967). Chinese occasional rites in Hong Kong. In M. Topley (Ed.), *Some traditional Chinese ideas and conception in Hong Kong social life today*. Hong Kong: Royal Asiatic Society of Great Britain and Ireland, Hong Kong Branch.

Toulmin, S., & Leary, D. E. (1985). The cult of empiricism in psychology and beyond. In S. Koch & D. E. Leary (Eds.). *A century of psychology as science* (pp. 594–617). New York: McGraw-Hill.

Traux, C. B., & Carkhuff, R. R. (1967). *Toward effective counselling and psychotherapy: Training and practice*. Chicago: Aldine-Atherton.

Traver, H. H. (1992). Colonial relations and opium control policy in Hong Kong,

1841–1945. In H. H. Traver & M. S. Gaylord (Eds.), *Drugs, law and the state* (pp. 135–149). Hong Kong: Hong Kong University Press.

Valliant, G. E. (1983). *The natural history of alcoholism: Causes, patterns, and paths to recovery*. Cambridge, Mass.: Harvard University Press.

Valliant, G. E., & Milofsky, E. S. (1982). The etiology of alcoholism: a prospective viewpoint. *American Psychologist, 37*(5), 494–503.

Van Kaam, A. (1966). Addiction: Counterfeit of religious presence. In *Personality fulfillment in the spiritual life* (pp. 123–53). Wilkes-Barre, PA: Dimension Books.

Van Limbeek, J., Geerlings, P. J., Wouters, L., Beelen, W., de Leeuw, M., Heinemeyer, M., Edelbroek, W., v. Rooyen, T., & Goris., A. (1990). The prevalence of psychopathology among drug addicts in an outpatient methadone maintenance and detoxification clinic in the Hague. In J. J. Plattt, C. D. Kaplan, & P. J. Mekin (Eds.), *The effectivness of drug abuse treatment: Dutch and American perspectives* (pp. 169–175), Florida: Robert E. Krieger Publishing Co.

Viney, L. L. (1981). Experimenting with experience: a psychotherapeutic case study. *Psychotherapy, 18*, 271–286.

Viney, L. L., Westbrook, M. T., & Preston, C. (1985).The addiction experience as a function of the addict's history. *British Journal of Clinical Psychology, 24*, 73–82.

Wakefield, J. C. (1996a). Does social work need the eco-systems perspective? Part 1. Is the perspective clinically useful? *Social Service Review, 70*(1), 1–32.

Wakefield, J. C. (1996b). Does social work need the eco-systems perspective/ Part 2. Does the perspective save social work from incoherence? *Social Service Review, 70*(2), 183–213.

Waldorf, D. (1973). *Careers in dope*. New Jersey: Prentice-Hall Inc.

Waldorf, D. (1983). Natural recovery from opiate addiction: Some social-psychological processes of untreated recovery. *Journal of Drug Issues, 13*, 237–280.

Wallace, E.R. (1990). Psychiatry and religion: A dialogue. In J. A. Smith (Ed.), & S. A. Handelman (Assoc. Ed.), *Psychoanalysis and religion* (pp. 195–221). Baltimore: Johns Hopkins University Press.

Walsh, R. N. (1990). *The spirit of shamanism*. New York: Putnam.

Walters, G. D. (1996). *Substance abuse and the new road to recovery — A practitioners' guide*. Washington, D.C.: Taylor & Francis.

Warfield, R. D, & Goldstein, M. B. (1996). Spirituality: The key to recovery from alcoholism. *Counselling and Values, 40* (3), 196–205.

Warren, B. (1993). The problem of religion for constructivist psychology. *The Journal of Psychology, 127*(5), 481–488.

Washton, A. M. (1995). *Psychotherapy and substance abuse — A practitioner's handbook*. New York: The Guilford Press.

Weissman, M. M., Slobetz, F., Prusoff, B., Mazritz, M., & Howard, P. (1976). Clinical depression among narcotic addicts maintained on methadone in the community. *American Journal of Psychiatry, 133,* 1434–1438.

Wells, B. (1990). Psychosocial interventions. In H. Ghodse, & D. Maxwell (Eds.), *Substance abuse and dependence — An introduction for the caring professions* (pp. 149–175). London: MacMillian Press.

Wheeler, B.R., Wood, S., & Hatch, R.J. (1988). Assessment and intervention with adolescents involved in satanism. *Social Work, 33*(6), 547–50.

Wheelis, A. (1958). *The quest for identity.* New York: Norton.

Wicks, R., Parsons, R. & Capps. (1985). (Eds.). *Clinical handbook of pastoral counseling.* Mahwah, NJ: Paulist Press.

Wieman, H. N. (1926). *Religious experience and scientific method.* New York: Macmillan.

Wikler, M. (1986). Pathways to treatment: How Orthodox Jews enter therapy. *Social Casework: The Journal of Contemporary Social Work, 67*(2), 113–18.

Wilkerson, D. (1963). *The cross and the switchblade.* Old Tappan, NJ: Fleming H. Revell.

Wilson, F.V. (1992). Health-protective behaviors of rural black elderly women. *Health in Social Work, 17*(1), 28–36.

Winter, D. A. (1992). *Personal construct psychology in clinical practice: Theory, research, and applications.* London: Routledge.

Witkin, S. L., & Gottschalk, S. (1988). Alternative criteria for theory evaluation. *Social Service Review, 62,* 211–224.

Womack, S. A. (1981). Therapeutic aspects of a Pentecostal church on alcohol and drug abusers (Doctoral dissertation, University of Texas at Austin). *Dissertation Abstracts International, 41,* 3172A. (University Microfilms No. 8100984)

Woo, S. Y. (1983). The spiritual approach in drug treatment. In L. MacQuarrie (Ed.), *Drug dependence in Hong Kong* (pp. 139–145). Hong Kong: Hong Kong Polytechnic.

Wood, K.M. (1990). Epistemological issues in the development of social work practice knowledge. In Videka-Sherman, L. and W. J. Reid (Eds.), *Advances in Clinical Social Work Research* (pp. 373–390). Silver Spring, MD: National Association of Social Workers.

Wu, D Y. H. (1982). Psychotherapy and emotion in traditional Chinese medicine. In A. J. Marshall & C. M. White (Eds.). *Cultural conceptions of mental health and therapy* (pp. 285–301). Dordrecht: Reidel.

Wurmser, L. (1974). Psychoanalytic considerations of the etiology of compulsive drug use. *Journal of the American Psychoanalytic Association, 22,* 820–843.

York, G. Y. (1987). Religious-based denial in the NICU: implications for social work. *Social Work in Health Care, 12*(4), 31–45.

Zastrow, C. (1999). *The practice of social work,* (6th ed.). Pacific Grove, California: Brooks/Cole Publishing Co.

Zinberg, N.E. (1974). The search for rational approaches to heroin use. In Bourne, P. G. (Ed.), *Addiction* (pp. 149–174). New York: Academic Press.

Zucker, R. A., & Gomberg, E. S. L. (1986). Of alcoholism reconsidered: The case for a biopsychosocial process. *American Psychologist, 41*, 783–793.

# Index